GREAT CATHEDRALS OF BRITAIN

GREAT CATHEDRALS OF BRITAIN

TIM TATTON-BROWN

BBC BOOKS

TO VERONICA

Published by BBC Books,
a division of BBC Enterprises Limited,
Woodlands, 80 Wood Lane, London W12 0TT
First published 1989

Set in $11\frac{1}{2}$/14 pt Garamond

Printed and bound in Great Britain by Butler & Tanner Ltd, Frome and London
Jacket printed by Belmont Press, Northampton

Contents

Foreword by the Archbishop of Canterbury

Our cathedrals welcome millions of visitors each year. Canterbury alone has over two million tourists and pilgrims passing through its doors. This is an age fascinated by cathedrals, and there has been no shortage of books written about them in recent years. In that literature there has been a particular gap. This volume succeeds admirably in filling it.

Tim Tatton-Brown describes our cathedrals from the angle of the archaeologist rather than the architectural or ecclesiastical historian. His radio talks, upon which this book is based, corrected the false impression of many listeners that archaeologists were only interested in excavating the sites of ancient, but long defunct, buildings. Our knowledge of how and when our cathedrals were built has been considerably extended by the attention of archaeologists to the evidence to be found in the rafters as well as in the crypts. Cathedral restorations are not only a twentieth-century phenomenon. Successive generations have produced layers of building in our cathedrals which provides a rich vein for archaeological investigation.

I am particularly grateful for the comprehensive character of this account. It includes those buildings which once served as cathedrals but are no longer used as such, as well as those churches which have only come late in their life into use as cathedrals. Scottish cathedrals also, too often neglected in books of this sort, are given a full treatment. All this, together with the clarity with which Tim Tatton-Brown writes, convinces me that this volume will enhance the appreciation many people have for the cathedrals of our land.

Preface

During the last few months of 1987 and the early weeks of 1988 I was privileged to visit many cathedrals in Britain with John Knight, a BBC Radio producer, so that we could make a series of six programmes for Radio 4's archaeology series *Origins*. Later we were joined by the series' presenter Malcolm Billings who did a splendid job of linking and introducing each of the sequences, and I was amazed by the way John Knight managed to create six 30-minute programmes from so many different topics. These programmes were duly broadcast during the latter part of January and during February 1988. In order to make them I had to call on the assistance of many friends and scholars, and try and persuade them at short notice to come to a particular cathedral when we were due to be there, to be interviewed on the spot about their work in the building. This they did in an extremely generous way.

When I was subsequently invited to write this book I had to call on some of them again for assistance in particular chapters and, in some cases, to help supply illustrations relating to their very recent work. Without their help this book would have been much more difficult to write. I would therefore particularly like to thank Martin and Birthe Biddle, Harold Taylor, Warwick Rodwell, Richard Morris (Leeds), Jim Gibb, Richard Bailey, Richard Gem, Derek Phillips, Eric Cambridge, John Crook, Julian Munby, Roy Spring, Richard Morris (Warwick), John Allen, David Stocker, Nicola Coldstream, Richard Fawcett, Thomas Cocke, Phillip Lindley, and the Dean of Ely, the Very Revd William Patterson. All of them have been extremely kind in giving advice and I can only apologise to them if I have not heeded them, or if, as in a few cases, I have wilfully gone my own way!

I have enjoyed visiting cathedrals all my life (I was baptised in Nairobi Cathedral!), and I have been particularly lucky in more recent years in being able to visit parts of cathedrals which are not normally open to visitors (scaffolds, towers, roofs, triforia, crypts). Climbing inside the spire at Salisbury and the octagon at Ely were special privileges. I am most grateful to the deans and chapters for their permission to do so, and to the many virgers who made these visits possible. I am particularly grateful to His Grace The Lord Archbishop of Canterbury for not only allowing me to crawl all over his two palaces looking for 'archaeological' remains, but also for finding time in an immensely busy life to write a foreword to this book.

In the decade or so that I have worked with John Bowen, I have admired not only his excellent draughtsmanship but also the way he understands what he is drawing, however complicated the structure. I hope his special drawings, which were made for this book, speak for themselves.

I am also grateful to the Society of Antiquaries of London for allowing us to photograph drawings and engravings from many eighteenth- and nineteenth-century books in their library.

In preparing this book for the press, I have been lucky in having the assistance of a splendid group of people from BBC Books. I am particularly indebted to Susan Kennedy for making my text much more readable, and to Heather Holden-Brown, Susan Martineau, Rachel Hardman, John Martin, Jennie Allen and Karen Willie for all their hard work, also to Mrs J. M. Jessup and Marie Cooper for typing and re-typing the manuscript.

Finally I have to say that without the immense support and help of my wife, Veronica, this book could never have been written. She gave advice, read and typed at many stages during the writing of this book, and encouraged me when I thought it would never be finished. She also kept quiet our three children, Hugh (8), Miranda ($5\frac{1}{2}$) and Lucy (4), and allowed me to 'take off' and visit cathedrals all over Britain at short notice while still doing her own job.

Tim Tatton-Brown
Canterbury, December 1988

Introduction

During the summer of 1860, at the very time that the famous debate between T.H. Huxley and Bishop Wilberforce, sparked off by Darwin's *Origin of Species*, was taking place a man called the Reverend Robert Willis, who was Jacksonian Professor of Natural and Experimental Philosophy (actually Engineering) at Cambridge, went to Lichfield cathedral. His purpose was to look at walls being uncovered under the presbytery area during a colossal restoration by the architect Sir George Gilbert Scott. To use Willis's own words:

I occupied myself with as careful an examination of these remains as my short stay would permit, for the purpose of endeavouring to discover their relation to the architectural history of the building.

A few months later, in March 1861, he published in *The Archaeological Journal* not only an account of the below-ground archaeology but also a complete architectural history of the building which brilliantly analysed its complicated history. In the same year the great central tower and spire of Chichester cathedral collapsed, and shortly afterwards Willis not only published a detailed architectural history of Chichester, but also a very careful account (with detailed diagrams) of how and why the tower had fallen.

Willis's work on cathedral 'archaeology' had started in 1841 with an account of Hereford, and its structural problems in particular. He then went on to produce masterly studies of some of our greatest cathedrals – Canterbury (1845), Winchester (1846), York minster (1848) and Salisbury (1849) – which, to use the words of a great twentieth-century scholar, Sir Nikolaus Pevsner, 'have not been bettered by any scholar since'.

Robert Willis, who was born in 1800 and died in 1875, was undoubtedly 'the father of British cathedral archaeology', and as such deserves to be better known. His work on our great mediaeval buildings was well ahead of his time, and it is only really in the last few decades that archaeologists have been building on it to move forwards to a new understanding of how, and exactly when, our great cathedrals were built. This present work is an attempt to give an account of the new work in progress, as well as the background to it.

In the nineteenth century, archaeology meant the study of all the material remains of the past, and much more of it was devoted to upstanding ruins and remains than to what was hidden below ground. In the twentieth century, excavation has developed greatly as a science, and consequently, to many, a 'cathedral archaeologist' is someone who wants to dig holes around a cathedral. I hope to show in this book that, while for the period before the Norman conquest of 1066, almost all our new knowledge of cathedrals has indeed been gained from below-ground archaeology, for the Norman and later cathedrals as much information has been found in the roofs as under the earth. This is largely a consequence of the many restoration programmes that have been undertaken this century, but also because the pioneering work of Robert Willis produced a much greater awareness of the stratigraphical sequences (successive fragments of the fabric of earlier phases) that are hidden in a great building, and a realisation that this evidence is gradually being eroded during restoration.

At the same time, many great advances have been taking place in related fields. Art and architectural historians have been studying cathedral buildings in much more detail, and their stylistic analyses of many of them (particularly those without surviving documented dates) have been of immense value in working out a chronological sequence. Equally engineers, geologists and others have been looking at constructional details, building stones, etc., and have added much to our knowledge and understanding. Of all such recent work, however, perhaps the most important has been the study of the mediaeval carpentry within our cathedrals, and, related directly to this, the study of dendrochronology or tree-ring dating. Oak dendrochronology has, for the first time, thanks largely to the use of computers, been able to produce independent dates for timber structures (roofs, doors and so on) which form an integral part of these buildings. Over the next decade or so, detailed new chronological sequences, in particular those obtained from roofs, should revolutionise our understanding of exactly when many of our cathedrals were built. At the moment, for example, we cannot give a precise date for the construction of the spire of Salisbury cathedral. All we can do is admit that any date between the end of the thirteenth century and about 1340 is possible. When dendrochronology is applied to the original timber scaffolding within the spire, we should get much closer to the real date.

In studying cathedral archaeology we must bring together the very many different strands that bridge the infamous arts/sciences divide. I have already mentioned structural analyses and dendrochronology on the one hand, and documentary history and art history on the other. We should not forget, however, that a cathedral was a place occupied and used by people (in particular bishops, monks and canons) and that a detailed knowledge of history (both national and local) is also required if the buildings are to be put into their context. The new Salisbury cathedral is very much a product of the thirteenth century in England, just as St Paul's cathedral is a product of seventeenth-century London or Liverpool's Roman Catholic cathedral is of the nineteen sixties. Even more important, perhaps, is a knowledge of pre-Reformation liturgy, and particularly of liturgical topography. The original positions of long-vanished shrines, or of much-moved choir stalls (as at Ely or Worcester), are of great significance. Many small clues to earlier furnishings can still be discovered even today in the architecture, particularly on the floors (if these have not themselves been removed). For example, it is still possible to see on the piers of the crossing area in Canterbury cathedral the ghost of the mouldings of the fifteenth-century rood-loft, and the place where a censor was fixed to a wall and swung. In many cathedrals, stone piscinas (basins for washing the chalice) and sedilia (seats for the priests) survive, but few people realise what they were for, or that they mark the site of a now-vanished altar.

Once a cathedral had been built it would have been profusely decorated with stained glass, sculpture and wall-paintings. At the Reformation, and again during the Cromwellian period a century later, such decoration was considered heretical and idolatrous, and was widely destroyed (a small amount only was covered up). Furnishings and fixtures, by and large, lie outside the scope of this book, but one fitting must be mentioned here: the bishop's throne or cathedra, for it is this one object which differentiates a cathedral from any other large church. The sheer size of the building alone does not make a cathedral: vast structures like Peterborough abbey or St Peter's abbey, Gloucester only became cathedrals at the Reformation, long after they had been built, while some of the Welsh and Scottish cathedrals are only the size of a large parish church.

In most cathedrals the bishop's throne is to be found on the south-east side of the choir, and usually consists of a very grandiose stall. However, nearly all of them are relatively modern; only rarely does an ancient throne or stall survive.

Anglo-Saxon thrones, not surprisingly, are rarest of all, and the complete 'Frithstool' in Hexham abbey is a unique survival. Elsewhere we are lucky even to have a broken fragment, as in Norwich. Surviving bishops' thrones are uncommon, even after the Norman conquest — two splendid exceptions are the early-thirteenth-century marble chair for the archbishop at Canterbury cathedral and the huge timber throne, with its 60–foot high, elaborately decorated canopy, at Exeter cathedral. This was built in 1312. There is another fine throne on the south side of the presbytery of Durham

The 'Frithstool' in Hexham abbey.

cathedral which has two pairs of seats for the bishop's chaplains on either side; the whole structure is built in a gallery above the chantry of Bishop Thomas de Hatfield (1345–81) whose alabaster effigy can still be seen on his tomb immediately underneath the throne. Finally, St David's cathedral in Wales boasts a fifteenth-century throne, also with chaplain's seat. Its canopy is 30 feet high, and it is no doubt based on the Exeter throne. Elsewhere there is a dearth of thrones in which any mediaeval work has survived intact.

In this book I shall be dealing only with buildings that were cathedrals. This allows me to refer to Glastonbury abbey during the brief period that it was added to Wells as the bishop's see, and means that Henry VIII's six new cathedrals (Westminster, Oxford, Chester, Gloucester, Bristol and Peterborough), although older buildings, are not discussed until chapter 7 which deals with post-Reformation events. In the first chapter, however, I have tried to bring together all that is known about all the Anglo-Saxon cathedrals, many of which were in places that were later abandoned as the bishop's see.

The greater part of this account covers the period 1070 to 1530 and is dealt with in chapters 2 to 5. Here I have concentrated on looking at how the cathedrals were built, drawing in particular on new evidence about the fabric. Many general books have already been written about cathedrals; worthy of especial mention are the descriptions of cathedrals by Sir Nikolaus Pevsner (and his collaborators) in *The Buildings of England* series which remain unsurpassed. My contribution will, I hope, fit in with these, and will show that the study of cathedrals is moving forward into a new era.

One point should not be forgotten when looking at a cathedral built in the Middle Ages: it was at the time of its construction only the most important building of many standing within a complex. There were broadly two kinds of cathedral foundations – secular and monastic. Although I shall be dealing only with the cathedrals themselves, even in this context the difference between the two is often important. In a monastic foundation, the bishop – or archbishop at Canterbury – was also the abbot of a monastery; his second-in-command, the prior, effectively ruled the monastery, hence the term 'cathedral priory'. From the later tenth century until the middle of the twelfth century, these bishops were often monks themselves. After this, however, they tended to be royal nominees with little interest in monastic life, and as a result were often in dispute with their monks. Henry VIII finally put an end to this anomalous, and uniquely English, situation in 1539–40 when he dissolved cathedral priories and replaced them with 'new foundations' of deans and canons.

The 'secular' cathedrals (after the time of Henry VIII, called the 'old foundations') consisted of a group of canons under a dean (called collectively the chapter), who followed no monastic rule. Each owned a house and garden in the

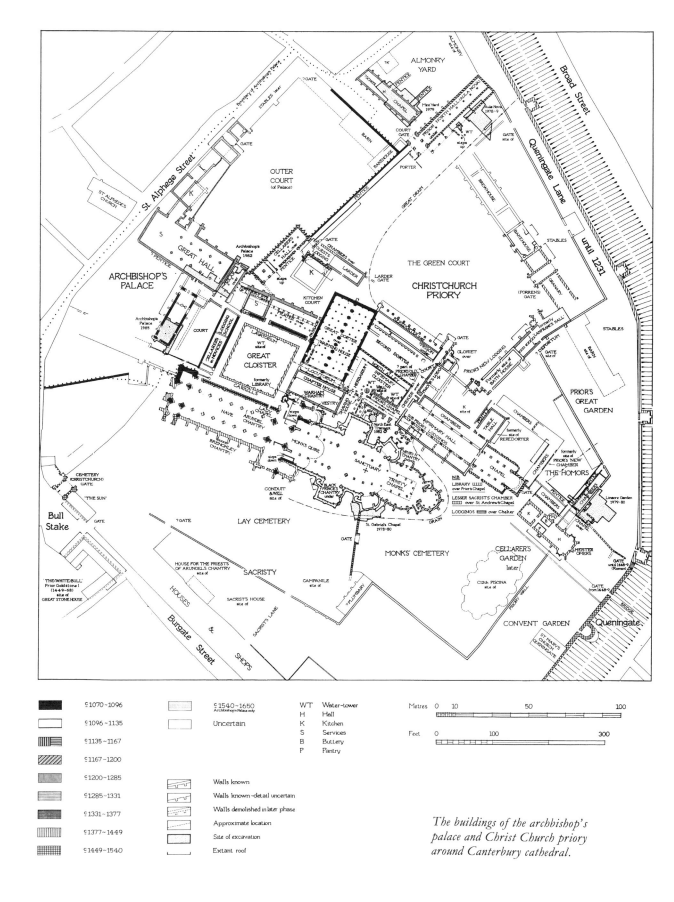

The buildings of the archbishop's palace and Christ Church priory around Canterbury cathedral.

close (the walled-in area around the cathedral) as well as having a 'prebend', that is a rural estate, to provide an income. Besides the dean, canons filled the posts of precentor, chancellor, treasurer, sub-dean and succentor, and the archdeacons of the diocese were also canons. The number depended on the size of the diocese – for example, there were only four archdeacons in Salisbury diocese, but seven in the huge diocese of Lincoln. By the thirteenth century, however, the richest cathedrals had endowed large numbers of canonries, many of which were non-residential and were given to royal servants. In the fourteenth century, canonries were frequently given to foreign church dignitaries (often cardinals) to supplement their income. This deprived the cathedral chapter of both a residential canon and his prebendal income. Many individual canon's houses survive within the grand seventeenth- and eighteenth-century houses in the cathedral closes of Salisbury, Wells and other places. In addition, there was a communal meeting place called the chapter house; in the later mediaeval period, this was connected to the cathedral by a large, often free-standing, cloister.

In the monastic cathedrals the cloister was at the heart of a complex of monastic buildings, of which the most important were the chapter house, dormitory and refectory. In a huge monastic cathedral like Canterbury, which had 150 monks by the twelfth century, there were two cloisters and the area of the monks' buildings covered well over twice the area of the cathedral itself. In fact, almost the whole area to the north of the cathedral was, until the Dissolution, covered by roofed buildings, the biggest of which was the vast great hall complex of the archbishop's palace, over 200 feet long. The story of how all these buildings, and those relating to the secular cathedrals, evolved would make another book.

A final word about the layout of the cathedral itself. As we shall see, the form of the earliest cathedrals, those of the Anglo-Saxon era, is still only now being re-discovered. The vast new cathedrals which were built all over England after the Norman conquest (and later in Scotland and Wales as well), however, although totally differing in detail from each other, had a common basic layout.

First there is the nave, which usually had aisles on either side (though not at the Norman York minster). In the earlier Norman cathedrals the area to the east of the nave, the presbytery or sanctuary, was often quite short, and the choir – that is, the place where the monks or canons sang the daily services – was often situated at the east end of the nave or under the crossing tower. On either side of the crossing, transepts were invariably built, many of them being likewise large aisled structures. By the end of the eleventh century, some immensely long naves, such as those at Winchester and Norwich, were being built, and at the same time large new eastern extensions had started to evolve: the biggest of these was the 'glorious choir' at Canterbury, as a contemporary described it. These eastern arms served not only as the place for the choir and

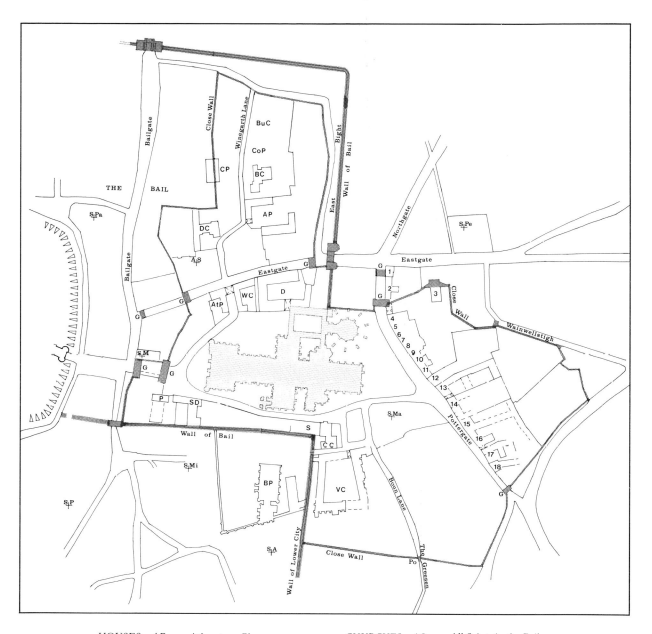

HOUSES	AP	Atherstone Place	CHURCHES	AS	All Saints in the Bail
	At P	Atton Place		SA	St Andrew
	BC	Burghersh Chantry		SMa	St Margaret in the Close
	BP	Bishop's Palace		SM	St Mary Magdalene
	Bu C	Burton Chantry (Burton Place)		SMi	St Michael
	CC	Cantilupe Chantry		SPa	St Paul in the Bail
	C	Chancery		SPe	St Peter in Eastgate
	Co P	Colby Place		SP	St Peter ad Vincula
	CP	Cottesford Place			(Stanthaket)
	D	Deanery			
	DC	Deloraine Court			
	P	Precentory			
	S	Sacrist's House			
	SD	Subdeanery			
	VC	Vicars' Court			
	WC	Works Chantry			

The close at Lincoln showing houses, walls, and gates.

sanctuary, but also as the site for many altars and shrines. By the thirteenth century many cathedrals were building large new presbyteries east of the choir to house a principal shrine; again, the most famous was that of St Thomas Becket at Canterbury. At the same time, there was a great increase in importance of the cult of the Blessed Virgin Mary, and the extreme east end of a cathedral usually acquired a magnificent new Lady Chapel. Exceptionally, at Ely, the Lady Chapel was a separate building on the north-east side of the cathedral, while at Canterbury (and later at Glasgow) it was in the vast crypt. Very unusually, at Durham, it was at the west end of the nave in what was known as the 'Galilee' – normally, as at Ely and Lincoln, a western porch used in the Sunday processions, which symbolised Christ going before the disciples into Galilee.

At the west end of the canons' or monks' choir, there was often a large stone screen, called the pulpitum, with a large central doorway and a gallery above it. Only much later, if ever, was this used for preaching (hence the post-Reformation word 'pulpit'). Further west again was a second, much thinner screen called the rood-screen. This had a nave altar on its western side flanked by a pair of doorways. Above it, on a beam or small loft, was the great rood – a large crucifix with the figures of the Virgin and St John below. These screens were usually destroyed at the Reformation, though the beautiful iron screen (but not the rood itself) survived at Canterbury until the eighteenth century. The pulpitum screen, however, has frequently survived and today often houses the cathedral's great organ case. East of the choir stalls was the presbytery and

Plans of Ely cathedral as it was in the early sixteenth century (below) showing the mediaeval liturgical topography, and as it is today (right) after G.G. Scott's mid-nineteenth-century reorganisation.

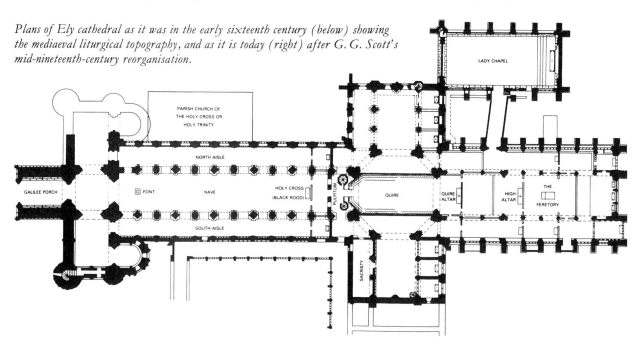

retrochoir. The high altar, often flanked by important tombs, stood at the centre of the former, while the retrochoir was usually the place that housed the cathedral's major shrine. It was separated from the presbytery by another screen, like the superb Neville screen in Durham cathedral, and was sometimes surrounded by an ambulatory for processions and to allow pilgrims to approach the shrine.

Very often these arrangements are not clear today because of the destructions which took place at the Reformation or during nineteenth-century refurnishings, and much detective work, using archaeological evidence, early drawings and, above all, the architecture of the building itself, is often required before the original liturgical plan and the position of shrines can be understood. At Winchester, for example, the wonderful eastern arm has a very clear presbytery and retrochoir on plan. The mediaeval shrine of St Swithin has, of course, been completely destroyed, but the four vast chantry chapels, still surviving, which were placed around it in the later Middle Ages indicate how sacred the area was. To the average visitor, however, this is a confusing site, despite the restoration of a modern 'shrine' to St Swithin, and scholars themselves are still trying to determine the exact position of the shrine between 1093 and the fifteenth century. The eastern arm of Canterbury cathedral was, until recently, equally hard to understand because the archbishop's marble throne, which had stood at the highest point of the extreme eastern end of the sanctuary, was removed in 1825 and replaced by a large high altar and reredos. Immediately east of this was the

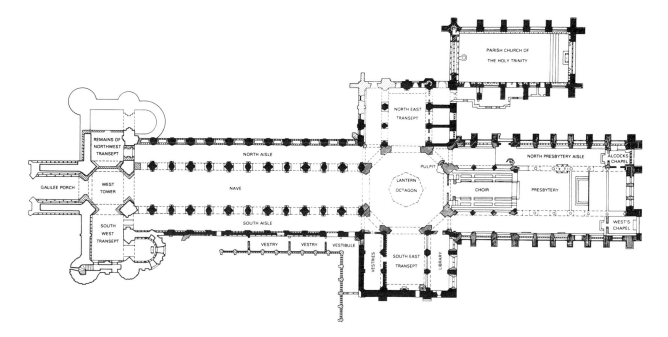

unique horseshoe-shaped Trinity Chapel which contained, until 1538, the shrine of St Thomas Becket and served as the retrochoir. In the mediaeval cathedral the high altar had been sited at a lower level further west, with the archbishop's throne above it on the central axis of the cathedral. Such a position for the cathedra was common in the early Middle Ages, and luckily in 1977 the dean and chapter decided to put the throne back in its original position. The wisdom of this decision has been fully vindicated on those occasions when the cathedral has been filled with bishops for enthronements and the Lambeth Conference services.

We should not forget that the cathedrals of Britain (except for a few ruins in Scotland) are still places of worship that are continuing to evolve. For example, Sunday Eucharist is often held around a new altar in the nave. As long as these new forms of worship fit in with the ancient architecture no harm can be done. However, no dean and chapter can overlook the need to study the architectural and liturgical topography of the past so that they understand the great buildings in their charge and avoid the disastrous 'improvements' of the past, when ancient furnishings and fittings were stripped out and replaced with over-confident 'modern' fittings in the 'wrong' place. Whatever the mitigating circumstances, the re-ordering of Salisbury cathedral and the re-building of the west end of Hereford cathedral in the late eighteenth century, or the demolition of the north-west tower at Canterbury cathedral in 1832, must represent the lowest point in the hazardous history of our cathedrals. Thanks to the work of Professor Robert Willis and of the architectural historians and archaeologists who are his successors, we have turned the corner. The study of cathedral archaeology is today an exciting and flourishing discipline as modern work reveals more and more of the extraordinary technological brilliance, as well as the artistic achievements, of the men who planned and made our cathedrals, surely the finest works of architecture ever built in Britain.

AUGUSTINE TO DUNSTAN

The Anglo-Saxon cathedrals

In [596], Gregory was inspired by God to send his servant Augustine with several other
God-fearing monks to preach the word of God to the English nation.

> Bede, *Ecclesiastical History of the English People* I,23

Having been granted his episcopal see in the royal capital [Canterbury], as already recorded, Augustine proceeded with the king's help to repair a church which he was informed had been built long ago by Roman Christians. This he hallowed in the Name of our Saviour, God, and Lord Jesus Christ, and established there a dwelling for himself and his successors.

> Bede I,33

In the spring of 596 a small party of about forty monks under the leadership of Augustine, prior of the monastery of St Andrew on the Coelian Hill, left Rome to go to England to re-establish Christianity. This daring scheme had long been in the mind of the pope, Gregory the Great, but it was by no means an easy mission. Gregory had wanted to undertake the mission himself, but as pope this was impossible, so he sent his companion, Augustine. After the Roman armies had left Britain about a century and a half before, eastern Britain had been invaded by pagan tribes (largely Angles and Saxons from Denmark and western Germany) and all forms of Christianity, which had probably been widespread in Roman Britain, had been driven westwards to Wales and the West Country, spreading from there into Ireland.

Augustine and his companions probably took a ship from Ostia to Provence. At an early stage they appear to have got cold feet at undertaking their perilous journey through France. Bede, the great historian, writing in the eighth century, who tells us almost all we know of this period, informs us that they 'were appalled at the idea of going to a barbarous, fierce and pagan nation, of whose very language they were ignorant'. They therefore sent Augustine back to Rome to try to persuade Gregory to call off the whole undertaking.

The pope, however, would have none of it. He appointed Augustine 'abbot' of the group and sent them a letter of encouragement as well as writing other letters, copies of which remarkably still survive, to bishops and local leaders in Gaul asking them to help and support the party in their journey. We can imagine the band of monks in the summer and autumn of 596 moving up the Rhône valley from Arles to Lyon and then on to Tours before proceeding northwards to the Channel coast, encouraged on their way by the local Christian communities.

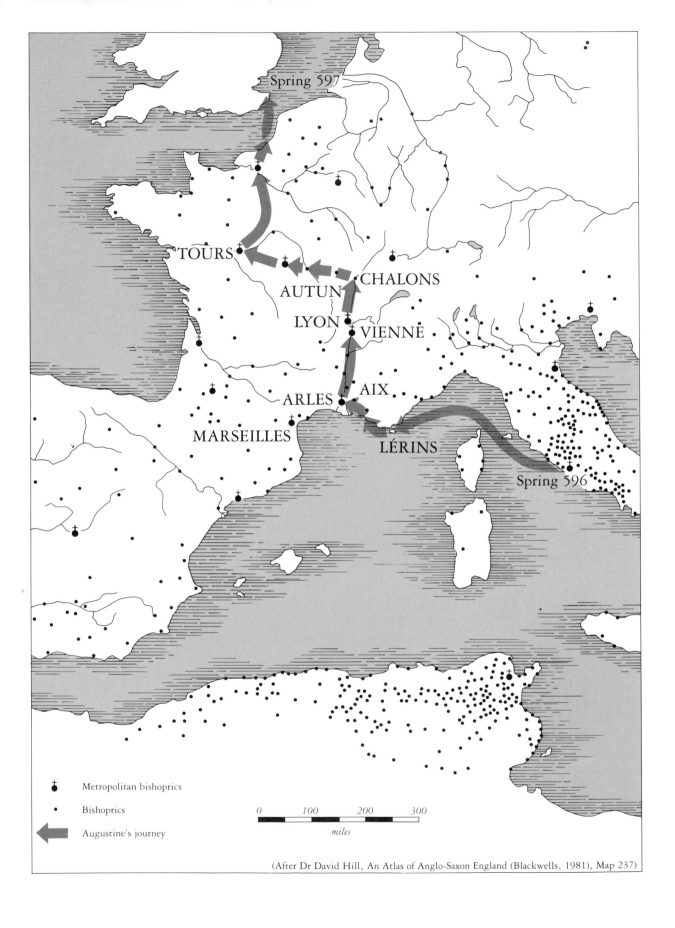

Spring 597

TOURS

CHALONS

AUTUN

LYON VIENNE

ARLES AIX

MARSEILLES

LÉRINS

Spring 596

✝●   Metropolitan bishoprics

•   Bishoprics

⬅   Augustine's journey

0   100   200   300

miles

(After Dr David Hill, *An Atlas of Anglo-Saxon England* (Blackwells, 1981), Map 237)

The bishoprics in Western Europe in the late sixth century, and the probable route of Augustine and his companions in 597.

The Anglo-Saxon cathedrals

21

Particularly important to them were the local bishops of the Frankish Church who sent priests with the group to act as interpreters.

At this time there were large numbers of bishops in Italy and north Africa (one in every town), and they in turn looked to the metropolitan bishops (only later called archbishops) as their superiors, with the pope as ultimate head. In France there were also bishops in most of the urban centres (Roman towns which by now had mostly declined to small towns) with a handful of metropolitan bishops at places like Arles, Vienne, Lyon and Tours. Bede tells us that Augustine was consecrated by 'Archbishop Aetherius of Arles' only a few years after his arrival in Kent, but this is probably a mistake. A surviving letter of Pope Gregory indicates that Augustine had been consecrated bishop with the pope's permission by the 'bishops of the Germanies'. This ceremony perhaps took place in northern France under the metropolitan bishop of Rheims, as there was no christianity surviving in the areas of the old Roman provinces of *Germania prima* and *secunda* along the Rhine.

In the following spring Augustine and his companions crossed the Channel and landed on the south side of the Isle of Thanet in north-east Kent. A few days later Augustine had a meeting with Aethelberht, the King of Kent, and after a short time the monks were allowed to cross to the mainland and were given a dwelling place in the city of Canterbury, which Bede calls the chief city of all Aethelberht's kingdom. England at this time was divided into a whole series of small kingdoms: Kent, Essex, East Anglia, Sussex, Wessex, Mercia and Northumbria. At Canterbury they were allowed to preach and before long had started to make some converts.

Outside the eastern walls of the city of Canterbury was an old church, dedicated to St Martin, which Bede says was built 'during the Roman occupation of Britain'. It was already being used by Bertha, the Christian wife of King Aethelberht, who belonged to the Christianised Frankish royal house in Paris. She had with her a priest, called Bishop Liudhard, and they were the only Christians in Kent at the time. It was at St Martin's that the little band first gathered to 'sing the psalms, to pray, to say Mass, to preach and to baptise'. This little church was therefore to become the first church in England since the Roman period to hold a bishop's seat or cathedra, and as such we can perhaps call St Martin's church a 'proto-cathedral'.

Quite remarkably, the church of St Martin's still survives to this day just outside Canterbury, and many traces of very early work can still be found in its walls. The western part of the chancel is made almost entirely of Roman bricks and on the south side there remains an original flat-headed doorway (now blocked) which would have led into a small room. This part of the church may well have been built in the Roman period (perhaps the later fourth century),

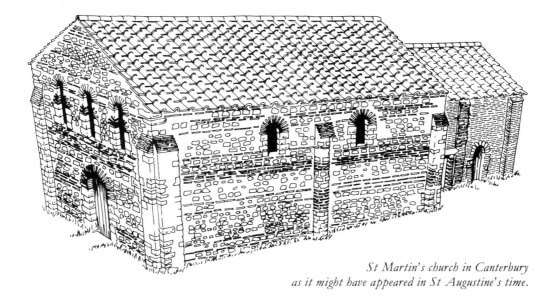

*St Martin's church in Canterbury
as it might have appeared in St Augustine's time.*

though it would be difficult to prove this without further excavation. Even more remarkable, however, is the surviving nave. Here we have all the walls, standing to their full height, of a structure that has been added to the chancel. At the outside corners of the nave were small pilaster buttresses, mostly made of blocks of a very unusual stone (called ditrupa limestone) that was almost certainly quarried in the area north of Paris. The walls themselves, which contain two original windows at the west end (now blocked), are full of re-used materials with irregular string-courses of re-used Roman brick. They are built in a way that closely parallels very late Roman work in Italy. Is it possible that we are still looking at the nave of St Martin's church which was built by Augustine and his followers? The limestone may have been sent by the Frankish royal family at Bertha's request, while the masons were the monks themselves who re-used the local Roman materials and building in the way they had done in Rome.

After a few years, King Aethelberht himself was converted and baptised, and as a result many other people in his kingdom were baptised as well. Bede tells us that Augustine then 'proceeded with the king's help to repair a church which he was informed had been built long ago by Roman Christians'. He was then 'established there with a dwelling for himself and his successors'. This was to be the first true cathedral at Canterbury, and from this time onwards the metropolitan bishop of Canterbury, which Augustine was soon to become, would keep his cathedra in this church.

Nothing of the Anglo-Saxon cathedral survives above ground at Canterbury cathedral today: all that we see now in that magnificent building was constructed between 1070 and 1500. In 1979–80, however, archaeological trenches were cut around the western and southern sides of the crypt chapel of St Gabriel before 'damp-proofing' for this part of the crypt was carried out. The area was found to contain a large Roman red tessellated pavement with a square mosaic panel having a blue and white chequer pattern at its centre. Associated finds suggested that this building may in origin have been a Roman temple. It is quite possible that after Christianity became the official religion of the Roman Empire in the late fourth century it then became a Christian church.

Could this building be part of the Roman church restored by Augustine to be his cathedral? Only further excavation in the area will answer this, though archaeology has already recovered for us the plan of the remarkable monastery church begun by Augustine just outside the city walls, dedicated to Saints Peter and Paul. That building, which was not completed until after Augustine's death

The pallium as worn by an archbishop.

was also to become the royal and archiepiscopal mausoleum, and the tombs of Augustine's three immediate successors as Archbishops of Canterbury, Laurence (died 619), Mellitus (died 624) and Justus (died c.630) can still be seen in the northern porticus of this church. Unfortunately, Augustine's own tomb was destroyed in the 1090s when the Norman abbey church was built, as were those of King Aethelberht, Queen Bertha and Bishop Liudhard in the southern porticus.

Pope Gregory the Great intended to establish in Britain a Christian church based on his knowledge of the old Romano-British Province; no doubt he was able to consult old documents and maps in Rome. In a letter sent to Augustine in 601, accompanying the pallium, the double Y-shaped band worn over all vestments, that made Augustine a metropolitan bishop, he outlined his plan:

You are to consecrate twelve bishops in different places, who will be subject to your jurisdiction: the bishop of the city of London will thenceforward be consecrated by his own synod, and will receive the honour of the *pallium* from this apostolic See which, by divine decree, we at present occupy. We wish you also to send a bishop of your own choice to the city of York, and if that city with the adjoining territory accepts the word of God, this bishop is to consecrate twelve other bishops, and hold the dignity of metropolitan. If we live to see this, we intend to grant him the *pallium* also, but he is to remain subject to your authority. After your death, however, he is to preside over the bishops whom he has consecrated and to be wholly independent of the Bishop of London. Thenceforward seniority of consecration is to determine whether the bishop of London or York takes precedence.

Bede I,29

23

Late Roman Britain had consisted of two provinces, *Britannia prima* and *Britannia secunda* with London and York as their capitals. Later these were subdivided to make four, then five provinces. In addition there had been about twenty-six walled towns each of which had probably had its own bishop in the fourth century. However, Gregory clearly did not know that the Anglo-Saxons were a totally non-urban people and that all the old Roman towns were in ruins. Nevertheless a few years later, in 604, a second Kentish see was established in a church dedicated to St Andrew at Rochester, and more importantly a church dedicated to St Paul was created in London for the East Saxons. Bede tells us that both churches were built by King Aethelberht, and that Augustine consecrated Mellitus and Justus, who had arrived from Rome in 601, bishops in London and Rochester respectively. No further bishops were to be created for over twenty years.

In the autumn of 1888, when holes were being dug immediately outside the west front of Rochester cathedral to underpin it, some remarkable discoveries were made. These were carefully recorded for us by Greville Livett, a minor canon and precentor of the cathedral. The west front dates from the middle of the twelfth century, but underlying it Livett saw the remains of the earlier and much plainer Norman west front. He describes his find:

Running under and through the foundations were discovered the foundations, and portions of the walls, of a building of much earlier date than the earliest of the Norman works. These older foundations underlie the northern half of the present west front ... They doubtless form part of the Saxon church.

Archaeologia Cantiana XVIII (1889), 261–2

Livett was able to record parts of an apse and the beginnings of the walls running westwards of the nave of a small church. Roman bricks had been re-used in the walls and the general plan of the building was similar to other seventh-century churches in east Kent, both at St Augustine's abbey in Canterbury and at Reculver and Lyminge where early monasteries were built. Later 'excavation and probing' done by Livett in the summer of 1894 revealed that the internal measurements of the nave of the church were 42 feet long by 28 feet wide, and it seems very likely that this is the original cathedral church of St Andrew. The position of these walls was subsequently marked out on the ground and can still be seen.

Bede mentions that when Bishop Paulinus (whom we shall meet again shortly) died in 644 he was buried in the 'sacristry' of the church while his successor Ithamar (644–c.655), the first native Kentish bishop, was buried 'in the body of his church'. About seventy years later, Bishop Tobias (692–726) was buried in the '*porticus* of St Paul' in this church. All of this suggests other additional parts to the building, but at present we only have the tantalising evidence for other walls and burials approximately recorded in the surrounding

✝ Carlisle

Aldborough ✝
✝ York

✝ Chester ✝ Lincoln

✝ Wroxeter ✝ Leicester ✝ Caister
✝
Water Newton

✝ ?Carmarthen ✝ Gloucester ✝ Colchester
✝ Cirencester ✝ St. Albans
Caeleon ✝ London
✝ Dorchester ✝
Bath ✝ Silchester ✝ Rochester ✝
✝ Canterbury
✝ Ilchester ✝ Winchester
Dorchester ✝ Chichester
Exeter ✝ ✝

0   50   100

miles

area. One day major excavations inside and outside the west front of Rochester cathedral will have much to tell us.

In London nothing has been found of the original church of St Paul built for the new diocese of the East Saxons in 604, and much of the archaeological remains of this church were probably destroyed by the great crypts of both the mediaeval and baroque cathedrals. There is, however, an area on the south side of Wren's great church (now a garden) which contains the foundations of the mediaeval chapter house and part of the cloister, and we might expect to find parts of the early building under here. Early maps of the city suggest that the original church of St Paul was on the south side of the mediaeval cathedral in the centre of a line of early Anglo-Saxon churches dedicated to St Martin (on Ludgate Hill), St Gregory, St Paul and St Augustine. The later mediaeval churches on these sites, which may still have contained some Anglo-Saxon work, survived until the Great Fire of London in 1666.

When King Aethelberht died in 616, Christianity had not advanced very far into England and for a short time it looked as though it would be snuffed out altogether. Bishop Mellitus was driven out of London and, with Justus of Rochester, fled to France, while Laurence of Canterbury, Bede tells us, was only stopped from following them by a vision of St Peter. In Kent this was only a temporary setback. Eadbald, the pagan son of Aethelberht and Bertha, was soon converted and Justus returned to Rochester. The East Saxon see, however, was to remain vacant for nearly forty years; as a result Mellitus succeeded to Canterbury and London never became the metropolitan cathedral that Gregory had planned.

The next great step in the establishment of the English church came about when Aethelburgh, the Christian daughter of Aethelberht of Kent, married Edwin, King of Northumbria in 625. She took north with her the monk Paulinus who had just been consecrated bishop by Justus of Canterbury. Bede's history of these events devotes several chapters to the story of the conversion of Northumbria which reached a climax in 627, when on the eve of Easter, Edwin:

with all the nobility of his kingdom and a large number of humbler folk, accepted the Faith and were washed with the cleansing waters of baptism.

Bede II, 14

Bede also specifically tells us that for this baptism the king 'hastily built of timber' a church dedicated to St Peter the apostle, and that soon after:

at Paulinus' suggestion, he gave orders to build on the same site a larger and more noble basilica of stone, which was to enclose the little oratory he had built before. The foundations were laid, and the walls of a square church began to rise around this little oratory; but before they reached their appointed height, the cruel death of the king left the work to be completed by Oswald his successor.

Bede II, 14

Here we have a splendid description of what was to become the first Anglo-Saxon cathedral in the north, and it is sad that all the excavation work that was carried out underneath York minster in 1967–73 (see chapter 2) failed to locate any trace of it. Bede's description suggests that the first building (the timber one) was a baptistery, so it might reasonably be expected to have had within it a large font (at this time a tank set into the floor). To date, only one font of this type has been found in England, at Richborough, Kent where there are remains of a hexagonal tank near a timber church in the north-west corner of the Roman fort. This must be a baptismal font. Many other early fonts in England no doubt await discovery (there would certainly have been one in the baptistery church of St John the Baptist built in c.750 just to the east of the early Canterbury cathedral), but the nearest examples that we can turn to at present are in Germany at Cologne and Boppard, where fine octagonal and heptagonal baptistry tanks have been identified in the last few decades.

27

The baptistery at York was hastily erected, we are told, and it is possible that this structure was in the courtyard of the Roman legionary headquarters building which lay to the south of the present minster. The 1967–73 excavations did find that parts at least of the Roman headquarters building, lying under the crossing and south transept of the present minster (now to be seen in the undercroft museum), were still standing at the end of the eighth century. Edwin's 'noble basilica of stone' may therefore have been a reconstruction of the Roman building.

Bede goes on to tell us that:

Paulinus also preached the word of God to the province of Lindsey, which lies immediately south of the Humber, and extends to the sea. His first convert was Blaecca, 'Prefect' of the City of Lincoln, with all his family. In this city he also built a stone church of fine workmanship, which today [i.e. in c.730], either through neglect or enemy damage, has lost its roof, although the walls are still standing ... It was in this church that Paulinus consecrated Honorius as bishop [of Canterbury].

Bede II, 16

Recent excavations on the site of the church of St Paul-in-the-Bail which lies in the very centre of the upper city of Lincoln, a few hundred yards north-west of the present Lincoln minster, have given us some tantalising new evidence of this building. In 1978–9 an early church was discovered in the middle of what had been the forum of the Roman city. The walls of this church had been completely robbed out, but the foundation trenches showed that it was very similar in plan to the seventh-century church at Rochester, having a simple rectangular nave with an apsidal chancel. At the east end in the centre of the nave of this church was a stone-lined grave. Although the body itself had been removed at a subsequent date, a magnificent seventh-century bronze 'hanging

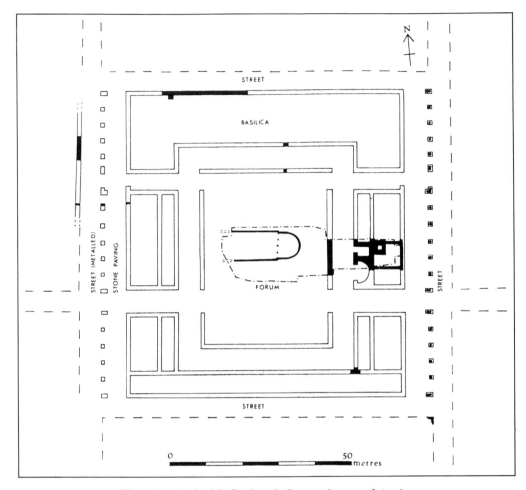

The early church of St Paul in the Roman forum at Lincoln.

bowl' had been accidentally left in the corner. It had some very fine decorative attachments, probably used to suspend it from the ceiling, as well as some beautiful enamel discs on the inside and outside of the base set with an elaborate decoration of millefiori glass rods. Three similar hanging bowls were found in the famous Sutton Hoo ship burial of c.625, which we know to have been that of an Anglo-Saxon king, and this very splendid object suggests that some important person was buried here in the centre of the church. Possibly his body was taken away at a later date, when the area was being raided by the Vikings. More problematical for the archaeologist are the remains of an early Christian cemetery found around the church. Recent Carbon 14 dating of some of the burials has thrown up the possibility that the church is even earlier than the seventh century, perhaps of late Roman date. Once again the archaeological excavations seem to have posed more questions than they can answer. However there still remains, in my view, a strong possibility that we are looking at the remains of Paulinus' church of c.628–9. Was the person buried in the centre of the church Blaecca, the Prefect of the City of Lincoln mentioned by Bede?

We do not yet have firm evidence to prove that Lincoln was a bishop's seat at this time. However, the fact that Paulinus consecrated Honorius to the vacant see of Canterbury here strongly suggests that it was, and we may assume that Paulinus was acting as a bishop both in Northumbria and in Lindsey (the Anglo-Saxon name for the region around Lincoln).

A few years later, in 632, all Paulinus' hard work was brought to a halt when King Edwin was killed in battle and Northumbria was devastated by King Cadwallon and a pagan Mercian army. Paulinus escaped to Kent, where he was appointed to the vacant see of Rochester. Of the Roman mission, only Paulinus' deacon, called James, remained behind in the north, and the new churches at York and Lincoln were left for many years without bishops (York till c.664 and Lincoln till c.677). Yet within two years there was a new bishop in Northumbria, Aidan.

Events in the aftermath of Edwin's death moved rapidly, so Bede informs us. Cadwallon was himself overthrown only about a year later, and in 633 Oswald, who came from Bernicia in the northern part of the kingdom, became King of Northumbria. He was a Christian, but had been converted by the monks of Iona, 'the chief of all the monasteries of the northern Irish and of all the monasteries of the Picts,' and once he was established as king, he sent to Iona for a bishop from the Celtic Church. The Celtic Church, which had sprung from the last remnants of Romano-British Christianity, had been driven into the west (particularly Ireland) in the fifth century when England was being overrun by the pagan Anglo-Saxons. In its isolated geographical position it had little contact with Rome. Before the close of 634 a group of Celtic monks under a man called Aidan had travelled south-eastwards to found a new monastery on the tiny island of Lindisfarne off the extreme northern coast of Northumbria. Over the next two decades Aidan and his fellow Celtic monks re-established their form of Christianity throughout the north of England. The Celtic bishops were ascetic evangelists who travelled around preaching both to the rulers and the ordinary people, and unlike the Roman church there was no tradition of their having cathedra in town churches, so that Northumbria (and Scotland and Ireland) can be considered as being without cathedrals at this time. We know that when Aidan came to Lindisfarne he did not even bother to build a church suitable for his seat.

Ultimately there was bound to be conflict with the Roman Church as the two groups were so different. Things came to a head in 663–4 at the Synod of Whitby when there was great disagreement over calculating the date of Easter. After much discussion King Oswiu of Northumbria ruled in favour of the Roman

NORTHERN
✝ Iona
IRISH

PICTS

Aidan 634

IRISH
CHURCH

NORTHUMBRIA

Lindisfarne ✝

✝ York

Bangor ✝   ✝ St Asaph
GWYNEDD

Lincoln ✝
LINDSEY

MERCIA

EAST
ANGLES

POWYS

MIDDLE
ANGLES

Dommoc ✝

✝ St Davids

DYFED

MIDDLE
SAXONS

EAST
SAXONS

BRITISH CHURCH

Llandaff
✝

Dorchester ✝

London ✝
Rochester ✝

WEST
SAXONS

Canterbury ✝
KENT

DUMNONIA

SOUTH SAXONS

Augustine
from France
597

0   50   100
miles

party. As a result, many Celtic monks, including the bishop of Lindisfarne, left Northumbria and returned to Iona.

During the period of the Celtic ascendancy in Northumbria, the church in southern England had rather stagnated under two obscure bishops at Canterbury, Honorius (c.627–652) and Deusdedit (655–663). Even the diocese of the East Saxons was under a bishop, Cedd, brought up in the Celtic tradition. However, two new bishoprics had been created for the East Angles and the West Saxons under the authority of Canterbury.

In about 630, Sigeberht, the King of East Anglia who was a Christian (he had been baptised in Gaul as an exile) asked for a bishop for his kingdom from Honorius who responded by sending him a Burgundian bishop called Felix, then in Kent. Bede tells us that Felix established his seat at Dommoc and ruled this diocese for seventeen years. Unfortunately we will never know for certain where Dommoc was. There are two possible sites – Dunwich and Walton castle at Old Felixstowe (Felixstowe means Felix's holy place or church). However, both sites, on the vulnerable Suffolk coast that is under constant erosion by the North Sea, have been totally destroyed.

The second new diocese was founded for a man called Bishop Birinus. He had been sent from Rome by the pope and was consecrated at Genoa by the metropolitan bishop of Milan before reaching England in 635 when he was given the old Roman town of Dorchester-on-Thames for his see. This West Saxon town, close to the boundary between Wessex and Mercia, was probably the place where Cynigils, King of Wessex, was baptised in the presence of King Oswald of Northumbria: we are told by Bede that both kings jointly gave Birinus the town. According to Bede, Birinus built and dedicated several churches there, but no archaeological evidence has yet been found for any of these churches, despite quite extensive areas of excavation in the southern and north-western parts of the old Roman town which uncovered seventh-century Anglo-Saxon timber buildings. The area around the later abbey and parish church, which, as we will see, was possibly the late Anglo-Saxon cathedral, in the eastern part of the town is, however, the most likely site of Birinus' cathedral as well.

Birinus died and was buried in Dorchester in about 650. In around 690 his relics were moved to Winchester, which had become the premier cathedral in Wessex. King Cenwalh of Wessex had first built a church in Winchester in about 648 'and consecrated it in St Peter's name' according to the Anglo-Saxon Chronicle. This building, probably at the core of the later Anglo-Saxon cathedral and mostly excavated by Martin and Birthe Biddle in 1962–9, at this time was most likely only a royal chapel, and did not become a cathedral until c.660 when a second bishopric was created in Wessex, in addition to Dorchester, with Wine as bishop. How this came about is amusingly described by Bede:

When Cenwalh had been restored to his kingdom, there arrived in the province a bishop from Gaul named Agilbert, who had been studying the scriptures in Ireland for many years. This bishop came to the king and voluntarily undertook to evangelise the country. Appreciating his learning and enthusiasm, the king asked him to accept an episcopal see in the province as his chief bishop [i.e. at Dorchester in c.650]. Agilbert acceded to the king's request and presided as bishop for many years. Later, however, the king, who understood only Saxon, grew tired of the bishop's foreign speech, and invited to the province a bishop of his own tongue called Wine, who had also been consecrated in Gaul; and dividing his kingdom into two dioceses, he gave Wine the city of Venta, known by the Saxons as Wintancaestir, as his see. This action gravely offended Agilbert, as the king had not consulted him in the matter, and he returned to Gaul, where he became Bishop of Paris and ended his days there at an advanced age.

Bede III,7

Despite the success of the Roman party at the synod of Whitby in 664, the church in England was still in a very disorganised state. The turning point came when the pope appointed Theodore as archbishop of Canterbury in 668. From Tarsus (in the south of modern Turkey, famous as the city of the apostle Paul), came Theodore who was sixty-six years of age at this time and living in Rome as a monk, with a great reputation as a scholar, philosopher and divine. After a year long journey through France (including a stay with Bishop Agilbert in Paris), he arrived in Canterbury in May 669 and immediately began a visitation of the whole of his province. Wessex, Mercia, East Anglia and Rochester in Kent were all without bishops and Bishop Wine, who had recently been turned out of Wessex by King Cenwalh, had bought the bishopric of London from Wulfhere, King of Mercia, a gross act of simony. In Northumbria, both Wilfrid and Ceadda (or Chad as he was called later) were nominally bishops, Ceadda based in York and Wilfrid at his monastery of Ripon. Theodore immediately made Wilfrid bishop of York, and Ceadda bishop of Mercia, based for the first time in Lichfield. He then appointed new bishops at Rochester and Dunwich, and in 670 consecrated Hlothere, nephew of Bishop Agilbert, to the see of Winchester.

In 672 a general council of the whole English church met at Hertford, and here for the first time we see that the archbishop of Canterbury was the undoubted ruler of the church in England. Among many things that were discussed at the council was the provision of new dioceses particularly for the largest kingdoms of Mercia, East Anglia and Northumbria. In 672 there were only seven dioceses in England, but during the later 670s, new dioceses were created based on North Elmham in Norfolk, Lindsey (perhaps based again in Lincoln), and in the south-west of Mercia in the sub-kingdoms of the Hwicce and the Magonsaettan, based at Worcester and Hereford respectively. The vast eastern area of Mercia (originally the land of the Middle Angles) was given a diocese based on Leicester, though this did not become a permanent cathedral until 737, and Dorchester-on-Thames, which was now in southern Mercia, was revived as a diocese.

During this time, with Wilfrid as its powerful bishop, the huge area of Northumbria remained undivided. In 677, however, Wilfrid had fallen out with King Egfrid and was deprived of his see and expelled. Archbishop Theodore had to accept the *status quo*, and on visiting the area decided to divide the see. York became the cathedral for the southern sub-kingdom of Deira, while Eata, the prior of the monastery at Lindisfarne, was ordained bishop of Bernicia and allowed to choose to have his seat in either Lindisfarne or in Wilfrid's new monastery of Hexham. He chose Lindisfarne.

Meanwhile Wilfrid spent several years in travelling to Rome to appeal to the pope against his expulsion. Although he was successful there, the King of Northumbria would not accept him when he eventually returned to England in 680. Wilfrid was imprisoned for a time and then expelled once again. This indomitable man then travelled south through Middle Anglia and Wessex to find refuge with Ethelwalh the Christian King of the South Saxons. Isolated behind the great forest of the Weald, these peoples were the last completely pagan tribes in England and between 681 and 686 Wilfrid and his small band of followers gradually converted them. He received the estate of Selsey from the king and this island off the south-west Sussex coast was to become the site for the cathedral. In the meantime, some more dioceses had been created by Theodore in the extreme north, the first at Abercorn, near the modern Edinburgh, which was created for the Picts, who were now subject to Northumbria (this see only lasted until c.685). A second bishopric in Bernicia was created at Hexham and finally, a bishop in the Anglian monastery of Whithorn in Galloway, in the extreme south-west of Scotland, may have been created at this time. This area was also now under the control of the kings of Northumbria, though it did not receive a permanent bishop until 731.

When Archbishop Theodore died in 690, this exceptional administrator had created dioceses for the whole of England (only Sherborne, in 705, was to be added later). Finding on his arrival virtually no bishops in England, he had in two decades roughly created on the ground the system that Pope Gregory the Great had envisaged. There was, to be sure, only one metropolitan bishop, Theodore himself, and he was still based in Canterbury rather than London, but considering the difficulties he encountered his achievement was immense. Theodore, rather than Augustine, should perhaps really be credited with founding the church in England.

It is entirely due to Bede's famous *Ecclesiastical History* that we know anything of the great missionary period in seventh-century England. Without this unique book, the Middle Anglo-Saxon period in England would be almost as obscure as the Dark Age that preceded it. Turning to the cathedral churches themselves, however, it is fair to say that archaeology, with the few exceptions

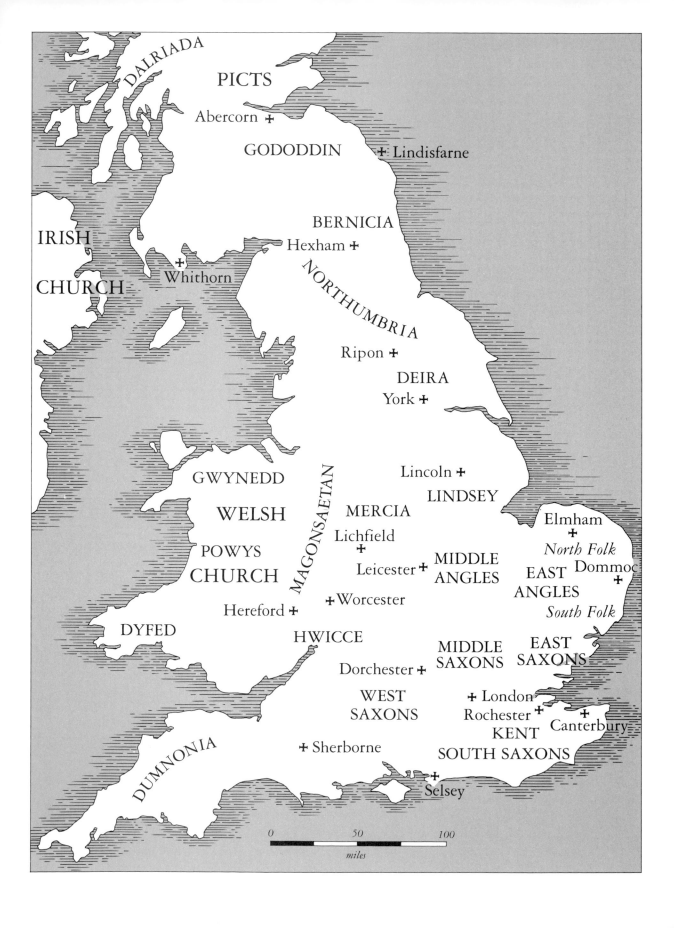

DALRIADA

PICTS

Abercorn ✝

GODODDIN

✝ Lindisfarne

IRISH

BERNICIA

Hexham ✝

CHURCH

✝
Whithorn

NORTHUMBRIA

Ripon ✝

DEIRA

York ✝

Lincoln ✝

GWYNEDD

LINDSEY

WELSH

MERCIA

Lichfield

Elmham

✝

POWYS

✝

North Folk

MAGONSAETAN

CHURCH

Leicester ✝

MIDDLE
ANGLES

EAST
ANGLES

Dommoc

✝

Hereford ✝

✝Worcester

South Folk

DYFED

HWICCE

MIDDLE
SAXONS

EAST
SAXONS

Dorchester ✝

WEST
SAXONS

✝ London

Rochester ✝

✝
Canterbury

KENT

✝ Sherborne

SOUTH SAXONS

DUMNONIA

✝
Selsey

0   50   100

miles

noted above, has to date thrown almost no new light on them. The plan, let alone the site, of the first cathedrals at Lichfield, Worcester, Hereford and Leicester is completely unknown, though no doubt those at the first three places lay close to the site of the later cathedral. There are however two exceptions to this: the two monastic cathedrals of Bishop Wilfrid, Ripon and Hexham. In both places, we have underlying the later church a crypt for relics that can without doubt be associated with Wilfrid. Recent archaeological studies have been limited, but the reassessment work of Dr Harold Taylor and Professor Richard Bailey has allowed these two remarkable spaces to be much more fully understood. To add to this, we have one other source of inestimable value to our study of Ripon and Hexham, the almost contemporary *Life of St Wilfrid* written c.710–20 by the priest Eddius Stephanus. About Ripon he records that between 671 and 678, Wilfrid:

35

> built and completed from the foundations in the earth up to the roof, a church of dressed stone, supported by various columns and side aisles or porches.
>
> Eddius Stephanus Ch.17

Although we know almost nothing about the church itself, the crypt at Ripon is still a remarkable structure made, as Stephanus tells us, of 'dressed stone'. It was entered by steps leading down into two narrow passages (that from the east was only reopened in 1974 – unfortunately with little archaeological supervision). The passage from the west turns through three right angles (perhaps deliberately, to disorientate the pilgrim) before entering the main chamber which faces east and is covered with a simple barrel vault about 9 feet high at the top of the vault. The walls are all well-built of fine dressed stone with five small

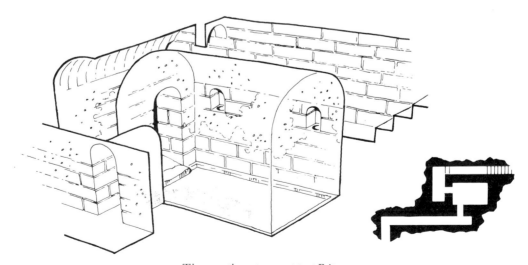

The seventh-century crypt at Ripon.

recesses for lamps. High up in the east wall was a larger recess which no doubt housed a holy relic; other relics were perhaps kept in free-standing chests. The pilgrims must have entered through one passage (in near darkness), prayed at the site of the shrine, and then passed out through the other.

The crypt at Hexham is even more remarkable, and was not rediscovered until 1726. Again we have an excellent near-contemporary description of the church of St Andrew at Hexham, which had been given to Wilfrid as another monastery by Queen Aethilthryth. This is what Eddius Stephanus says:

> My feeble tongue will not permit me here to enlarge upon the depth of the foundations in the earth and its crypts of wonderfully dressed stone, and the manifold building above ground, supported by various columns and many side aisles, and adorned with walls of notable length and height, surrounded by various winding passages with spiral stairs leading up and down; for our holy bishop, being taught by the spirit of God, thought out how to construct these buildings; nor have we heard of any other house on this side of the Alps built on such a scale.
>
> Eddius Stephanus, Ch. 22

This church was started just after Ripon in about 672 and the crypt is again made of very finely dressed stone, almost certainly robbed from the nearby Roman fort at Corbridge. Quite a large number of stones still have Roman inscriptions on them, though no doubt these were covered by plaster in the seventh century.

One can enter the crypt today only by going down a steep flight of steps from the west and straight into the ante-chamber. In the seventh century there were two other entrances, now blocked, from the north-east and south-east. That

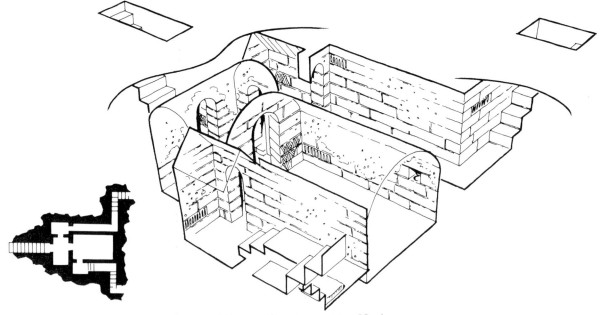

The seventh-century crypt at Hexham.

from the north-east turned through two right angles before reaching a second ante-chamber on the north of the principal ante-chamber, while the south-east entrance (which is more heavily blocked) leads to another small chamber which connects directly with the south side of the main chamber. This latter passage was perhaps the main way out for the pilgrims. The main chamber, which is bigger than that at Ripon, is again barrel-vaulted with recesses in the side and end walls for lamps. There is no eastern recess so we must suppose that the relics were in a special chest or casket in the centre of the chamber. Again, as at Ripon, one can still get a strong impression here of what it was like to be a late-seventh-century pilgrim in underground passages and chambers that are reminiscent of the catacombs of Rome. No doubt Wilfrid himself saw some of the catacombs when he had been in Rome as a young man twenty years earlier.

Above ground little is known of the form of Wilfrid's church. When the present nave was being constructed in 1908 various walls and other fragments were uncovered and roughly recorded by a local man, C.C. Hodges, but sadly no systematic excavation was carried out first. Re-excavation is badly needed. A start has been made, albeit on a small scale, by Professor Richard Bailey. Inside the present church a collection of Anglo-Saxon sculpture is displayed, including a group which has its closest parallels in the western Mediterranean area, bearing out what Eddius says about its being the most splendid house 'on this side of the Alps'. Perhaps the most extraordinary survival of all is the so-called 'Frithstool', which is almost certainly the original cathedra of the Anglo-Saxon church.

The eighth century was in many ways a 'golden age' for the English church, though apart from Sherborne in 705 no new sees were created. Consolidation was the rule, and in 731 and 737 respectively we hear of the first permanent cathedrals at Whithorn and Leicester. Fragments of the cathedral at Whithorn are probably incorporated into the ruins of the east end of Whithorn priory where some small excavations were carried out in 1949, and where current excavations (about 70 yards south of the probable cathedral site) are finding out a great deal more about the early history of this very important site. The site of the cathedral at Leicester is totally unknown, but of the later mediaeval churches in that Roman city those of St Mary de Castro and St Nicholas may be possible candidates for an early origin. During the Viking period, however, all traces above ground of the early cathedral were probably destroyed.

Of greater significance during the same period was the elevation of Egbert, bishop of York, to archbishop in 735. Egbert was far the most important churchman of his time in England, and is famous above all else for his founding of the school in York which was to be one of the greatest centres of learning in western Europe. This is also the time when the Venerable Bede was writing his great history, and when Boniface – the quite remarkable West-Saxon missionary, possibly from Crediton – was founding new dioceses all over Germany. In 732 he had received his own pallium from the pope (he was to become archbishop of Mainz). Many of the great churchmen of the period were international in their outlook, and so we find men travelling frequently to Rome from England, or to help Boniface in central Europe. It is also for us, rather sadly, a period when we know almost nothing about the actual cathedral buildings used by these men.

Towards the end of the century, when Offa, King of Mercia, was the most powerful ruler in England, a new archbishopric was created, based on Lichfield. This, however, only lasted from 787 until about 799 (though it was not formally declared void until a council held in 803), and by this time the first Viking raids were already taking place on the English coast.

The successive inroads into England of large armies of Norsemen from the middle of the ninth century brought about the destruction of the whole of the diocesan organisation in northern England. By the 870s cathedrals all the way down the east coast, at Lindisfarne, Hexham, Lindsey, Leicester, Elmham and Dunwich, had been abandoned and almost certainly left in ruins, and the same thing had probably happened at York by the end of the century. With the eventual defeat of the Vikings by Alfred the Great, and the reconquest of northern England by his successors as kings of Wessex and, for the first time, kings of England, dioceses were again established. There were, however, fewer cathedrals. In the northern province, apart from York itself, Chester-le-Street was the only other diocese created when the monks of Lindisfarne settled there in 883 with the body of St Cuthbert which they had carried from their vulnerable island in 875. After a brief period at Norham, they had wandered right across northern England before establishing the bishop's cathedra at Chester-le-Street, apparently in a wooden church. Just over a century later, in 995, they made their final move to Durham. The dioceses of Lindsey and Leicester were never re-established and, as we have seen, Dorchester-on-Thames became the cathedral for a vast diocese extending from the Thames to the Humber. In East Anglia, Elmham cathedral had been re-established by the middle of the tenth century, but its diocese now covered the whole of both Norfolk and Suffolk. Only in the west of England, at Lichfield, Hereford and Worcester, did the situation return to much as it had been a century or so earlier.

In southern and south-western England, the heartland of Wessex, there were just two large dioceses, Winchester and, 'west of Selwood forest' (as it was described at the time), Sherborne. In 909, under King Edward the Elder, these great dioceses were divided, with new cathedrals at Ramsbury for Berkshire and Wiltshire, Wells for Somerset, and Crediton for Devon and Cornwall. Winchester became the cathedral for Hampshire and Surrey, while Sherborne just served Dorset. To the east, the smaller dioceses of Selsey, Rochester and Canterbury

CHESTER-LE-STREET

TO DURHAM 995

YORK

LICHFIELD

TO YORK 956

DORCHESTER

ELMHAM

RE-ESTABLISHED
BEFORE 956

HEREFORD

WORCESTER

RAMSBURY

LONDON

WELLS

SHERBORNE
ADDED
1058

WINCHESTER

ROCHESTER

CANTERBURY

SELSEY

ST. GERMANS and CREDITON
HELD IN PLURALITY
FROM C. 1027

SHERBORNE

TO EXETER 1050

0   50   100

miles

(After Dr David Hill)

remained unchanged. In the 930s Devon and Cornwall were divided, with the creation of a new see of St Germans. This was to last only for just over a century; by 1050 Devon and Cornwall had joined together again, and the cathedral had moved from Crediton to Exeter. Ramsbury and Sherborne had also been joined together in 1050 as one diocese, due to the poverty of each of these diocesan bishops whose endowments were not adequate for their needs. These were to be the last diocesan changes before the Norman conquest, and we see that the dioceses no longer relate to tribal areas, but to the shires of England which had also been created in the tenth century.

What about the archaeology of the later Anglo-Saxon cathedral? In recent years four cathedral sites have been excavated: Sherborne, Wells, Exeter and, most important of all, Winchester. As a result we do now know something more about the size and plan of the buildings that were replaced at the Norman conquest. At three of these places the buildings were totally demolished, but at Sherborne some parts of the Anglo-Saxon cathedral still survive within the fabric of the mediaeval abbey.

During the summer of 1965 I went to work as a volunteer digger on the cathedral green at Winchester. Here, immediately outside the cathedral on the north, Martin and Birthe Biddle were conducting their fourth major season of excavations on the Anglo-Saxon cathedral. My main task that summer, along with many others, was to dig out very large trenches which had once contained the walls and foundations of the Anglo-Saxon cathedral, all the masonry from which had been robbed out and re-used by the Norman builders in the new cathedral after 1093. The plan of the Anglo-Saxon cathedral could therefore only be obtained by very carefully digging out these robber-trenches, and then making accurate plans of the foundation trenches. Within the building itself a few of the old floor and construction levels had survived, but these had been very badly cut into by burials in the later mediaeval cemetery.

Plan of the excavated robber-trenches
and foundations of the Anglo-Saxon cathedral
at Winchester.

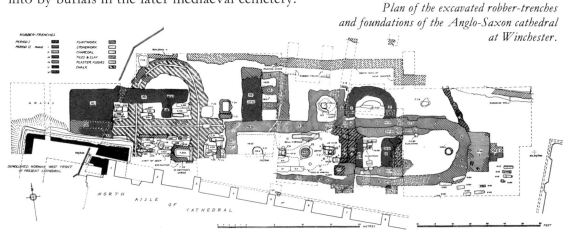

The Biddles' work had been inspired by a very detailed study of all documentary (and particularly topographical) evidence relating to the pre-Norman cathedral undertaken by the historian Roger Quirk. A series of trial trenches were cut in 1962–3, in the area north of the cathedral, which were then expanded into larger excavations in the following year. By the end of 1965 the east end of the Anglo-Saxon cathedral had been found and fully excavated, and after four more seasons the west end was finally located, after most of the northern half of the cathedral had been fully dug. (Much of the southern half was found to be under the north aisle of the present cathedral.)

This excavation was one of the most important of its kind ever undertaken. It pioneered many new techniques, and showed for the first time that much can still be found out and understood of a building even if it has been very thoroughly demolished and robbed out. The excavation finished at the end of the 1969 season, but since then a huge amount of research work has been carried out on all aspects of the discoveries (both the structural remains and the finds). By studying depths and thicknesses of wall foundations, construction levels (containing tiny fragments of the stone and mortar used for walling), and the many related finds (of window glass, floor tiles, a few sculptural fragments, etc.), Birthe Biddle has painstakingly tried to reconstruct the various buildings and how they developed. She has also carefully studied surviving contemporary buildings on the continent, and made use of some very modern techniques (for example computer-generated images which allowed her to 'get inside' the building visually) to make a whole series of reconstruction drawings of the building. When the final report is published in a year or so it will be a landmark in British archaeology.

Let us now try to summarise what has been found out about the history of Winchester cathedral between its mid-seventh-century origins and its final rebuilding at the very end of the tenth century. The sites of the various walls have now been marked out in modern brick on the grass to the north of the present cathedral, and it is well worth a visit, just to get an idea of the buildings. The whole complex in its final form was over 230 feet long, and its great western tower may have reached a height of 150 feet – a little higher than the present crossing tower.

The key to understanding the building sequence is a sentence in an early-fifteenth-century history of the cathedral by Thomas Rudborne. In it he says that outside the north door of the nave there was a 'modest chapel' in the place in which St Swithin (the later patron saint of the cathedral) had *originally* been buried. The chapel has gone, but the 'north door' is still there, and, sure enough, the Biddles found the foundations there of a small chapel surrounding the remains of a monumental tomb. There was no doubt that this was the original tomb of

St Swithin, the miracle-working bishop of Winchester who died in 862 at the height of the Viking invasions.

We are told by another earlier chronicler that he was buried outside the west door of his cathedral. This again ties in with the archaeological evidence: excavations to the east of this tomb have revealed the foundations of a church that was about 100 feet long and cruciform in plan with a square east end, and there can be little doubt that this was the church of St Peter and St Paul built by Cenwalh in c.648 and raised to cathedral status in the 660s. It was later known as the Old Minster. At the east end of the nave of this church (and ironically found in the first trial-trench in 1963) was the original altar base which was surrounded by four post-holes, perhaps for a canopy (or baldachino) to cover the altar. The square chancel of this church was found to have been reconstructed with an apse in the eighth century, and then in the late tenth century was reconstructed yet again to make a new high altar on a podium above a small *confessio* or relic crypt. Just over a century later after the saintly Swithin's death, on 15 July 971, Bishop Aethelwold moved his coffin, at which many miracles had taken place, to a new site inside the cathedral in the midst of a torrential downpour (hence the later legend that if it rains on St Swithin's day it will rain for a further forty days).

Bishop Aethelwold, who was later canonised, was along with St Dunstan and St Oswald one of the great reforming bishops of the tenth century, and it was he who introduced Benedictine monks to the cathedral. After translating St Swithin's body, he went on to build a very large western extension to the cathedral around the site of the original burial place. Excavations showed that this was originally to be a huge memorial building with large north and south apsidal chapels (the vast chalk foundations for these were excavated), but after only a few years plans were changed and a great 'westwork' was built instead, still focusing on the original tomb of St Swithin. The very large west front of this building, which incorporated an earlier tower, St Martin's Tower, was roughly in line with the present west front of the cathedral. It, too, had massive foundations, and the Biddles have suggested that it may have looked like the great 'westwork' of the church of Corvey on the Weser in Germany (built c.873 to 885). Inside this building were found a series of important tombs, all set in neat rows around St Swithin's shrine. These were almost certainly the original tombs of later kings of Wessex and England, like Cnut (died 1035), and of bishops of Winchester. It is even possible that one of them is that of King Alfred, who died in 899, and was probably later translated here from another part of the building.

The final rebuilding work started by Bishop Aethelwold, but unfinished at his death in 984, was at the east end of this cathedral. This work was eventually finished by his successor Bishop Alphege in 993–4. It created a much larger east end with apses on the north, south and east surrounding a raised high altar, with a small crypt beneath, while further to the east was a well (perhaps for liturgical uses) with beyond it a small projecting crypt, or *aussencrypta*. Around this eastern crypt were found some fine late Saxon burials with carved grave-slabs.

By the end of the tenth century Winchester cathedral was perhaps the greatest in the land. It was being used for four principal functions. It was the place where Benedictine monks sang all their daily offices; it was the cathedral for a see that extended from the Isle of Wight to the Thames south of London; it was a place of pilgrimage to the shrine and tomb of St Swithin; and finally it was a church in which kings and bishops were consecrated and buried. Thanks to the large-scale excavations we now know as much about this great church as will ever be possible.

In the years following the completion of the pioneering Winchester excavations, two more major Anglo-Saxon cathedral sites were partially excavated, Exeter in 1971–6, and Wells in 1978–80. The site at Exeter, which produced spectacular Roman remains, was just west of the west front of the later cathedral. Unfortunately much of the Anglo-Saxon remains were totally destroyed by the massive foundations of the Victorian church of St Mary Major (built in 1865 and demolished in 1970). Some very important discoveries were made, however, including parts of a northern porticus and of an eastern apse to a church that was at least 110 feet long. East of the apse and perhaps extending as far as the present cathedral (an area yet to be fully excavated) is a sunken area which may be part of a later crypt like that at Winchester. These must be parts of the later Anglo-Saxon minster church which acquired cathedral status in 1050, and was finally destroyed after the Norman cathedral was consecrated in 1133.

At Wells excavations carried out by Warwick Rodwell in 1978–80 have proved once and for all that the Anglo-Saxon minster church of St Andrew, which became a cathedral in 909, lay under the present cloister on a different alignment from the later cathedral. These excavations uncovered only the eastern tip of an apse which must have been the extreme east end of the cathedral (the rest of the cathedral church awaits excavation under the cloister garth), but the excavations did show that east of the cathedral was an earlier middle Saxon mortuary chapel of St Mary, which, in turn, overlaid a Roman or sub-Roman mausoleum, and that the whole complex was aligned on the holy well of St Andrew which gave the place its name. There is some documentary evidence that the early cathedral, which survived until the twelfth century, had lateral apses (*hemicyclii*) as at Winchester in which the last two Saxon bishops, Dudoc (died 1060) and Giso (died 1088) were buried. The whole cathedral complex in its final Norman form was perhaps about 300 feet long.

Plan showing the relationship between the old and new cathedrals at Wells.

Another cathedral site which ought to be mentioned is that at North Elmham. The massive ruined stone church here has long been called the 'Anglo-Saxon cathedral'. However, a recent reassessment has shown that this is almost certainly incorrect, and that this stone church was built for the bishop after 1071 when he had transferred his see to Thetford. This ties in with thirteenth-century documentary evidence which describes the wanderings of the see two centuries before it finally settled at Norwich in the late eleventh century. This account says that the see moved from a 'timber chapel' at Elmham to a 'borrowed church' at Thetford. In 1954, when the ruined church at North Elmham was being partially excavated, traces of earlier floors and of a timber building were found below the masonry structure. This is more than likely to be part of the later Anglo-Saxon cathedral. Only further excavation, however, will tell us whether both the cathedral of 673 to c.870 and the later tenth- and eleventh-century 'timber' cathedral were on this same site.

The final Anglo-Saxon cathedral to be considered is that at Sherborne. Here uniquely we have above-ground surviving remains of the Anglo-Saxon cathedral. Now incorporated within the walls of Sherborne abbey (a parish church since 1540), these remains have recently been studied by J.H.P. Gibb. Ironically the first discoveries of Anglo-Saxon work were made in the later nineteenth century by R.H. Carpenter after his father had restored the west front of Sherborne abbey. Carpenter senior extended the west (perpendicular) window downwards in 1849 and in so doing discovered and destroyed a 'double row of small pillars

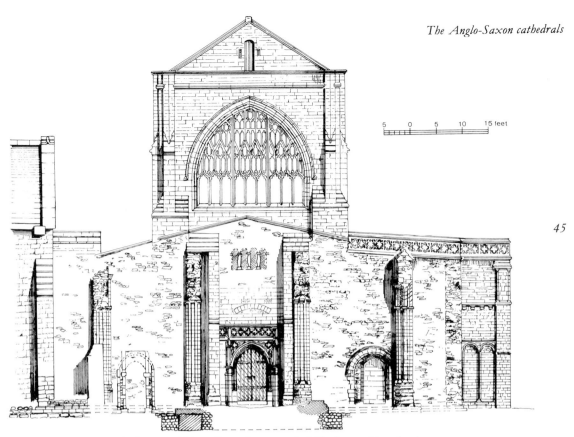

*Anglo-Saxon rubble walls at the west end of Sherborne abbey showing
the c.1050 doorway (bottom left). The late mediaeval great west window was
lowered in 1850 destroying the window with baluster shafts in it.*

and arches of an early date'. These must have been an upper floor opening,
perhaps into a tower. In the 1870s, R.H. Carpenter dug holes outside the west
front of the abbey, exposing a 'strangely' moulded plinth running westwards,
which was bonded into the west wall of the abbey. Further small-scale work by
Sir Alfred Clapham in 1949 and J.H.P. Gibb in 1964 showed that the surviving
west front had also been the east wall of a large Anglo-Saxon tower with flanking
north and south transepts. Further east, the crossing area of the mediaeval abbey
church was also shown to reflect probably the earlier Anglo-Saxon plan.

Careful analysis by Jim Gibb of all that has been found to date suggests that
the late Anglo-Saxon cathedral was a double church with the original church,
that was founded in 705 by St Ealdhelm, the first bishop, on the west. During
the eighth and ninth centuries this was an important church, and several kings
of Wessex were buried here, including the two elder brothers of Alfred the Great.
Nothing of this original church has yet been found, though parts of it may have
been incorporated in the parish church of All Hallows, which was rebuilt in the
late fourteenth century and occupied the area immediately west of the present
west front. That church was unfortunately demolished at the Dissolution.

The present abbey (parish) church has four massive crossing piers, which
were reconstructed in the Norman period. These perhaps indicate a large

46

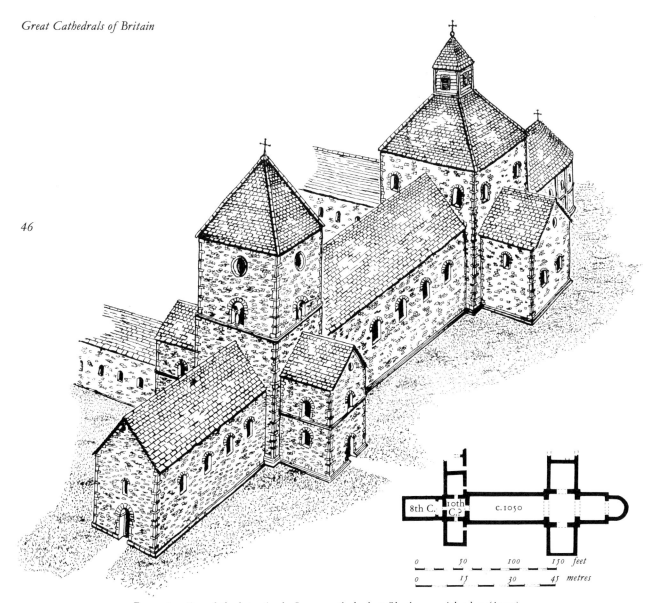

Reconstruction of the late Anglo-Saxon cathedral at Sherborne with plan (inset).

cruciform church, which was presumably added to the earlier church. Documentary evidence suggests this was built by Bishop Aelfwold (1045–58). By this time the cathedral had become a monastic settlement (like Canterbury and Winchester), and the tomb of an earlier bishop, Wulfsige (died 1001/2) had become the focus of miracles. His body was translated to the north side of the high altar and this was probably under the present crossing. By the Norman conquest, Sherborne cathedral was at least 160 feet long (its probable total length was about 250 feet, similar to Winchester's), and dominated the small village that had grown up around it. To the Normans this was an anomaly: their cathedrals were the focal points of large centres of population and, as we shall see, it was soon to lose its bishop's throne. William of Malmesbury, writing in the early twelfth century, says:

Sherborne is a small village, agreeable neither for the density of its population nor for the attraction of its position, in which it is a cause for wonder and almost shame that an episcopal see lasted so many centuries.

De Gestis Pontificum Anglorum

As we have seen, two of these Anglo-Saxon cathedrals, Winchester and Sherborne, had become 'monastic cathedrals', and the same was true of Canterbury and Worcester. This was an uniquely English phenomenon, and meant that the bishop (or archbishop) of the diocese was also the abbot of the monastery. A large body of monks lived communally in buildings around a cloister attached to the cathedral, and sang all the daily services. The founding genius of this system, and the man most responsible for the tenth-century monastic revival as a whole, was St Dunstan, who was archbishop of Canterbury from 959 to 988. The revival started in 940 when Dunstan became abbot of Glastonbury, and reached its high point in the 970s under the patronage of King Edgar.

When Dunstan died his tomb quickly became a place of pilgrimage in his own cathedral at Canterbury. Unfortunately, archaeology has not yet recovered anything of the late Anglo-Saxon cathedral, which was destroyed by fire in 1067. We do, however, have a description of the cathedral dating from the late eleventh century, written by a monk of Canterbury, Eadmer, who had seen it as a boy. From this, and a few other scraps of documentary evidence, many people have tried to reconstruct the plan of this building, starting with Professor Robert Willis in the 1840s. What is now needed is large-scale excavation on the south side of Canterbury cathedral along the lines of the Biddles' 1962–9 excavations at Winchester. Only then will we come near to forming an accurate picture of what must have been the greatest cathedral of its day in England.

THE ANGLO-SAXON CATHEDRALS

EARLY CATHEDRALS		*Bishop's seat held*	*Excavations*
1	Canterbury	597–	1979–80
2	Rochester	604–	1888 and 1894
3	London	604–616, c.650–	•
4	York	627–33, 664–	1967–72
5	?Lincoln (Lindsey)	c.628–33, 677–c.870	1978–9
6	?Dunwich or Old Felixstowe	c.630–c.870	Site destroyed
7	Lindisfarne	634–664, c.678–c.875	•
8	Dorchester	635–c.660, c.680–c.779 c.870–	•

MIDDLE PERIOD CATHEDRALS

9	Winchester	c.660–	1962–9
10	Ripon	668–c.669, 686–709	1932 and 1974
11	Hexham	668–c.669, 680–c.875	1978
12	Lichfield	669–	1856 and 1860
13	(North) Elmham	673–c.870, c.950–	1954
14	Worcester	c.679–	•
15	Hereford	c.679–	•
16	Leicester	(c.679), 737–	•
17	Abercorn	c.680–5	•
18	Whithorn	(c.680), 731–c.870	1949
19	Selsey	681–	•
20	Sherborne	705–	1870s, 1949, 1964–73

LATE CATHEDRALS

21	Chester-le-Street	883–995	•
22	Wells	909–	1978–80
23	Crediton	909–1050	•
24	Ramsbury	909–1058	•
25	St Germans	c.930–1032, 1046–50	•
26	Durham	995–	•
27	Exeter	1050–	1971–6

2

LANFRANC'S REVOLUTION

The Norman cathedrals

Although 1066, the year of the Norman conquest, is probably the most famous date in English history, so far as the history of the church is concerned, its importance is overshadowed by the year 1070. In the spring of that year, Ermenfrid, a papal legate, came to England with William the Conqueror's approval to set in motion a much needed root and branch reform of the English church, which was very insular and Anglo-Saxon in its outlook. William wanted not only a new Norman aristocracy in England but also a new Norman hierarchy in the church. Councils were held at Winchester and at Windsor at which Stigand, the pluralist archbishop of Canterbury and bishop of Winchester, along with several other bishops, was deposed. This was immediately followed by the appointment of Thomas of Bayeux to the vacant archbishopric of York, and the two royal chaplains, the Normans Walkelin and Herfast, as bishops of Winchester and Elmham. Rather unusually, an Anglo-Saxon, another Stigand, was appointed to the see of Selsey at the same time. Later that summer Ermenfrid crossed the channel to Normandy in company with William the Conqueror and there he appointed Lanfranc, abbot of the monastery of St Etienne that William had founded at Caen, the new archbishop of Canterbury. This was done on 15 August. Two weeks later Lanfranc was welcomed at Canterbury, consecrated archbishop, and enthroned.

At this time, Lanfranc, a northern Italian by birth, was nearly sixty years old. A close friend of William the Conqueror, he was one of the greatest Benedictine monks and teachers in Europe, and his choice as archbishop of Canterbury was a natural one. Lanfranc himself, however, did not want the job. He had turned down the opportunity of being archbishop of Rouen three years earlier, and within a few months of his appointment he was writing to the pope, Alexander II, asking to be released from the job on the grounds of his own inadequacy. The pope and the king stood firm, and Lanfranc consequently spent the next nineteen years totally reorganising and rebuilding the English church. Like Archbishop Theodore four hundred years earlier, his influence on it was enormous.

The first action of his reign was to travel to Rome with Thomas of Bayeux so that both could collect their *pallia* from the pope. They took the opportunity while they were there to argue the relative importance of Canterbury and York (the primacy dispute) in front of the pope, and the matter was finally settled at a meeting in Winchester castle at Easter 1072, when Lanfranc was made primate of all England, retaining possession of the three disputed sees of Worcester, Dorchester and Lichfield, which had also been claimed by York. The original document recording this, with the signatures of all the parties concerned, still survives, and is one of the priceless treasures of Canterbury cathedral library.

At Whitsun the same year at Windsor, Lanfranc held the first of a series of great councils in which he completely reorganised the English church. Unfortunately, records of these have only partially survived, but it is clear that the policy of removing cathedral sees from villages to towns was to be continued (Crediton had moved to Exeter as early as 1050). The first post-Conquest move was that of the cathedral at Dorchester-on-Thames to Lincoln under its bishop, Remigius. Bishop Herfast of East Anglia, meanwhile, left Elmham for the urban centre of Thetford. Just over twenty years later the see moved on again to Norwich and became another new monastic cathedral, following Rochester which had become monastic in about 1082 under its new Norman bishop, Gundulf, and Durham in 1083.

The most important of Lanfranc's councils was that held at St Paul's cathedral in London in 1075. Both archbishops and all the bishops in England (except Durham) attended as well as many abbots. The transference of three more sees was agreed: Sherborne to Salisbury (Old Sarum), Lichfield to Chester, and Selsey to Chichester. About a dozen years later, the bishop of Wells was to move to Bath and become yet another monastic bishop, while the see of Chester moved again at the end of the century to Coventry, also a monastery. As Benedictine monks, therefore, Lanfranc and his successor Anselm (1093–1109) were extending the unique English system of monastic cathedrals which, as we have seen, was started in the later tenth century at Winchester, Worcester, Canterbury and Sherborne. (It is an anomaly that Bishop Remigius of Lincoln, a monk, should have been in charge of a new secular cathedral.) By the end of the eleventh century, of the fifteen sees in England eight were monastic and seven were secular.

Monastic sees	*Secular sees*
Canterbury	Exeter
Rochester	Chichester
Winchester	Salisbury
Coventry	London
Norwich	Lincoln
Durham	York
Bath	Hereford
Worcester	

To them were added Ely in 1109 (another great monastery) and Carlisle in 1133 (unique as a house of the Augustinian canons ruled by a bishop).

Most remarkable of all, from our point of view, is the fact that in the half century after Lanfranc's arrival in 1070 every single cathedral was rebuilt (or built anew) on a far grander scale than its Anglo-Saxon predecessor. Not only this, but whereas the Anglo-Saxon cathedrals (as far as we know them) were a hotch-potch of agglutinated buildings, all the new cathedrals were massive uniform structures in the brand new Norman style of Romanesque architecture. Lanfranc was therefore not only responsible for the reorganisation of the English church, but also for a renaissance of architecture in England on a grand scale.

In studying these new Norman buildings, we find that the vast majority of them have left sizable portions of their fabric within or below (as crypts) our surviving cathedrals, and over the last century and a half architectural historians and archaeologists have been disinterring these remains from the later fabric. Only in rare cases, like Durham, is the majority of the Norman fabric still visible and unaltered.

Let us now look, in roughly chronological order, at this rebuilding programme and see what we can find out about the size and form of these early Norman cathedrals in England.

Lanfranc arrived in Canterbury at the end of August 1070, and according to a contemporary source, the monk Eadmer, he was able 'within the space of seven years to restore the church to use, almost complete from the foundations'. Another chronicler suggests that it was done in only five years. Between the spring of 1071 and 1076–8, therefore, we can imagine a rapid programme of construction taking place that certainly involved the completion of all of the eastern arm and much of the nave (where the monks' quire was then situated). Most of the plan of the church still survives in the nave and transepts of the present cathedral, and a careful examination of the fabric shows that many of the fragments of Lanfranc's cathedral are still visible, particularly in the crossing area. This was first recognised by Professor Robert Willis as long ago as 1844, and it was he who pointed out the close resemblances between Canterbury cathedral and Lanfranc's own monastery of St Etienne in Caen, where building had begun in c. 1064. Both buildings, which have similar dimensions, were completed in c. 1077 and it is very likely that Lanfranc brought over his own Caenais master mason to construct what was to be nearly a 'carbon copy' of St Etienne. Once that work had been completed, as we have seen, exceptionally quickly, Lanfranc went on to rebuild all the main claustal buildings of his monastery, which adjoined the cathedral on the north, as well as his own palace (attached to the north-west tower of the cathedral) before his death in 1089.

Lanfranc's cathedral at Canterbury is the first truly Norman building in

Britain that we know anything about. Its surviving fragments have been recorded in detail, and have recently been subjected to careful new analysis by Dr Richard Gem, so that we now have a fairly exact idea of what the building looked like. The earliest recording work was done in 1821–2 when sections of the cathedral were made for Britton's *History of Canterbury*. We are fortunate that in 1832 a magnificent draughtsman called J. C. Buckler drew the Norman north-west tower of the cathedral in detail just before it was scandalously demolished by the dean and chapter and replaced by a replica of the fifteenth-century south-west tower. Just over a decade later Professor Willis arrived on the scene and gave us his brilliant analysis of the way the cathedral had developed.

Buckler's measured drawings of the north-west tower are of great importance for our understanding of the levels in the cathedral. This tower was directly connected to Lanfranc's palace on the north-west (a door leading west from the first floor of the tower can be seen in the drawing), and it is probable that in this earliest Norman cathedral (as in the Anglo-Saxon one) the archbishop had a throne in the gallery at the west end. Norman fragments survive at either end of the nave aisles above the vaults, and these probably relate to the clerestory level of the cathedral. Originally in the aisles below this, galleries connected the western gallery with the transepts at first-floor level. This was a common feature of large early Norman cathedrals. The north transept, later made famous as the place where Thomas Becket was murdered, was rebuilt in the mid-fifteenth century but it still contains many fragments of the earlier building trapped within its walls. These fragments were planned and measured in 1978–9 after it was discovered that much more of the Lanfranc fabric survived above the vaults than was hitherto realised. Most important of all was the discovery of the south wall and vault springing of the upper chapel east of the transept. It was found to be much longer than earlier thought, showing that the first-floor chapels in the transepts were small chapels in their own right with a 'nave' (in the transept) and two-bay 'chancel'. The 'nave' had direct access from the ground via a stair-turret in the north-west corner of the transept which still survives intact. The door into the gallery is now blocked.

In March 1979 the floor at the extreme west end of the huge Norman crypt was dug up to make new brick foundations for showcases for a treasury. Beneath the floor at the west end were found the foundations of Lanfranc's crypt cut by those of the c.1096 crypt (see p.66). The west wall of Lanfranc's crypt still survives intact and can be seen today by those visiting the cathedral treasury. In the north-west and south-west corners are original columns surmounted by the earliest 'cushion' capitals in England. Almost exactly 80 feet vertically above them are the remains of the two eastern clasping buttresses for the base of Lanfranc's central tower which can still be seen above the late twelfth-century choir vault and below the base of the present 'Bell Harry' tower. Similar pilaster buttresses, with *in situ* nook shafts, also survive on the west side, and it is clear that about 80 feet of the core of Lanfranc's crossing piers remains below another 120 feet of the huge 'Bell Harry' tower, a remarkable comment on the solidity of early Norman building work.

At Canterbury, as elsewhere in early Norman England, a complete new technology for constructing massive new structures was being introduced, and so we find similar building methods being used both for large new churches and for the vast stone castle keeps that maintained Norman political might. It is interesting to note that when Lanfranc came over from Normandy in 1070 he brought with him his friend Gundulf, the prior of St Etienne in Caen, as his personal assistant. This remarkable man, who became bishop of Rochester in 1077, not only rebuilt his cathedral at Rochester (and introduced monks there) but also supervised the building of the castle at Rochester and the White Tower at the Tower of London. He is described by a contemporary as being 'very competent and skilful at building in stone'. We can therefore conjecture that Gundulf had earlier been in charge of the building work at St Etienne between 1064 and 1070 and of Lanfranc's works at Canterbury cathedral.

At Rochester cathedral, only the western part of the crypt survives from this earliest Norman period. All the rest of the Romanesque work, including the wrongly named Gundulf's Tower (in fact a mid-twelfth-century detached bell tower), dates from after Gundulf's death in 1108. The two bays of the crypt, however, are more complete than the earliest crypt at Canterbury cathedral, and the two massive freestanding columns with flat cushion capitals are very fine examples of early Norman work. The stone used here is from the Marquise quarries just south of Calais in France, and this and two other good quality stones – Caen from Normandy, and Quarr from the Isle of Wight – was being imported into Kent in large quantities in the late eleventh century for ashlar masonry. The rest of the walling which was massively thick at this time,

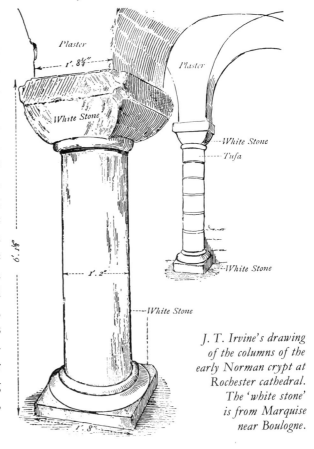

J. T. Irvine's drawing of the columns of the early Norman crypt at Rochester cathedral. The 'white stone' is from Marquise near Boulogne.

was made of local materials, particularly sandstone and flints in the south-east. The usual method was to use small ashlar blocks (which at this time had thick mortar joints between the blocks) for quoins, pilaster buttresses, and so on, and roughly coursed local materials for the rest of the face. Into the middle of the walls were poured masses of rubble and mortar which often took a long time to dry. The outside of the walls were then usually plastered over. Within about twenty years, however, the quality of ashlar work improved enormously, and we find very beautiful ashlar with hardly any mortar visible in many Norman buildings of the second generation.

55

One of the best places to see early Norman ashlar work is in the west front of Lincoln cathedral (or minster as it has always been called), where it is embedded in the vast thirteenth-century facade. As we have seen, Lincoln was one of the group of secular cathedrals started on new sites in the mid 1070s. The main church (now destroyed) was in plan, at least, similar to Canterbury. Bishop Remigius's new foundation is described only half a century later in these words:

Having, therefore, bought lands in the upper city itself, next to the castle which was distinguished by very strong towers, he constructed a strong church in that strong place, a beautiful church in that beautiful place, dedicated to the Virgin of virgins; it was to be both agreeable to the servants of God and also, as suited the times, invincible to enemies.

Henry of Huntingdon, *Historia Anglorum* VI,41. Trans. R. Gem

Reconstruction of the late-eleventh-century west front of Lincoln cathedral.

Only the west front, dating from about 1092, survives of the early Norman cathedral, but a recent detailed study of its fabric by Dr Richard Gem has allowed its original form to be partially reconstructed. This shows a most unusual structure, something between a monumental arch and a castle, and this is apparently exactly what it was – a monumental entrance to the cathedral and a castle for the bishop. The cathedral stood opposite Lincoln castle inside the Roman city walls of the upper city, which also acted as the outer bailey of the castle. The 1070s were very insecure times (especially in the north), and Dr Gem has shown that the surviving parts of the early Norman work reveal several features more akin to military than ecclesiastical use. Perhaps the most obvious of these are the machicolation slots in the western arches, and the possible garde-robe chute on the north side (now partially visible, though walled-up, in the 'Morning Chapel' of the minster). In 1140, during the civil war between Stephen and Matilda, Stephen 'made a castle of the church of the blessed Mother of God in Lincoln [the minster]', in order to invest the castle. There can be no doubt that he was using the 'westwork' of the minster for this. A little later during the same quarrel the minster was burnt, and in the rebuilding that followed, the west front was refashioned with the two tall western towers later remodelled to form the towers we see today. The twelfth-century towers at Exeter (see below) may also have had a military use in the siege of 1136.

Another new cathedral of the later 1070s also placed inside the outer bailey of a castle was that at Salisbury, where Bishop Herman's new cathedral was built inside the Iron Age hillfort and Roman town of Sorviodurum (now Old Sarum, see plan on p. 213). William of Malmesbury describes the site as:

a castle instead of a town, situated in a high place surrounded by no mean wall; and though being strong in one way or another with other provisions, yet is troubled with scarcity of water.

De Gestis Pontificum Anglorum, 182–3

Yet again, defence considerations seem to have been more important than the desire to move to a centre of population in relocating the see, and it should not be forgotten that many of the Norman bishops, like Herman, were great secular lords in their own right. This cathedral, erected from c.1075 to 1092, and the twelfth-century building which succeeded it on the same site, were totally demolished in the later Middle Ages to provide stone for the close wall of the thirteenth-century cathedral in Salisbury itself. The foundations at Old Sarum were partly exposed and measured in 1834–5, and the site later completely excavated in 1909–15 under the general direction of Sir William St John Hope when the foundations of the cloister, canons' houses and the bishop's palace, as well as the inner bailey of the castle, were also dug out. William of Malmesbury tells us that the twelfth-century cathedral of Old Sarum was made of exceptionally fine ashlar masonry which made it look as if whole walls were carved from a single stone, and the excavators uncovered the remains of a large church of this date with western towers, an eight-bay nave, aisled transepts and a long choir. Beneath its fine, decorated pavements, the much smaller east end of the original Norman church was found, which appeared to have had towers on either side. A recent study, however, by Dr Richard Gem suggests that the transepts never had towers above. The foundations have now been marked out on the ground in coloured concretes and some of the fine architectural fragments that were found are on display in Salisbury museum.

The decision to move the cathedral of the South Saxons from the very exposed island of Selsey to the Roman walled city of Chichester seems much more in line with the needs of the eleventh-century population. A late Anglo-Saxon burh (fortified town) already existed within the Roman city walls and though the town also had a Norman castle, it was well away from the cathedral. Much of the early Norman cathedral survives within the later fabric, and has been studied in detail by Professor Robert Willis. To see the early fabric, however, one has to disinter it from a great deal of the later fabric, as the plan makes clear. The eastern arm of the cathedral, which was probably built in the late 1070s, was originally a large apse with an ambulatory around the inside. On the outside of the apse were three small semicircular chapels, and fragments of the foundations of these were discovered in the late 1960s during rescue excavations in advance of underpinning work. The plan of this area is very similar to that of St Augustine's abbey in Canterbury (built c.1077–87), and was widely copied in early Norman churches.

A devastating fire in 1187 left much of the inside of the building heavily scarred by the collapse of burning timber and lead roofs. We shall see that the monks of Canterbury, with the vast resources available to them, were able to rebuild lavishly after a similar fire in 1174, but at Chichester the decision was taken merely to reface the burnt inner faces of the nave and choir where necessary. The refacing work was done very skilfully with Caen stone and Purbeck marble (the latter for the shafts and string courses), and this contrasts quite strikingly with the earlier work which uses only Quarr stone. One can also see how the fire did most damage just below the ceiling, and at the lowest level, from burning timbers on the floor. More of the face work (that above the main arches) had to be replaced in the four eastern bays of the nave than in the four western bays, perhaps because there were more timber stalls and other furnishings here.

Another place where the contrast between the early Norman Quarr stone and the later Caen work can be seen is the Norman south-west tower. Documentary evidence records that in 1210 a great storm brought down 'two towers' at

Chichester. One of these was clearly the south-west tower. Not only is the upper stage of thirteenth-century masonry of Caen stone, but a great split up the centre of the west wall has been repaired in Caen. This contrasting stonework can be seen both inside and outside the tower, though the original pilaster buttresses on the south and south-west are covered by larger thirteenth-century buttresses.

Enough survives of Chichester's original fabric, once the later work has been mentally stripped away, for Professor Willis to reconstruct elevations and sections with almost complete certainty. One virtually 'unknown' area of the eleventh-century cathedral are the windows lighting the triforium gallery of the nave, now buried under the thirteenth-century roofs. It's possible, however, to crawl through them, with a torch in hand, from the triforium and stand on the thirteenth-century vaults. From this vantage point a marvellous row of Norman decorated corbels is revealed at the top of the eleventh-century walls. Most are in very good condition because they were only washed by (unpolluted) rain for just over a century.

On the Welsh border, the cathedrals of Hereford and Worcester were also rebuilt in the early Norman period. At Hereford, the Anglo-Saxon cathedral had been 'utterly burned' by the Welsh in 1055 and work on the new cathedral was probably started soon after the appointment in 1079 of Robert de Losinga as bishop. Much of the plan of the early Norman cathedral can be reconstructed, and early fabric can still be seen in the choir and south transept area. Unfortunately, the notorious restorer, James Wyatt (known as 'Wrecker' Wyatt) rebuilt the nave area very drastically after the fall of the western tower in 1786; he swept away the triforium and clerestory completely, leaving only the massive cylindrical piers of the early twelfth century.

At Worcester the situation was very different. The remarkable Bishop Wulfstan (1062–95) was the only Anglo-Saxon bishop to survive the Norman conquest for any length of time, and as prior of his monastery, he had earlier been involved in building work there. When he became bishop there were only twelve monks in the monastery, but by 1084 the number had risen to fifty and with Archbishop Lanfranc's encouragement he decided, albeit reluctantly, to rebuild in the new style. By 1089 the first part was complete, and William of Malmesbury in a very revealing passage describes the situation at the time:

When the work of the main church, which he had begun from the foundations, had advanced to that stage of growth that now the monks might move into it, the old church which blessed Oswald had built was ordered to be unroofed and destroyed.

Wulfstan is then quoted as saying:

We miserable people have destroyed the work of the saints, that we may provide praise for ourselves. The age of that most happy man did not know how to build pompous buildings, but knew how to offer themselves to God under any sort of roof, and to attract to their examples their subordinates. We on the contrary strive that, neglecting our souls, we may pile up stones.

William of Malmesbury, 283

This is a very telling summary of what an elderly Anglo-Saxon prelate felt about the new Romanesque style, which he was forced to adopt.

At Worcester today only the north and south transepts retain large parts of the shell of the early Norman church (there is a particularly fine eastern arch in the south transept). However, underneath the choir are the fairly complete remains of a magnificent crypt which was certainly finished by 1092 when Wulfstan held a synod there. Small-scale excavations in 1975 and 1986 (when a new south-east entrance was made to the crypt) were able to show that there was an unusual polygonal chapel on the south-east side of the ambulatory, and the plan of the crypt as a whole clearly reflects the plan of the presbytery above. The monks' quire, as in other early churches, was at the east end of the nave and under the crossing. Between the fourteenth-century work and the late twelfth-century work at the end of the nave, parts of the early Norman round shafts have been left *in situ*. They are mostly of alternating green and white stone, and show that Wulfstan's cathedral must have had a striped effect. This can best be seen today inside the nearby chapter house.

In 1088 Bishop Giso of Wells died, and William Rufus appointed a man called John de Villula (or John of Tours as he is also called) as bishop. At the same time the abbacy of Bath was vacant, and at Archbishop Lanfranc's suggestion, John de Villula transferred the Somerset see to Bath, creating yet another monastic cathedral. After the official confirmation of this in 1091, work started on the new cathedral and abbey church, which was another fine Norman building with an apsidal eastern arm with three semicircular chapels. The whole of this eastern arm was demolished in the sixteenth century, and excavation, the most recent in 1979, has recovered only fragments of the plan. Parts of the west wall of the eastern arm do, however, survive in the east wall of the present abbey, and it is clear that these fragments were originally on the west side of a great central crossing tower (see p.152). When Bishop John died in 1122, we are told that his church had been finished 'up to the lower vaultings'. Does this indicate that, as at Durham, the new abbey was acquiring a ribbed vault, and was this over the nave, or only over the eastern arm? Beneath the nave, fragments of the Norman west front as well as some pier-bases were recorded during reflooring work between 1863 and 1872. One of these piers can still be inspected in a pit below the floor at the east end of the present north aisle.

By far the most imposing of all these early Norman cathedrals, however, was the truly vast building put up at Winchester. At the time work started on

Great Cathedrals of Britain

The Norman north transept of Winchester cathedral
in 1817 showing the fifteenth-century roof
before it was covered by a ceiling.

the new cathedral in 1079, Winchester was still a powerful centre of government (as it had been under the last Anglo-Saxon kings), and the setting of many royal councils, so when the new cathedral was planned, it was to be on a really monumental scale with its principal dimensions based on the basilica of St Peter in Rome (it was also dedicated to St Peter). Just to the west of the cathedral was the royal palace, and as Dr Richard Gem has shown, it is probable that the huge length of the nave was planned from the beginning. Bishop Walkelin may have acquired the dimensions for his master mason to use from Rome itself. The length of the nave up to the west side of the crossing is about 350 feet, and this is almost exactly the same as the total length of St Peter's in Rome. The width of the nave and aisles together at Winchester was about 85 feet, which compares with the width of the great central nave of St Peter's, while the total width of St Peter's was 208 feet, which is very close to the width across the transepts at Winchester.

Taking the cathedral as a whole, from the eastern apse to the west side of the now demolished Norman westwork, it measured about 530 feet, which made it by far the largest Romanesque building in Europe, and probably the largest structure since Roman times. Soon it was to be rivalled by the incredible abbey church at Cluny in France, as well as, perhaps, by St Paul's cathedral in London. However, at the time it was completed, at the beginning of the twelfth century, it was clearly in a class of its own, and it is worth noting that at exactly the same time William Rufus was putting up at Westminster palace in London the longest mediaeval hall (c.240 feet long) ever built, another sign of the power and wealth of the early Norman kings in England. The new Winchester cathedral must therefore be seen as a great royal church, as it was in the Anglo-Saxon period. William Rufus was buried here after his death in 1100 in the New Forest.

The finest surviving parts of the Norman cathedral are the two magnificent transepts where only the windows have been enlarged and filled with tracery at a later date in the fourteenth century. The large numbers of semi-circular arches and many cushion capitals, as well as the rough masonry in these great spaces give at least a flavour of what the whole cathedral was once like. The large first-floor galleries here are also very impressive. Indeed, in the original church it was probably possible to walk all the way round the cathedral on these large galleries, except perhaps at the east end, in just the same way that one can walk around the very spacious galleries at St Sophia in Constantinople. But for the large crypts which are still complete (though unfortunately often flooded due to a rising of the water table in the last 900 years) nothing has survived of the eastern arm of the Norman church. There is an unusual smaller eastern crypt which Dr Gem has suggested may roughly copy the earlier Anglo-Saxon *aussencrypta*, which lay outside and beyond the east end of the cathedral at a lower level (see p.40).

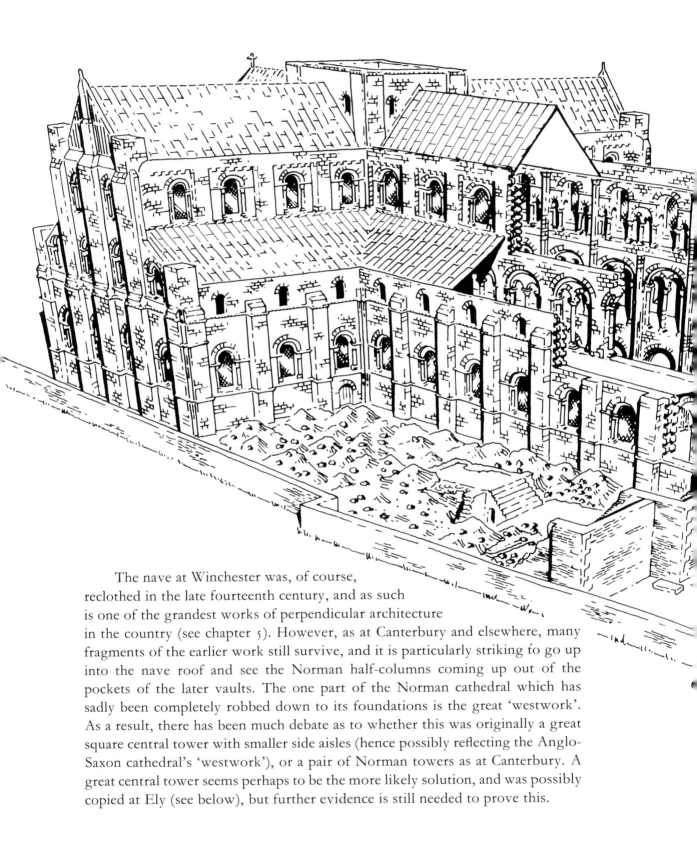

The nave at Winchester was, of course, reclothed in the late fourteenth century, and as such is one of the grandest works of perpendicular architecture in the country (see chapter 5). However, as at Canterbury and elsewhere, many fragments of the earlier work still survive, and it is particularly striking to go up into the nave roof and see the Norman half-columns coming up out of the pockets of the later vaults. The one part of the Norman cathedral which has sadly been completely robbed down to its foundations is the great 'westwork'. As a result, there has been much debate as to whether this was originally a great square central tower with smaller side aisles (hence possibly reflecting the Anglo-Saxon cathedral's 'westwork'), or a pair of Norman towers as at Canterbury. A great central tower seems perhaps to be the more likely solution, and was possibly copied at Ely (see below), but further evidence is still needed to prove this.

The crossing tower of the original Norman cathedral collapsed in 1107 and was replaced soon afterwards, and as Professor Willis has shown, the masonry of the four crossing piers (and the adjoining piers in the north and south transepts) is of much better work. The ashlar on the piers is more closely jointed, as well as in the arches above, and it is quite clear that this is all post-1107 work. Willis's investigations revealed that the free-standing piers in the corners of the transepts had also been strengthened at a later Norman date, and there is other evidence to suggest that four smaller towers were to be constructed at the corners of the transepts, though they were apparently never completed. The intention at Winchester, therefore, was that it would soar upwards in a whole series of towers, impressing by its height as well as its very great length. In the event, however, only the rather squat early twelfth-century crossing tower has survived.

Until quite recently, it was thought that almost nothing had survived of Archbishop Thomas of Bayeux's cathedral at York. The very extensive campaign of excavations carried out from 1967–72 beneath the minster has changed all that. The excavations, directed by Derek Phillips, were carried out under very difficult circumstances, during the underpinning of the central crossing tower and the western towers to save them from collapse. As we have seen in the first chapter, nothing was revealed of the Anglo-Saxon cathedral, but to compensate for this the Norman discoveries were of exceptional interest. The foundations were found over large areas, giving us an almost complete plan of Thomas's cathedral, and on top of these many fine fragments of the walls were found standing to 5 feet

Winchester cathedral from the north-west, as it might have appeared in 1095. In front are the robbed-out ruins of the Anglo-Saxon cathedral. In the foreground is the shrine-tomb, from which St Swithin's remains have recently been removed, surrounded by the tombs of late Anglo-Saxon kings and bishops. The large pit to the west (right) is where the bones, disturbed by the new foundations, are being reburied.

high. In several places the rough ashlar work was still covered by its original plaster on which were painted red lines in imitation of large blocks of stone. Norman ground level was about 6 feet below the present floor level of the minster, thus preserving the lowest parts of the walls. Below the walls themselves, in the tops of the foundations, were found an ingenious system of slots into which a timber grillage had been set. In some places the timbers have rotted, leaving voids in the masonry, but elsewhere oak timbers were well preserved. Some of these, with some of the *in situ* foundations, can still be seen in the undercroft museum of the minster. Enough of this timber grillage, part of the constructional system, has been found to allow us to reconstruct how it worked. Once the oak grillage was in place, retaining walls were built on either side and a mortared rubble core then poured in to cover the whole thing. This dried, to give an immensely strong foundation on which could be built the massive 70 to 90 feet high walls of the building. We know this was the height, because fragments of the superstructure have been preserved (just as at Canterbury and Winchester) above the vaults of the later minster on the north-west and south-east sides of the central tower.

In its overall plan Thomas of Bayeux's cathedral was about 365 feet long, and though it would have been dwarfed by the later minster, which was over 500 feet long, it was still a very large building. It was, however, unusual in

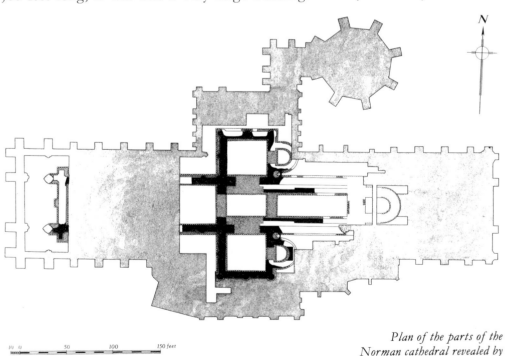

N

Plan of the parts of the Norman cathedral revealed by excavation at York minster.

having no aisles to the nave and no western towers (these were first added in about 1200). The eastern arm of the church projected some 140 feet from the large central tower, and in its original form it appears to have had no crypt, or else only a very small crypt under the eastern apse. This was apparently replaced within about fifteen years of its completion by a square east end; and then, only a few decades later, under archbishop Roger of Pont l'Eveque (1154–81), a large new crypt and presbytery were built with smaller eastern transepts. Parts of the exceptionally beautiful decorated masonry of the piers of this crypt (in Magnesian limestone which is easily carved) were first uncovered in the nineteenth century after the disastrous fire of 1829 which gutted the minster choir. They, too, can still be seen in the 'Victorian' part of the undercroft museum, and are clearly reminiscent of the marvellous piers of Durham cathedral of half a century earlier, to which we must now turn.

Durham cathedral is the finest and most complete of all the Norman cathedrals surviving in Britain. Only its east end (the incomparable 'chapel of the nine altars') and its towers are later. Not only that, but its magnificent setting high up on a rock in a great U-shaped bend in the River Wear makes its situation both secure and very striking. The contemporary Chronicle of Simeon of Durham tells us that Bishop William of St Calais decided to build a new cathedral in 1092 and ordered the whole of the existing church, which had been built nearly a century before, to be demolished. Then, on 29 July 1093, in the presence of the bishop and the prior, the first foundation trenches for the new church were dug. Just under a fortnight later, on 11 August, the first stones were ceremoniously laid. Bishop William died in 1096 but the monks carried on the work, and when Rannulf Flambard was made bishop in 1099 we are told that the church was 'made as far as the nave'. On 29 August 1104 the coffin of St Cuthbert was translated to its new resting place within the eastern apse, and William of Malmesbury tells us that there was a premature but harmless collapse of the centring upon which the vault over the east end was erected. When Bishop Flambard died in 1128 the walls of the nave were complete 'up to the covering' (presumably the vault), and during the next five years the work was completed. Thus, in a period of forty years, the whole of this magnificent structure was put up. As far as we know, it was the first great cathedral in Europe to be vaulted throughout, a truly remarkable achievement.

Before turning to the vaults, however, let us look at the rest of the structure. The complete plan of the Norman cathedral has long been known (parts of the wall of the demolished eastern apse can be seen under the trapdoors close to St Cuthbert's shrine), and it is almost exactly 400 feet in length. The plan is uniform throughout with alternating compound and cylindrical piers giving a series of double bays, and though it is ultimately based on the plan of Lanfranc's cathedral at Canterbury of twenty years or so earlier, it has already moved on very far to embody a new concept, the technological high point of English Romanesque architecture. The main arches, which are very carefully made, are extremely tall, and the famous cylindrical columns have incised into them their splendid decorated patterns, spirals in the eastern arm of the cathedral and lozenges, chevrons and fluting in the nave. The galleries, which are high up, are a much less important element in the cathedral. Walking in them, it is quite clear that their main function is to carry the proto-flying buttresses which take the thrust of the high vaults.

The earliest vaults in Durham must, from the known chronology given above, have been in place before 1100. These were probably those in the choir side aisles and they are already ribbed rather than groined vaults. These consist of diagonal ribs (in the form of round arches) which form a framework into which the infilling (called the webs) were laid. The really bold step, however, came with the construction of the high choir and nave vaults. These span over 30 feet, and though the diagonal ribs are semicircular (as in the aisles), the main transverse ribs, which come in every other bay (between the compound piers), were pointed. This was a remarkable innovation, years ahead of its time in England, and it has even been suggested that the masons got their ideas for this new vaulting technique from the great buildings of the Islamic east. This was after all the period of the First Crusade, which had culminated in the fall of Jerusalem in 1099, and it was certainly a time when many new ideas were reaching north-west Europe from the east.

As they survive today, the high vaults of the choir at Durham date from the thirteenth century; they had to be replaced in c. 1235 when they started to crack. It is, however, still possible to see the scars marking the place of the original vaults high up on the choir walls on either side of the clerestory windows. The nave vaults, the originals of c.1128–33, remain perfectly sound today.

The last few years of the eleventh century are in many ways a turning point in English Romanesque architecture. Not only are ribbed vaults being introduced as general building techniques are becoming much more skilful, but the buildings themselves are changing from the massive solid early Norman structures to the much more decorated and beautiful buildings of the High Romanesque of the twelfth century. Archbishop Lanfranc had not been very keen on the cults relating to the Old English saints, particularly in his own cathedral at Canterbury, but when the saintly Anselm became archbishop in 1093, all this was to change. At Canterbury another extraordinary architectural development was to take place, the building of the new 'Glorious Choir'.

Within three years of the work starting at Durham, the short eastern sanctuary at Canterbury had been pulled down and from 1096 to c.1107 a vast new choir was built on an exceptionally large crypt (see p. 124), almost doubling the length of the cathedral, bringing its total to about 450 feet. This vast choir was built to contain, first, the stalls of the 150 monks of the cathedral priory (Lanfranc's choir was in the nave) and, secondly, a whole host of new chapels and shrines, the most important of which were the tombs of St Dunstan and St Alphege, placed on either side of the high altar. Of this choir, only the huge crypt and the lower parts of the upper walls survive today as it was completely rebuilt after the disastrous fire of 1174, but at the time of its final completion and dedication in 1130 it was considered to be one of the great wonders of England. As William of Malmesbury recorded:

Nothing like it could be seen in England either for the light of its glass windows, the gleaming of its marble pavements, or the many coloured paintings which led the wondering eyes to the panelled ceiling above.

De Gestis Pontificum Anglorum

Virtually nothing survives of this decoration (there are still some contemporary wall paintings in the crypt chapel of St Gabriel), but there is sufficient of the architecture for us to get some idea of the form and proportions of the building which were totally different from that at Durham. At Canterbury the crypt was groin-vaulted and the high choir clearly had a flat timber ceiling (the covering of the aisles is unknown). This allowed thinner walls with much larger windows – hence the lightness of the building where surface decoration was all important.

In the middle years of the twelfth century Canterbury cathedral was finally completed with the building of a series of towers and turrets, only some of which survive today. These were highly decorated (whole surfaces were covered with carved ornament), and for the first time coloured marble shafting was used, particularly Onyx marble and Purbeck marble, albeit very sparingly. The cathedral at this time is depicted in a unique contemporary drawing of c.1160, which emphasises its great length and its towers. Similar decorative work was being added at this time to other cathedrals, and two of the best examples of this are the splendid applied west fronts at nearby Rochester and at Lincoln.

The 'Glorious Choir' at Canterbury and Durham cathedral are perhaps the two most famous buildings of the time, but they were in fact only a part of a quite extraordinary programme of building that was going on all over England at the close of the eleventh century and the beginning of the twelfth. This was the final flowering of Benedictine cathedral monasticism before the Cistercians and others took over the initiative in spiritual matters and started to build churches in a very different way. We have already seen how Durham and Rochester became monastic cathedrals and how Bath abbey became a cathedral in 1091. A few years later in 1095, the bishop of Chester moved his see to St Mary's abbey in Coventry and the bishop of Thetford moved to Norwich.

67

Nothing has yet been found of the Norman cathedral at Coventry (it was sadly the only cathedral in England to be totally destroyed at the Reformation), but at Norwich we still have a marvellous cathedral where work started in 1096. The bishop was a man called Herbert de Losinga (in an extraordinary act of simony he had bought the see for the huge sum of £1900 in 1091), and when he started his new cathedral he attached to it a priory of Benedictine monks. The eastern arm of the cathedral is an enlarged version of the ambulatory plan which we have seen at Chichester and Worcester cathedrals, and it also in part gained its inspiration from the abbey church of Fécamp where Herbert de Losinga had been prior. The chapels off the ambulatory all have unusual shapes, the eastern one (later demolished, but the plan is known from excavation) was horseshoe-shaped, while the two others were in plan double segments of circles. Work on the eastern arm was complete by about 1120, and the monks then turned their attention to the nave where building was to be carried on for the next twenty-five years. It is of great length (over 260 feet and fourteen bays long) and was clearly inspired in the first instance by Durham cathedral. The first six bays had alternating cylindrical and compound piers with spiral decoration on them, though the main arches did not achieve the great height of Durham. After this all the remaining bays were in compound form only, but with more decoration added. Finally, after a fire in 1171, the eastern two pairs of cylindrical piers were encased to make them into compound piers as well. Almost the whole of the Norman shell at Norwich has survived, though pierced by many later windows and covered by some wonderful late mediaeval vaults. Outside, the most striking thing is the great central tower which is the tallest Romanesque tower in England and covered in characteristic late Romanesque decoration. It was originally capped, as many of the twelfth-century towers were, by a squat wooden spire. This was, however, blown over in a storm in 1362, and the stonework of the tower had to be extensively renewed before the present stone spire was added.

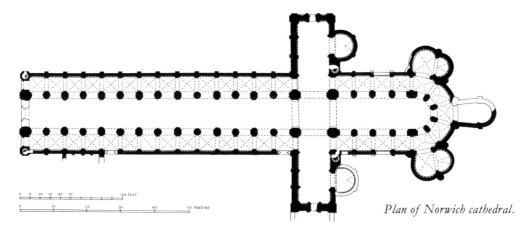

Plan of Norwich cathedral.

Perhaps the finest Norman towers to have survived almost complete are the two which clasp the cathedral at Exeter. Transept towers are most unusual, and are usually found, if anywhere, in churches not cathedrals. Exeter is also unusual in that it was not apparently rebuilt in the Norman period until c.1114–33, after the arrival of William Warelwast as bishop (1107–36). This was long after most other cathedrals. Little is known about the form of the Norman cathedral except the towers (the plan of the east end is unknown) because of the extensive later mediaeval rebuilding. Norman walling up to the window-sill level is still visible in the nave and just east of the crossing. The towers, however, which have been drawn and studied in detail since work started in 1982 on restoring the southern one, are covered in tiers of blind arcading. The main decorative element of the upper parts is a chevron or zig-zag pattern, and almost all the original masonry was of Salcombe stone. Lower down, particularly on the north tower, where the work is plainer, Caen stone is often used. Work on the north tower probably started in about 1120. During the anarchy of 1136–7 construction was perhaps halted for a time, at the level of the strange circular and semi-circular panels, before being completed by about 1170. The nave was not completed until the final years of the century when we are told that Bishop Marshall (1194–1206) 'finished the building according to the Plan and Foundation which his predecessors had laid'.

The last of the great Benedictine abbeys to become a cathedral see was Ely in 1109. Its Norman rebuilding, however, had started in c.1081 under Abbot Simeon, who had previously been the prior of Winchester cathedral priory and was the brother of the bishop there, Walkelin. The plan of Ely (p.16) clearly shows its indebtedness to that of Winchester, though the scale is not quite so large (the whole cathedral was just over 400 feet long). There is roughly the same shaped presbytery (though without the crypt) and the large double aisled transepts and very large nave are also similar. The presbytery and crossing have now disappeared above ground, but much of the great transepts remain, and the nave is perhaps the most complete and beautiful of the early twelfth century in England. Its thirteen bays are over 200 feet in length; like Winchester, Old St Paul's and Norwich, it was never vaulted, and the present (nineteenth-century) wooden ceiling gives an impression of what the original may have been like.

The only cathedral to have rivalled Winchester in length was the now vanished cathedral of St Paul in London whose total length in the later Middle Ages was about 600 feet. The destruction of this truly stupendous building in the Great Fire of 1666 was one of the greatest tragedies in English architecture. However much one may admire Sir Christopher Wren's replacement, one cannot but regret the disappearance of its predecessor. The plan (p.197) and drawings of Old St Paul's that Wenceslas Hollar made about ten years before the Great Fire

are our chief evidence for its appearance, and they show that the nave – the so-called 'old fabric' of 'Paul's Walk' – was another very long nave. Like Ely, it was made entirely of compound piers. The eastern arm of the Norman cathedral was replaced in the thirteenth century by the 'new work', but excavations to the south and east of Wren's choir may one day rediscover the foundations of the earlier as well as the thirteenth-century building. We know that the west front of Old St Paul's was just to the west of the base of the steps leading up to the present west door. Attached to the south side of this was the church of St Gregory, which was almost certainly Anglo-Saxon in origin. Maybe one day the 'sacred' paving behind Queen Victoria's statue could be temporarily removed for a research excavation.

The nave of St Paul's cathedral in the mid-seventeenth century.

The Norman cathedral of St Paul's was started in about 1087 and not completed until about the middle of the next century. As at Winchester, the cathedral was probably planned from the first to be a very large building. Bishops of London at this time were still hopeful that the metropolitan see would be transferred from Canterbury to London; early in the twelfth century Bishop de Belmais petitioned the pope that the Primacy should be moved to London, as Pope Gregory had directed five centuries earlier. Archbishop Anselm in Canterbury had much greater influence in Rome, however, and the metropolitan see remained where it was.

At this time the province of Canterbury had fourteen sees while York had only two (three once Carlisle was added in 1133). It was, however, a time when the English king was expanding his domains, and in 1101 the pope ordered the Scottish bishops to profess obedience to York and to be consecrated by him. Glasgow refused and disputes ensued for many years until in 1188 the pope declared the Scottish Church independent. We will look at the Scottish twelfth-century cathedrals in chapter 6.

In Wales, the church had come under the control of Canterbury by the mid-twelfth century. The process was started as early as 1092 when Herve, a Breton, was forcibly made Bishop of Bangor. His episcopacy was shortlived, but in 1107 the see of Llandaff was refounded, followed in 1115 by St David's, in 1120 by Bangor, and finally in 1143 by St Asaph. All these sees claimed, with some justification, to have been founded in the middle of the sixth century (that is, a half-century before Canterbury), and St David's was considered a metropolitan see from which the other bishops received consecration. It was part of the political programme of Henry I that the sees of Wales should come under the authority of the province of Canterbury. Initially this was accepted by the Welsh bishops, but during the anarchy under King Stephen, Bishop Bernard of St David's argued his case for an independent archbishopric with Archbishop Theobald of Canterbury at the papal court at Meaux in 1147. He lost, as did two later attempts for independence in 1176 and 1198, and from that time the cathedrals of Wales were effectively under the control of Canterbury.

The refounding of the Welsh sees coincided with the period of Norman rebuilding, and the earliest remains in the cathedrals of Bangor and Llandaff date from this time. We are told in *The Book of Llandaff* that when Urban was made bishop in 1107 the 'Little Minster' he found was only 28 feet long, 15 feet wide and 20 feet high. It had very small transeptal annexes and an apsidal chancel 12 feet long and 12 feet wide. Shortly afterwards (c.1120) Urban started to rebuild his cathedral totally; behind the high altar a large, highly decorated round arch of Bishop Urban's new cathedral can still be seen. In the nearby south wall of the sanctuary, the top of a second arch can be seen, cut through by a later arch.

These were probably parts of the eastern arm of the cathedral, and the building of the nave no doubt followed on sporadically after this. The beautiful, highly decorated doorways on either side of the nave perhaps date to the completion of the work in c.1160–70. In 1188 Baldwin of Canterbury came on a tour of Wales to exert his supremacy and preach the Second Crusade. He was accompanied by the Welsh historian, Gerald (who ten years later himself tried unsuccessfully to become archbishop of St David's), and we can imagine them on the green outside the newly constructed cathedral standing with the Welsh on one side, and the English on the other.

The other Welsh cathedral which retains visible traces of its earlier Norman fabric is Bangor. The present building still reflects the cruciform plan of Bishop David's (1120–39) church. It was about 130 feet long with a triapsidal east end, and a blocked-up Norman window, as well as a pilaster buttress, can still be seen on the south side of the choir. The foundations of an apse south of this were excavated in 1946. The nave of the Norman church was probably two bays shorter than the present nave and it seems likely that it was unaisled.

The finest and largest of the Welsh cathedrals is that at St David's. The present church was not started until about 1180 under its third Norman bishop, Peter de Leia (1176–98). The whole of the nave, as well as the western parts of the crossing and transepts, all date from the last twenty years of the twelfth century, and in many ways they reflect the high Romanesque style, but the pointed arches in the last two bays of the nave, as well as in the triforium, clearly look forward to the Gothic style. All the arches, however, are typical mid-twelfth-century round arches with some fine decoration carved on them. There is also a series of unusual decorated arches on the upper walls framing the whole of the triforium and clerestory, and it is likely that some of the inspiration for this work came from Wells and Worcester. The twelfth-century roof was clearly of timber, and was replaced at the end of the fifteenth century by another amazing timber roof with dropped pendants. The west front at St David's has a large decorated doorway with flanking pronounced turrets similar to the west fronts of Rochester, Norwich and Hereford (the last destroyed in 1786).

By the middle decades of the twelfth century, the initial building of most of the great English cathedrals had been finished. The century after the arrival in England of Archbishop Lanfranc had been one of the most remarkable periods of building work ever undertaken in England, and never again would such ambitious construction programmes be undertaken by the church. In virtually every case, Lanfranc's bishops had started with a 'clean slate'. After this time, although almost all the cathedrals would be refashioned at one time or another, the work would be carried out in stages, leaving in most cases the shell or skeleton of the Norman cathedral (Salisbury is the only major exception). As we have seen in this chapter, it is within this shell or skeleton that so much of the evidence lies that archaeologists are now rediscovering and examining. By combining detailed study of these remains with below-ground excavation, it is now possible to reconstruct on paper much more of the original form of these remarkable structures.

74

THE NORMAN CATHEDRALS

CATHEDRALS REBUILT ON THE SAME SITE

Main dates of building

1	Canterbury	1071–7, and c.1096–c.1160
2	Rochester	c.1077–83 and c.1130–60
3	Winchester	1079–93, 1093–c.1107, and c.1108–20
4	Hereford	1079–1100, and c.1100–45
5	York	c.1080–1100, c.1137–40, and c.1154–75
6	Worcester	1084–9, 1089–c.1120
7	London	c.1087–1110, and c.1110–30
8	Durham	1093–1104, and 1104–1133
9	Exeter	c.1114–c.1160

CATHEDRALS MOVED TO NEW SITE

10	Lincoln (from Dorchester, 1072–5)	c.1074–92
11	Norwich (from Thetford, 1095, from Elmham, 1072–5)	c.1096–1120, and 1121–45
12	Chichester (from Selsey, 1075)	c.1078–c.1108
13	Salisbury (Old Sarum, from Sherborne, 1075)	1078–92, and c.1103–39
14	Coventry (from Chester, 1095 from Lichfield, 1075)	c.1100–
15	Bath (from Wells, 1091)	c.1091–1122, and 1123–c.1130

NEW CATHEDRAL SEES

16	Ely (1109)	c.1083–1106, and c.1109–c.1130
17	Carlisle (1133)	c.1092–1123

3

REACHING UP TO HEAVEN

The Early English Gothic cathedrals

On 29 December 1170, Thomas Becket, Archbishop of Canterbury was murdered in his own cathedral. The event shocked the whole of Christendom and led to Becket's canonisation in less than three years. Eighteen months later, on 5 September 1174, the whole of Archbishop Anselm's 'Glorious Choir' at Canterbury was gutted by fire. The new choir and Trinity Chapel (designed as a shrine for St Thomas) that rose like a phoenix out of this shell in only a decade were built in the new French so called 'Gothic' style, the first time it had been used in England. It was a marvellous achievement. But more important from our point of view is the fact that, uniquely for mediaeval building work, the whole of this rebuilding is described year by year in great detail by an eye witness, the monk Gervase. All of this work is still visible in Canterbury cathedral, where is has remained almost untouched for over 800 years.

The building of the new choir at Canterbury between 1175 and 1184 is a turning point in English architecture, and its unique documentation repays careful study for the light it throws on how cathedrals were erected in Europe during the high Middle Ages. The whole of Gervase's account, written in Latin, was translated and then analysed in detail by Professor Robert Willis in the last century, and remains one of the great classics of architectural history. Since Willis's time, studies have been made of many details of the fabric (and of the sculpture and stained glass), but no new overall survey and analysis has been undertaken.

Gervase's narrative begins with a full account of the fire of 1174 and the destruction it wrought. He then tells us that 'French and English artificers' were summoned for a conference and after much disagreement as to what could be done, the monks chose a man called William of Sens, 'a man active and ready, and as a workman most skilful in wood and stone', and dismissed the others. William first made a detailed survey of the burnt shell, and started to plan the new choir, pulling down all the damaged stone walls including the heavily calcined pillars. Gervase goes on:

And now he addressed himself to procuring stone from overseas. He constructed ingenious machines for loading and unloading ships and for drawing cement and stones. He delivered moulds for shaping the stones to the sculptors who were assembled, and diligently prepared other things of the same kind. The choir thus condemned to destruction was pulled down, and nothing else was done in this year.

The eastern arm of Canterbury cathedral
in the summer of 1175, prepared for the
rebuilding work to start.

The Early English Gothic cathedrals

After describing the earlier cathedral of Lanfranc and Anselm, Gervase returns to his narrative:

In the following year, that is, after the feast of St Bertin [5 September 1175], before the winter, he erected four pillars, that is, two on each side, and after winter two more were placed, so that on each side were three in order, upon which and upon the exterior wall of the aisles he framed seemly arches and a vault, that is three *claves* [keystones or bosses] on each side. I put *clavis* for the whole vault because the *clavis* placed in the middle locks up and binds together the parts which converge to it from every side. With these works the second year was occupied.

Here we have a marvellous description of how the ribbed quadripartite vaults at the west end of the north and south choir aisles were seen being built. In the next year the rest of the columns and arches of the choir were erected as far as the eastern crossing and then the triforium gallery and clerestory above were built 'intermingled with many marble columns'. Gervase then describes how the high vaults were built from the central tower to the eastern crossing, 'all which things appeared to us and to all who saw them, incomparable and most worthy of praise'. Clearly the monks were beginning to see what a splendid new building they were getting.

If we look at the choir today, we can still see exactly what William of Sens did in these first two years. The lower parts of the outer walls are of early twelfth-century masonry, but higher up larger, better-cut blocks can be seen, and we are clearly into new work. The old windows have been heightened and above them is a new gallery in front of a series of unusual large trefoil-headed windows. Partly covering these windows is the first of William's new vaults. In the main arcade, the first things to be noted are the magnificent large carved capitals, the work of great sculptors who had come from north-eastern France. Similar capitals can be seen at St Denis in Paris, and at Sens and Laon cathedrals. Above the capitals, and especially in the triforium gallery, which is a mass of round and pointed arches, there are many shafts of Purbeck marble, just as described by Gervase. This vertical marble shafting, used in England for the first time at Canterbury, was soon widely taken up in new building work, and by the beginning of the thirteenth century it was ubiquitous. Salisbury cathedral is perhaps the best known example.

Springing from the upper walls are the ribs for the high vaults, which were the first really large vaults to be built in the cathedral. Right from the start they are managed with great virtuosity, and it is no wonder that the monks were impressed by William of Sens' work. The main vaults are sexpartite, which means they are in six sections (i.e., with six areas of webbing), and their beautiful curves, as well as the striking 'nailhead' decoration on the ribs and the carved bosses, are a perfect match for the splendid capitals and great shafts down below. But

Great Cathedrals of Britain

*The first four stages of the rebuilding
of the eastern arm of Canterbury cathedral
as described by Gervase.*

what about the technology required to achieve this? To see this best, we must go up into the triforium galleries above the aisle vaults.

In the first bays to be built on the south we find a series of transverse arches under the roof running from north to south. A series of barrel vaults rests on them, and between each vault a triangular-shaped buttress rises up through the roof to support, on external pilaster buttresses, the upper clerestory wall. Remarkably this upper wall sits in part, not on the triforium arches, but on the haunches or shoulders of the aisle vaults below. This very complicated situation, used to spread the great weight of the high vaults, can best be seen and understood in the diagram. On the north side of the choir aisle, we can see that a similar system of transverse barrel vaults was started, but never completed. Here William of Sens changed his mind very soon after beginning the work, and put in instead an upper semicircular buttress, which sits on the wall over the lower transverse arch and supports the upper clerestory wall. This upper semicircular buttress soon becomes separate (supporting itself under its own weight), and is the first true 'flying buttress' to be used in the rebuilding. From then on, they become standard for the rest of the work, and can be seen above the sloping aisle roofs all the way round the Trinity Chapel. Prototype flying buttresses had first been used in England at Durham a few decades earlier, but these were hidden under the triforium roofs.

During the summer of 1178 Gervase tells us that ten more pillars (five on each side) were erected, and on to these William of Sens:

placed the arches and vaults. And having, in the next place, completed on both sides the triforia and upper windows, he was in the act of preparing with machines for the turning of the great vault, when suddenly the beams broke under his feet, and he fell to the ground, stones and timbers accompanying his fall, from the height of the capitals of the upper vault, that is to say, of fifty feet.

The columns and aisle vaults erected in 1178 in the presbytery area, were much more difficult to place because here William of Sens was constrained by the existing curving outer walls of Anselm's 'glorious choir' which had on either side two large clasping 'tower chapels' (which Gervase calls the towers of St Andrew and St Anselm). Furthermore, the most easterly of the new columns, which was placed over the old crypt ambulatory, had to have a pair of columns underneath for support. For this a pair of Anselm's old choir columns (considerably shortened) were used, and they are still a fine sight in the crypt. The vaulting of the aisles was an equally complicated operation because of the irregular area to be covered, and the first bay has an unusual five-part vault.

William of Sens fell as he was supervising putting up the largest of the vaults, a quadripartite vault, over the eastern crossing. Each of the diagonal ribs had to span more than 50 feet, and they are locked together with a huge boss

WINTER 1175

WINTER 1177

SUMMER 1176

SUMMER 1179

over 2 feet wide (Gervase's *clavis*) on which was carved the Paschal lamb carrying the flag of victory (the symbol of the Resurrection).

William was badly injured, but tried to continue to supervise the work from a sick bed. He got no better and returned to France that winter. The following spring of 1179 a new master mason took control; he was an Englishman, also called William. He finished the transept vaults and then erected the splendid sexpartite vault over the high altar. He also laid the foundations for the enlarged Trinity Chapel around the then still-existing Norman Trinity Chapel (Becket's body was buried in the crypt of this chapel). To do this, Gervase tells us, he had to dig in the cemetery, and all the bones that were disturbed were carefully collected and put in a large trench on the north. Gervase goes on:

Having, therefore, formed a most substantial foundation for the exterior wall with stone and cement, he erected the wall of the crypt as high as the bases of the windows.

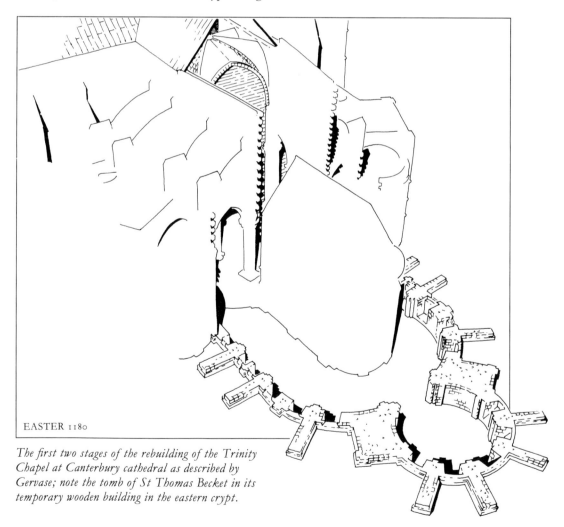

EASTER 1180

The first two stages of the rebuilding of the Trinity Chapel at Canterbury cathedral as described by Gervase; note the tomb of St Thomas Becket in its temporary wooden building in the eastern crypt.

These were the first totally new foundations and outer walls to be built, and today we can still see the large blocks of Marquise stone at the base (no doubt re-used from the earlier building), with new blocks of Caen stone on top. These blocks are larger in size than the earlier Norman ones, and onlookers in the autumn of 1179 must have been amazed to see the old two-storied Trinity Chapel surrounded by the horseshoe-shaped new lower wall with its huge buttresses. To the east was the base of an almost circular chapel called the Corona with vast square bases (later to hold stair-turrets) in the angles between the two parts.

In the early spring of 1180, the monks decided that they must be able to move back into the choir by Easter. Accordingly, William made a temporary wooden wall just behind the high altar (with three windows in it, we are told), and the new altars were made ready, as well as new tombs on either side of the high altar for the bodies of St Dunstan and St Alphege. A detailed account is then given of the translation of the remains into new 'wooden chests, covered within and without with lead and strongly bound with iron'. They were then 'enclosed in stone-work that was consolidated with melted lead'. St Dunstan's tomb was opened for inspection 328 years later in 1508, after the abbot of Glastonbury abbey claimed that his abbey had the remains of St Dunstan, and though the upper part of the tomb was destroyed at the Reformation, the coffin may still be *in situ* under the present floor. The position of the tombs of St Dunstan and St Alphege were once again marked on the floor in May 1988 on the millennium of Dunstan's death.

WINTER 1180

Once the monks had moved into the new choir, other altars and tomb shrines were made ready in the double apsidal chapels of the eastern transepts. All the relics and coffins were moved there from the eastern Trinity Chapel (including the coffin of Archbishop Lanfranc), except the most important shrine

81

of St Thomas Becket in the crypt. This was covered with a temporary wooden structure while the whole of the surrounding Norman building was 'levelled to the ground'. Eight new double columns were then erected in a horseshoe-shape (around Becket's tomb) for the new crypt, and a new entrance was made from the old crypt to the new before work stopped at the end of a momentous year.

At this point Gervase pauses in his narrative to enumerate the differences between the old and new work:

> The pillars of the old and new work are alike in form and thickness but different in length. For the new pillars were elongated by almost twelve feet. In the old capitals the work was plain, in the new ones exquisite in sculpture. There the circuit of the choir had twenty-two pillars, here are twenty-eight. There the arches and every thing else was plain, or sculptured with an axe and not with a chisel. But here almost throughout is appropriate sculpture. No marble columns were there, but here are innumerable ones. There in the circuit around the choir, the vaults were plain, but here they are arch-ribbed and have keystones. There a wall set upon pillars divided the crosses [i.e. transepts] from the choir, but here the crosses are separated from the choir by no such partition, and converge together in one keystone, which is placed in the middle of the great vault which rests on the four principal pillars. There, there was a ceiling of wood decorated with excellent painting, but here is a vault beautifully constructed of stone and light tufa. There, there was a single triforium [wall passage], but here are two in the choir and a third in the aisle of the church. All which will be better understood from inspection than by any description.

These last words are just as true today, 800 years later. We can still see, exactly as Gervase described them, the twenty-eight tall pillars and exquisite capitals, the high-quality chiselled sculpture (the earlier 'axe work' can still be seen in the lower parts of the outer walls), the masses of vertical shafts of Purbeck marble, and the beautifully constructed rib-vaults of stone and light tufa. It is an astonishing piece of work and was clearly immediately considered a masterpiece. Whether the whole design was that of William of Sens, or whether it was modified by William the Englishman is still a subject for debate, but what matters is the overall harmony of the work. Stand today at the western entrance to the choir (or in the organ-loft), and you cannot fail to be impressed with the unity of design in one of western Europe's great architectural masterpieces.

The last four years of William the Englishman's work (1181–4) are dealt with rather rapidly by Gervase. He tells us that in 1181 'the new and handsome crypt was completed' and the outer walls of the upper Trinity Chapel were finished up to the marble capitals, but the windows were not turned, nor were the interior pillars erected because of the approaching winter rains. The following year William:

> erected the eight [double] interior pillars and turned the arches and the vault with the windows in the circuit. He also raised the tower [i.e. Corona] up to the bases of the highest windows under the vault. In the ninth year no work was done for want of funds. In the tenth year the

upper windows of the tower, together with the vault, were finished. Upon the pillars was placed a lower and an upper triforium [gallery], with windows and the great vault. Also was made the upper roof where the cross stands aloft, and the roof of the aisles as far as the laying of the lead. The tower was covered in, and many other things done this year.

At this point Gervase's narrative stops suddenly, and he goes straight on to tell us that in that year (1184) Baldwin was elected archbishop. For the next thirty or so years the priory was to go through the most difficult period in its history with constant disputes between archbishops Baldwin and Hubert Walter, and then with King John. From 1207–13 the monks were in exile in France, and only after 1215 did a new era dawn; the translation of St Thomas Becket's body finally taking place at a great ceremony in July 1220.

A close examination of the Trinity Chapel adds much to Gervase's brief narrative. First we can see that just after the old Trinity Chapel was demolished in 1180 an apparent modification to the plan was made which involved raising the level of the upper chapel (and surrounding ambulatory) by about 8 feet. This can be seen most clearly at the extreme east end of the north choir aisle where the steps up to the Trinity Chapel progressively bury an earlier lower arcade which was originally to have led to an ambulatory at a lower level. Just off these same steps a door leads southwards into a little-known chamber called the 'Wax Chamber' (now the Vesturer's office) which lies beneath the archbishop's throne. Here a pair of very fine rib vaults of the same kind as the aisle vaults can be inspected at close quarters, but these have been roughly inserted, with no capitals beneath, and with the bosses left uncut, after the change of plan. No doubt some of the stones which were intended for the vault of the ambulatory were used. This chamber, which was later used to store candles and so on, has windows into the eastern crypt. It could, therefore, have acted as a watching-chamber for the earlier shrine of St Thomas in the crypt.

The most striking thing to notice in the Trinity Chapel is the use of double columns of polished marble around the sacred area of the shrine itself. This marble is of two kinds, Purbeck marble (here used in horizontally-bedded drums) and a pink marble of a very unusual kind whose source (it is not English) has not yet been identified. The pink marble is only used in the area immediately around the shrine, and it can also be seen in the capitals, shaft-rings and bases of the very tall free-standing columns of the outer aisle and in the lozenge pattern on the floor on either side of the shrine. The shrine itself was totally destroyed by Henry VIII in 1538, but a few fragments of it have survived and are now kept in the cathedral library: these are also of pink marble. The shrine was on a low podium of three steps and when this, too, was broken up in 1538, the steps were laid flat in the middle of the floor. These slabs still bear the pattern worn by countless pilgrims' feet on them, and a few years ago I was able to reconstruct the shape of the podium exactly from them. To the west of the shrine was a magnificent Italian marble-inlay pavement; this still survives.

The final part of William the Englishman's rebuilding concerned the most unusual round tower called the Corona, later to hold the shrine for Thomas Becket's head. It is covered (as is the area above the main shrine) by a wonderful octopartite vault into which masses of light penetrates from the large clerestory windows. Above this, however, some sort of tower was planned that was never finished, and the bottoms of the windows of an upper chamber can still be seen, though now surrounded by brickwork of Tudor and eighteenth-century date. On either side of the Corona are large stair-turrets (much used today by visitors to the cathedral in the summer), and it seems likely that quite a large chamber was planned here, with perhaps a short spire above it. In the event nothing further was ever built, except the crenellated parapet raised in 1748, though George Gilbert Scott and other nineteenth-century architects suggested various plans which were never taken up.

It should be apparent that the rebuilding of the Canterbury choir was a work of great importance and it directly influenced the building of other cathedrals, though nothing like the same documentation survives elsewhere.

Until 1238 the bishopric of Rochester was directly under the control and patronage of the archbishop of Canterbury, and close contact always existed between both establishments of monks. Gervase, the same monk who described the rebuilding of the Canterbury choir, tells us that on 11 April 1179 'the church of St Andrew [at Rochester] with all its offices was burnt and reduced to cinders'. Virtually no other documentary evidence survives except that we know that windows were glazed and the roof of the great church leaded early in the thirteenth century. However, Rochester cathedral today has a magnificent eastern arm, raised on a large crypt that must date from circa 1180–1200. It consists of a large presbytery (uniquely without aisles and having only a two-storied elevation-arcade and clerestory), with flanking eastern transepts which each have double chapels with an unusual chamber above. What is so striking, however, is the close connection between the vertical shafting, the windows and the vaults here and the work of William the Englishman at Canterbury. Sir William St John Hope made a careful study of this work in 1898 and suggested it was built from circa 1200–1215. But the detailing is so similar to the Canterbury work of the early 1180s that there can be little doubt that the whole eastern arm at Rochester, including the choir, was rebuilt soon after the fire of 1179 by masons who came from William's team at Canterbury.

As mentioned in chapter 2, Chichester cathedral also suffered a devastating fire, in 1187, and the nave and choir were recased afterwards. However, not long after this the eastern apse was breached and a start was made on a new presbytery.

This, too, was strongly influenced by the work at Canterbury. Here we find what is a continuing trend in 'Early English' architecture, the replacement of rounded Norman east ends by squared-off east ends, often in a tripartite form with a Lady Chapel in the centre. At Chichester the piers that were built to bridge the old ambulatory are a magnificent pair of round columns made of horizontally bedded drums of Purbeck marble, surrounded by four vertical Purbeck shafts. At the top is a very fine composite capital. In the triforium above are some fine double arches, and they are joined together in a high east wall of the same form, but with rich sculpture of grotesque animals running after each other in the hollows of the mouldings. Above this is a trio of lancets which can be seen down the full length of the choir, while below is the entrance to the Lady Chapel. Here all the styles of architecture from late twelfth century to early fourteenth century can be made out in a unified whole.

During the thirteenth century Chichester, like other cathedrals, was to acquire many fine but small-scale additions, notably the porches and outer chapels on either side of the nave. It is again archaeology that can disinter such features from later work and show, for example, that the chapels on either side of the nave were originally covered on the outside with unusual transverse gables, only later replaced by a continuous parapet (see p.216).

At Winchester, Bishop de Lucy began work on a retrochoir as early as 1190. The detailed study of the fabric carried out by Professor Willis and more recently by Dr Peter Draper makes clear that it was built as a setting for a new shrine of St Swithin. Later works in the area, the building of huge chantry chapels, and the destructive work of the Reformation have all done much to obscure this, but we should not forget that many of the rebuilt east ends of cathedrals were erected in the thirteenth century to house large new shrine-tombs.

The rebuilding of the whole eastern arm of Lincoln cathedral at this time was the most extensive of all. This work was started in 1192 by Bishop Hugh of Avalon (later St Hugh). The disaster that led to it was not a fire this time, but an earthquake which took place on 15 April 1185 and was said to have 'split the minster from top to bottom'. No earthquake is recorded elsewhere, and what probably happened was a collapse of the central crossing tower, though whether this was in fact triggered by an earthquake, or whether it was just caused by a fault in the earlier work, there is no way of telling. The result, however, was the decision to rebuild on a very large scale, yet again no doubt influenced by the new choir at Canterbury. Much money had to be collected and permission had to be sought from the king to breach the old Roman city wall which hemmed in the cathedral on the east. It was seven years before this was obtained, and work could start on the remarkable new eastern arm later known as St Hugh's choir (he died in 1200, and was canonised in 1220). The extreme east end of this

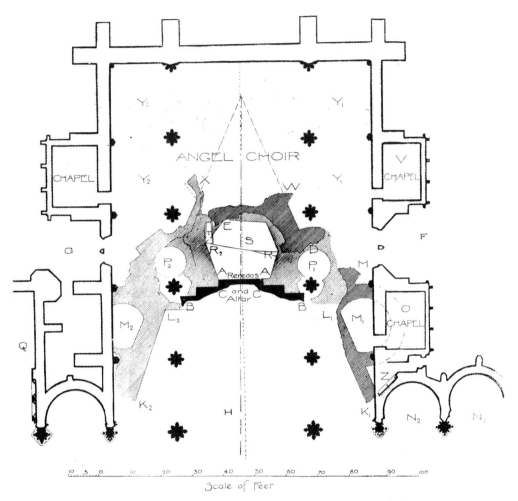

*Plan of the foundation of the east end of St Hugh's cathedral
at Lincoln uncovered in 1886.*

building was demolished only just over sixty years later when the Angel choir
was built, but a brief excavation carried out in November 1886 uncovered a
rough plan which shows that the new cathedral ended in a polygonal ambulatory
terminated by a hexagonal chapel with flanking spiral staircases. This is reminiscent of the Corona area at Canterbury, as are the eastern transepts with double
chapels ending in apses.

But in many other ways Lincoln is totally different and the master mason
here, Geoffrey de Noiers (apparently an Englishman) created many 'strange and
unexpected' things, to quote Sir Nikolaus Pevsner, which are unique to Lincoln.
Perhaps the strangest, and certainly the most famous, are the vaults above the
main choir, which some years ago were christened the 'crazy vaults'. Here we
find, not the usual quadripartite or sexpartite vaults with a central boss, but two

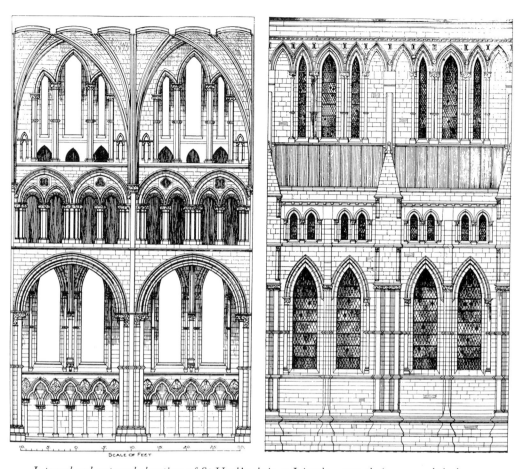

Internal and external elevations of St Hugh's choir at Lincoln – note the 'crazy vaults' above.

bosses on a ridge-rib at the centre of each bay, from which alternating Y-shaped patterns of ribs run back to the clerestory wall giving a syncopated effect. This has the advantage, if nothing else, of allowing more light in from the clerestory windows, and though these vaults were a one-off experiment, they led the way to all the vault patterns created in the later thirteenth- and fourteenth-century work at Lincoln, involving the use of tiercerons and ridge-ribs (in the nave and Angel choir), and liernes (under the tower). All these developments in vaulting are something that is quintessentially English, and we shall meet it again at other cathedrals.

At Lincoln some small-scale below-ground archaeology has recently been carried out by David Stocker which has allowed the foundations of the demolished north chapel in the north-east transept to be re-examined, as well as establishing the position of the demolished Roman city wall that runs under the minster. This can still be seen outside the south side of the retrochoir. The most important recent work, however, has been up in the roofs where detailed examination of the surviving mediaeval roof trusses has been undertaken.

The study of the great timber roofs of our cathedrals has only really begun in the last two decades, as the result of the pioneering work on structural carpentry by Mr Cecil Hewett and of the very great advances made recently in mediaeval oak dendrochronology (tree-ring dating). Lincoln cathedral, as Mr Hewett first recognised, has more original timber roofing surviving than any other cathedral in Britain, and during 1979 and 1980 extensive repair and releading of the roof was undertaken. This allowed a team from Nottingham University to make a detailed study of all the carpentry and to take samples for dendrochronology. The results from this work are still being analysed, but already it is clear that a great deal of new light has been thrown on the dating of the various parts of the cathedral.

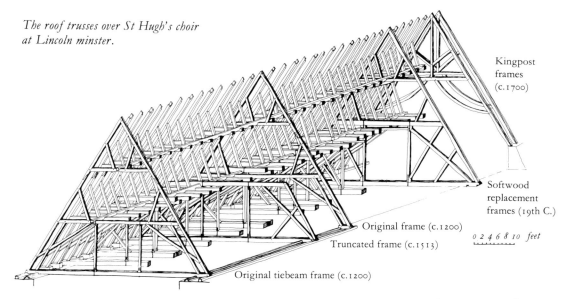

The roof trusses over St Hugh's choir at Lincoln minster.

Kingpost frames (c.1700)

Softwood replacement frames (19th C.)

Original frame (c.1200)

Truncated frame (c.1513)

Original tiebeam frame (c.1200)

0 2 4 6 8 10 *feet*

The earliest roofs, as one might expect, are those over St Hugh's choir and the inner parts of the north-east and south-east transepts, and the dates from the tree-rings suggest that they were erected between the end of the 1190s and 1209 at the latest. An exact date, though theoretically possible, cannot be given because most of the outer rings of the trees (the sapwood) was removed by adzing during construction. It is also probable that some of the trees were stockpiled for a short time after felling, and it seems very likely that the whole of the eastern arm of the cathedral was roofed in the first decade of the thirteenth century, immediately after the death of Bishop Hugh in November 1200. Though documentary evidence to confirm this is scarce, there is one letter from King John, dated January 1209, to a local official asking that the canons of Lincoln be allowed to take from the forest (probably Sherwood Forest) the timber that they have acquired and also the lead they had bought for the building of their church. Shortly after this the king was excommunicated by the pope and between 1209–13 all work must have stopped while the whole country was placed under papal interdict.

The study of the carpentry has also shown that the first area to be roofed was the presbytery (i.e. over the original polygonal east end described above). Some of the timbers from this were reused in the later roof of the 1270s over the Angel choir, and tree-ring dates, as well as constructional details, can be obtained from them. The south-east transept was next, and then the north-east transept roofs were raised from south to north. This was followed by the building of the main roof over the choir from the eastern crossing westwards to the central tower. All of this can be deduced from the joints and surviving carpenters' marks, and in looking at the roofs carefully, it can be seen that only later were longitudinal timbers and truncated frames put in to stop the roof raking (i.e. tilting sideways). The last few trusses immediately to the east of the central tower were certainly destroyed in the fall of the tower in 1237–9 (as was the vault beneath), and the later thirteenth-century roof here, which was less well built, was replaced again early in the eighteenth century.

The vaults beneath the roofs could only have been constructed once the roof was finished and covered in lead, so we can be certain that when St Hugh died in 1200 all the walls of the eastern arm were virtually complete and roofing work was starting. The 'crazy vaults' over the choir, however, cannot have been built until the first decade of the thirteenth century.

The study of carpentry is now taking place in several other cathedrals, most recently at Exeter and Ely, and in conjunction with dendrochronology is, for the first time, allowing independent dates to be obtained for construction work. This is extremely important where, unlike Canterbury, only very sketchy documentary evidence survives for dating major building works – in the past much dating of the architecture has been based on stylistic comparisons with other buildings, and can only be very approximate. As we shall see, roof carpentry has been of great use in this respect at Wells cathedral, thanks to the pioneering work of Cecil Hewett.

Reginald Fitz Jocelin de Bohun, member of a great Norman family and son of the then Bishop of Salisbury (the latter had apparently taken priest's orders and been made bishop only about a year after Reginald's birth in 1140–1), was consecrated bishop of Bath and Wells in Savoy on 23 June 1174. On his way back to his enthroning in Bath, he happened to pass through Canterbury on 4–5 September and actually witnessed the disastrous fire which gutted the cathedral choir. Later he was no doubt informed of the splendid rebuilding work there under the direction of Willliam of Sens, and determined to build a new cathedral for himself. (Ironically he was himself nominated archbishop of Canterbury just before his death in 1191).

This was a time when bishops were challenging the independence of Benedictine monks, particularly those belonging to cathedral monasteries, and attempting to establish their ecclesiastical authority over them. For this reason, Reginald must have been keen to move his see away from Bath and return to the former cathedral at Wells. No documentary evidence exists to tell us when the rebuilding work started at Wells, but Dr John Harvey has argued persuasively that it began between 1175 and 1180, and continued for about the next twenty-five years until halted by the papal interdict incurred by King John in 1208–9. As we shall see, there is a clear indication that halfway down the nave the work paused and this almost certainly occurred between about 1209 and 1215. Reginald de Bohun's successor was his cousin Savaric (bishop 1192–1205) who was a crony of King Richard I, and one of the negotiators for Richard's ransom after his capture on the way back from the Crusades. This gave him great power and Savaric managed to persuade the German Emperor, Henry VI, that one of the conditions of Richard's release was that Glastonbury abbey, the richest monastery in the country, should be added to his see. This was sanctioned by the pope, but bitterly opposed by the monks of Glastonbury and by King Richard after his release. Several violent scenes occurred which came to a head in 1200 when Savaric came to Glastonbury, broke down the doors of the abbey church, and had himself enthroned there with the active assistance of the dean and canons of Wells. The claim was only finally given up nearly twenty years later in 1219 by Savaric's successor, Jocelin (bishop 1206–42).

Only five miles down the road from Wells, Glastonbury had suffered a disastrous fire in 1184. Shortly afterwards, when the abbacy was vacant and the abbey in the hands of the king, Henry II had issued a charter declaring:

> because that whatsoever a man soweth, that shall he also reap, I, in the act of laying the foundation of the church of Glastonbury (which, being in my hands, has been reduced to ashes by a fire), do decree, by the persuasion of Heraclius, the patriarch of Jerusalem, Baldwin, archbishop of Canterbury and many others, that God willing, it shall be magnificently completed by myself or by my heirs.

The work had been put in the hands of the royal chamberlain Ralph Fitzstephen who was permitted to spend all the abbey's enormous revenues on rebuilding. After completing the western Lady Chapel by 1186, work started on the foundations of a huge new church which, we are told, was '400 feet in length, and 80 feet in breadth'. This vast royal structure was clearly to be the greatest church in the whole of western Britain, but after Henry II's death in 1189, its great wealth, as we have seen, made it the prize for much unseemly scrambling by greedy secular clerics. Hence its brief period as a cathedral see from 1195 to 1219.

Soon after Henry VIII's Dissolution of the monasteries, most of the great abbey of Glastonbury was demolished, but enough of the ruins survive to give us at least some idea of its size and architecture. Best preserved is the shell of the Lady Chapel, at the west end of the great church which is in late Romanesque style and must have been begun well before the 1184 fire, and completed after it. Adam of Damerham's Chronicle, written about a century later, says the Lady Chapel was built 'of squared stones of the most beautiful workmanship, omitting no possible ornament', and today it is still covered with some exceptionally fine sculptures, particularly on the north and south doorways. This chapel was dedicated in 1186, as we have seen, and is very different in style from the great church.

Only parts of the outer south walls of the nave and presbytery of this building survive, as well as remnants, 70 feet high, of the east side of the main crossing and transepts. Compared with Wells, these fragments are much more conservative in style, with chevron and other Romanesque features being used. This is very similar to the near contemporary building work at St David's cathedral in west Wales, as well as the retrochoir at Hereford cathedral, and the perhaps slightly earlier work at Worcester cathedral, seen in the two western bays of the nave. Apart from Wells, the only cathedral in the west where English Gothic is used is in the new nave at Llandaff (c.1193–1229). Furthermore, we know that Christ Church cathedral in Dublin (1172–1215), which is also in the new Gothic style, was entirely designed and built by men from Somerset. All of this suggests that the great new 'proto-cathedral' at Glastonbury, if we may be allowed to call it that, was built in the conservative style current in the west of England and Wales in the 1170s and 1180s. It looks as if this huge new structure was built very rapidly between about 1185 and 1200, and it is interesting to note that at this period the principal quarry at Doulting, eight miles from Wells, was reserved exclusively for the use of the monks of Glastonbury as so much stone was needed by them, so that the canons of Wells, who had been making use of this quarry, were forced to go elsewhere for stone. Sure enough, we find that Chilcote conglomerate starts to be used in the transepts and easternmost bay of the south aisle of the nave at Wells in the 1190s. Chilcote is much harder and less easy to cut, but it came from a quarry that belonged to the canons and was only two and a quarter miles away. It is used in the upper parts of the transepts along with Doulting stone (no doubt obtained earlier) for the carved work.

Wells cathedral, though quite small, is one of the great masterpieces of English architecture. It seems remarkable that it was being built at exactly the same time as the huge abbey of Glastonbury in a completely different style. Started in about 1180, it was the first cathedral to have pointed arches everywhere, and in every way can be considered the first truly 'English Gothic' building in Britain. Sadly, documentary evidence for the building of Wells is extremely poor, and we have no idea who the master mason was or where he came from. After a close study of all the available evidence, Dr John Harvey has concluded that 'the master of Wells has to be envisaged as a young man already showing genius in or very soon after 1175, and capable of producing the complete plan and at least quire elevations, by or before 1180'.

The building and architectural history of Wells was first studied in detail by Dean Armitage Robinson and John Bilson in the 1920s. Their masterly surveys have been the basis for the later work of John Harvey, Linzee Colchester and others, so that it can be said that in many ways the fabric of Wells is better known than at most cathedrals. The building stones, masons' marks, mouldings, and roof carpentry have been studied (though dendrochronology has not yet been carried out), and extremely detailed measured drawings have been made of the west front and its famous sculpture during the conservation and restoration work of recent years. The eastern arm of the cathedral, where work started in about 1180, was rebuilt and enlarged in the late thirteenth and early fourteenth century, but from the second bays of the choir westwards the structure is remarkably uniform, as careful study reveals. We have already seen how Doulting stone alone gives place to Doulting and Chilcote conglomerate in the transepts, and examination of the bay elevations (first undertaken by Bilson) shows that the size of the blocks used in the later ashlar work of the nave increases considerably. When standing in the nave, it is very noticeable that there is a continuous triforium of arches here, whereas in the choir and transepts the shafts holding the vaults come down to the stringcourse above the main arcade, and therefore break up the triforium. The other detail to notice is the carving on the stiff-leaved capitals which contain many delightful little scenes.

Construction of the nave probably started just before 1200, and by the end of 1209 (when the country was under an interdict, the king had been excom-

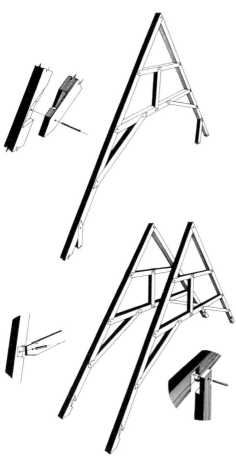

Cecil Hewitt's drawings
of the nave roof trusses at Wells
showing the 'secret' (top) and
'open' (above) notched-lap joints.

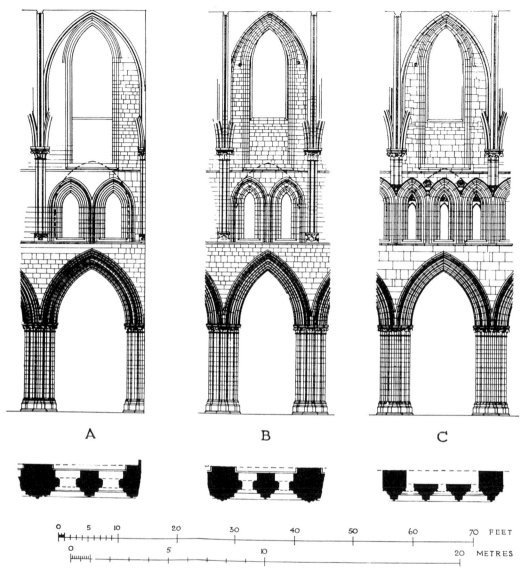

A   B   C

municated, and the bishop had fled overseas), work had almost certainly reached the fourth from last bay in the nave. Looking closely at this bay, it is apparent that there is a large diagonal break here, with changes in the cutting and tooling of the blocks, and in the masonry size. There is also a lack of the small corbelled heads above the main arcade capitals in the last three piers. It was in the roofs above the vaults that Cecil Hewett also noticed a 'break' in the carpentry, with the introduction of 'secret' (i.e. hidden) notched lap-joints in the roof trusses only in the last bays of the nave. Earlier, the notches in the lap-joints, which stop the subsidiary timbers from withdrawing from the main rafters, were all visible. The 'secret' notched lap-joint is a small but important technological advance on the 'open' ones, and it is hoped that before long dendrochronology will confirm the later dating of this part of the roof.

The interdict ended in 1213, but it is unlikely that work on the nave recommenced until at least 1215, and possibly not till 1220. By this time new plans for the west front were certainly evolving, and the construction of this great wall with its hundreds of niches for sculpture was probably carried out by a new team of masons between about 1230 and 1243, although all the 400 or so pieces of sculpture were probably not in place till 1257. Many details of the west front are different from the nave, and we find here vertical shafts of blue lias limestone (which could be polished like Purbeck marble) being used in profusion. As first built, the west front was just a rectangular facade (a horizontal double square) broken up by six large buttresses. Behind it, on either side of the nave aisles, were the bases of two towers, but the towers were not completed until the fifteenth century and even today they do not seem to fit in with the rest of the facade. The original design is still being hotly debated by architectural historians, and what the thirteenth-century builders' intentions were for the crossing and western towers remain completely unknown.

In summary, what we have at Wells is a building put up in two main stages, between 1180 and 1260, and between 1285 and 1345, with several sub-phases. The final result is magnificent in detail but unsatisfactory as a whole. At Salisbury the reverse seems to have been the case. This great building was in all probability constructed from start to finish (including the spire, cloisters and chapter house) in less than a century, an astonishing achievement, but one which could only have taken place in the thirteenth century.

By the middle of the twelfth century the site of the cathedral on top of the hill at Old Sarum was becoming inconvenient, but it was not until about 1198 that a bold decision was taken to move the cathedral down to the water-meadows a few miles to the south. The site was soon chosen, the king's permission obtained, and plots of land were being assigned to each canon in a vast new close to surround the new cathedral. Because of the troubles of King John's reign, however, work did not start for another two decades, and only in 1217 were the dean and chapter able to petition the pope for permission to move the cathedral. At this time, Richard Poore (brother of the previous bishop who had initiated the move) was appointed bishop and he brought a new spirit of energy to the work. In 1219 a new churchyard was consecrated and a temporary wooden chapel built, and at last, on 28 April 1220, five foundation stones at the extreme east end were laid. Work went rapidly ahead, and by 1225 the three eastern altars had been consecrated.

The following year the body of Bishop Osmund (the first Norman bishop, who had died in 1099) was placed in a new tomb in the centre of the eastern or Trinity Chapel. It is clear that, following the translation of St Thomas's remains in Canterbury cathedral in 1220 and the rising fame of his great shrine, the canons of Salisbury were hoping to claim an important new saint for their cathedral. Unfortunately for them, the process of Osmund's canonisation took another 230 years and cost them a very great deal of money: only in 1456 did the pope finally pronounce Osmund a saint. However, the incipient cult was fostered from 1226 and the space created for the shrine is still today the most beautiful part of Salisbury cathedral, with its incredibly tall shafts of Purbeck marble. The architect may well have been a very remarkable canon of Salisbury called Elias de Dereham. The Historian Matthew Paris tell us that he was one of the two 'incomparable *artifices*' (craftsmen) who designed Becket's shrine in Canterbury, and he is known to have been in charge of the king's works at Winchester and Clarendon palace (close to Salisbury) in the 1230s. In earlier days he had been a personal friend of two archbishops of Canterbury and of the bishops of Winchester, Lincoln and Wells, and no doubt he carried out various building projects for them. At Salisbury he is known to have built one of the first stone canonical houses in the close, and is described as 'Rector of the new fabric' from 1220 until his death in 1245.

The master mason was a man called Nicholas of Ely who with Elias probably planned and built much of the eastern half of the cathedral. No detailed study of the ancient fabric has ever taken place at Salisbury, but though at first sight the building looks uniform, there are many smaller details which indicate breaks in

Plan of Salisbury cathedral in the eighteenth century before the destructive reordering of Wyatt.

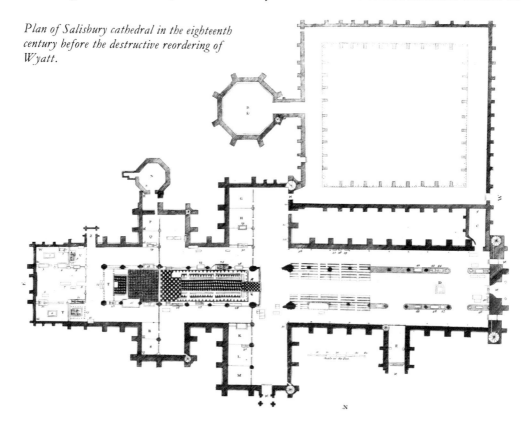

construction. For example, the simple quadripartite vaults over the Trinity Chapel and the first two bays of the flanking chapels are all uniform and without bosses, as are those over the eastern chapels in the north-east and south-west transepts, suggesting that these were the first vaults to be built (they were probably all in place by 1225). The vaults of the north and south presbytery aisles both east and west of the transepts appear to be later and have bosses, and the construction of these vaults no doubt preceded the building of the high vaults over the presbytery and choir, which was going on in the 1230s. Many other details indicate the approximate order of construction but, as at Lincoln, it will be the dendrochronology of the original roofs, where they survive, which will give us the closest dates in the future. Documentary dates are scarce, and in some cases contradictory, but we do know that the whole cathedral was consecrated in 1258, and that the final leading of the nave roofs (and no doubt the construction of the final nave vaults) was in hand in the mid-1260s. At the same time a large detached bell-tower (demolished in 1790, see p. 203) and the beautiful cloisters and octagonal chapter house were also going up, and all was perhaps finished by about 1280.

Work at the east end was heavily influenced by the new Canterbury choir and the retrochoir at Winchester, and Elias de Dereham was almost certainly the connection here. After his death in 1245, influences from elsewhere meant that the nave in particular is a purer form of English Gothic than the eastern arm: for example the use of nailhead decoration in the vault ribs and arches disappears. The west front of Salisbury is smaller than the west front of Wells (completed about twenty years before), and has flanking turrets only: the whole front was completed more quickly. Despite the later destruction of most of the sculpture, the west front at Salisbury is a more satisfying structure to view than Wells.

By the late 1270s, the whole of the cathedral, chapter house and cloisters were finished, and the bishop's palace and many canons' houses had probably also been built. A final and most remarkable project was now being mooted which would complete the cathedral and make it in due course one of the best-known cathedrals in the world. This was the building of a two-stage tower and a stone spire that would be over 400 feet high. Once again, documentary evidence is unfortunately very poor, but the suggestion that there was a contract for Richard Farleigh to build the tower and spire in 1334, which many books have referred to, is based on a misreading. Richard Farleigh was probably only demolishing the cathedral at Old Sarum at this time and building a strong close wall, as Roy Spring has recently suggested. It is more likely that the tower and spire were begun in the years before 1297, a golden age for Salisbury. During this period three exceptional scholars, Robert de Wickhampton, Walter Scammell, and Henry de Brandeston were successively dean, and then bishop, and presided over what was virtually a third university in England, after Oxford and

Cambridge. By the close of the century the academic reputation of Salisbury had died, and from then on most deans, and many precentors and treasurers, were non-resident foreigners with no interest in the cathedral (the jobs were often sinecures for French or Italian cardinals).

When the cathedral was finished in the 1270s there would have been a very low lantern tower (probably capped by a low pyramidal roof). The inside of this lantern would have been visible from the crossing floor, but since the fifteenth century, when the crossing vault was built, the fine interior Purbeck marble arcading has been hidden. At the top of this first stage a remarkable system of iron ties and braces were put in, which Sir Christopher Wren, who was carrying out a survey of the spire for the dean and chapter, thought was possibly the finest ironwork of its time in Europe. In his report on the tower and spire he recommended the insertion of further iron ties, and this was done in 1740. In the nineteenth century more ironwork was put in to bind up the corners of the lowest stage and to stop it spreading. Above this lowest stage two more stories were built which are characterised by their use of many decorated elements, particularly the carving of thousands of ball-flowers. This decoration, which is very costly to carve, is commonly found in the west of England in many of the finer buildings built on either side of the year 1300.

The great new tower was to rise to a height of 220 feet above the ground, and to this the masons added a spire of 180 feet – an amazingly daring undertaking which can best be appreciated by standing on the parapet at the top of the tower and first looking down at the cathedral roofs and then looking up one of the very attenuated faces of the spire to the capstone at the top. In the four corners of the tower, squinch arches were built to form the base of the octagonal spire. On top of these squinches, four pinnacles were contrived, covered in ball-flower decoration, while the four angle-turrets are capped with small spirelets. At the base of the spire on the four main sides are a pair of low doorways leading on to the parapet, surmounted by a long pinnacled gable also covered in ball-flower.

Anyone climbing up the inside of the tower will find that the top stage of the tower contains a timber frame. This was probably added in the late seventeenth century to support the main frame, and it is only inside the spire itself that we find the original timber frame. At the base of the spire are two massive tie-beams running north-south and east-west which cross at the centre and are partly supported from below by large braces. These tie-beams are like the cross-trees of a mediaeval post-mill, and on to them a central post was erected, as well as four other posts which support the first stage of the mediaeval scaffolding. This first stage is then turned through 45° and strengthened by a series of braces and horizontal diagonals. A series of planks was placed on top of this to form the first working stage, and above this are two more stages, each built as work

The spire of Salisbury cathedral showing the original internal timber framework. All later timbers have been omitted.

98

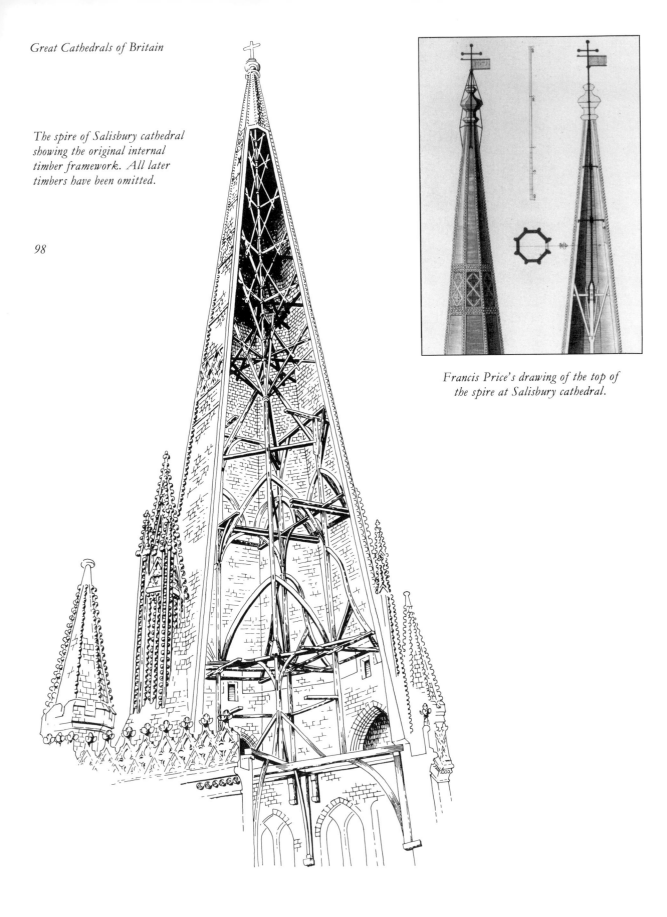

Francis Price's drawing of the top of the spire at Salisbury cathedral.

progressed to their height. It is quite clear that the whole of the spire, except the very top, was built from the inside outwards. After all, it would have been quite impossible to erect the high external scaffolding, between 200 and 400 feet, required. The timber framing itself is incredibly complex, containing pegged tenon-and-mortice joints as well as iron forelock bolts and iron spikes to hold it together, and the situation is further complicated in the lower stages by the addition of more timbers (struts, etc.) at various later dates. At the base of the spire there is a surviving mediaeval treadwheel windlass which, until comparatively recently, was used to haul up all the materials for repairs from the crossing floor over 200 feet below.

99

In most of the upper part of the spire the scaffolding was constructed by building a series of radiating struts, like the ribs of an upside-down umbrella, out from the central mast. There are six of these 'umbrellas', each one more closed up than the last, and as well as acting as scaffolding they were also used to touch the masonry walls and damp down wind pressure. At the top of the last 'umbrella', the spire has got very narrow, and at about 40 feet below the capstone on the top, there is a small door in the north face of the spire (called the weather door) which allows access to the outside and to a series of iron rungs which takes one to the top. This last section was built with an external scaffold, and it is still possible to see where the holes (called putlog holes) to hold it were. Stone plugs with iron handles were later inserted into them, which were removed when scaffolding for repairs was required.

The masonry of the spire itself is built of Chilmark stone blocks placed in a series of ascending octagonal rings which are all joined together by iron clamps surrounded in lead. Chilmark stone, which comes from quarries only a few miles west of Salisbury, was used for almost all of the cathedral. For the lowest 20 feet of the spire the stones are 2 feet thick. Above this they are only 8 inches thick, and at three levels, where lozenge-shaped panelling is cut into the spire, they are even thinner. The capstone at the top, which is made of four courses of stone each containing several pieces, is $5\frac{1}{2}$ feet in diameter and surmounted by an iron cross. From the base of the cross a wrought-iron rod runs down through the capstone and on for about 30 feet to join the top of the mast at the centre of the timber scaffold. The two are joined together in such an ingenious way that it is possible to tighten-up the joint. As Francis Price, the clerk-of-works at Salisbury cathedral, wrote in the mid-eighteenth century:

the timber-frame, though used as a scaffold while the spire was building, was always meant to hang up to the capstone of the spire, and by that means prevent its top from being injured in storms, and to add a mutual strength to the shell of stone.

A Series of ... Useful Observations ... on the Cathedral-Church of Salisbury (1753)

Price's book on Salisbury cathedral, published in 1753, is the earliest detailed analysis of any cathedral to be written. It is a masterly account by a man who knew his building very well after years of practical experience.

The great spire at Salisbury was probably finished by 1300 although a detailed modern analysis of it has yet to be undertaken. Today it is a rare survival but in the late thirteenth and early fourteenth century, spires were being put up on many cathedrals and churches in western Europe, literally as a way of reaching up to heaven. Sadly most of these spires, the majority of which were made of timber and lead only, have not stood the test of time, and we can only guess what they were like from early views of the building, if we are lucky. The two greatest spires in England, both probably over 500 feet high, were those over the central crossings at Lincoln and Old St Paul's cathedral. The former, which sat on the still surviving 270-foot-high tower, was destroyed in 1548, while the spire on Old St Paul's came down in 1561, just over a century before the whole cathedral was destroyed in the Great Fire of London. Many cathedrals boasted three spires (a central and two western ones), and the two western spires at Lincoln actually survived until 1807. Western spires at Durham cathedral survived until 1657, Hereford and Wells had slender central spires, and Ely a western central spire, and there is some evidence that other cathedrals such as Worcester and Winchester also had spires at some stage. The spire on the north-west tower of Canterbury cathedral is documented as having been built in 1317. It finally came down as a result of the great storm in 1703.

Of surviving spires, perhaps the finest are the three stone spires at Lichfield cathedral. These, though, were extensively restored after withstanding heavy bombardment during the Civil War. The central crossing tower and spire at Rochester was demolished in 1830 but replaced with a copy in 1904, and that at Chichester was also replaced after it telescoped in on itself during restoration work in 1861. For the rest, the 320-foot-high tower and spire on Norwich cathedral (the latter of a fifteenth-century date) is exceptionally fine.

By the close of the thirteenth century the Gothic style of architecture was in full swing, and English architecture had reached another peak. Not only were the masons and carpenters making great technical advances, but sculptors in stone and wood were producing some quite exceptional carved work, as was probably true of painters as well. There must have been a vast labour force of stone cutters of all types available at this time, in order to cut the thousands of ball-flowers, crockets and so on that were required. Within half a century, though, all this was to change. As a result of the Black Death it is estimated that up to half the population of western Europe disappeared or was uprooted, and it was a time of great social upheaval. The architectural consequences of this will be dealt with in the next chapter.

4

A Calamitous Time

Cathedral building in the fourteenth century

At the beginning of the fourteenth century, England was an extremely pros-
perous country ruled by a very strong king, Edward I, who had conquered Wales
and was in process of trying to conquer Scotland as well. The population had
been increasing rapidly and the church's rich income from the land had allowed
many enormous building projects to take place; some of the greatest cathedrals,
like Salisbury and Lincoln, were nearing completion with immensely tall spires.

Less than a century later western Europe suffered a sequence of cataclysmic
events which have perhaps not been paralleled in scale until the present century.
There was a series of famines and plagues, the worst being the Black Death in
1348–50, which, in England, reduced the population by half. There were many
years of dreadful wars, particularly in Scotland and France (the so-called Hundred
Years War). There were political acts of terrible violence, like the murder of
Edward II in 1327, and there were uprisings and civil wars, of which the Peasants'
Revolt in 1381 was the most bitter and widespread. In short, between 1300 and
1400 western Europe changed from a mediaeval society to one where the ideas
of the renaissance humanists that man was at least as important as God were
beginning to take shape.

In spite of all this, some remarkable building work was undertaken at many
cathedrals, particularly during the first half of the century. In 1326 the translation
of the relics of St Erkenwald (an early bishop of London who died in 693) to a
magnificent new shrine in the eastern arm of Old St Paul's in London marked
the completion of about half a century's building. This exceptional work has, of
course, totally disappeared except in the engravings of Wenceslaus Hollar, but
we know it was on a large scale, bringing the total length of the cathedral to
about 600 feet. The tracery of the windows, particularly the great rose window
in the east front, was very striking and can perhaps be attributed to one of the
great master masons of the period, Michael of Canterbury. Apart from St
Erkenwald's shrine the main focus of this new eastern arm of St Paul's was the
Lady Chapel. During the later twelfth and thirteenth centuries the cult of the
Blessed Virgin Mary had grown enormously and special chapels to the Virgin
were built in many cathedrals and great abbey churches, usually at the east end,
where an increasingly complicated liturgy could be performed. There were
exceptions to this practice: the eastern chapel of Salisbury cathedral, itself dedicated to the Virgin, was dedicated to the Trinity, and this was also the case at

Canterbury, as we have already seen. However here there was a very large early chapel dedicated to the Virgin in the centre of the crypt (later to be copied at Glasgow cathedral) and this was refurbished later on in the fourteenth century: as we shall see, it was here that the Black Prince wished to be buried.

At the beginning of the fourteenth century a fairly small and architecturally unadventurous eastern Lady Chapel was being completed at Chichester cathedral, being no more than a rectangular elongation of an existing chapel. Within the next two decades, however, Lady Chapels had been constructed at Wells and Lichfield which were masterly new polygonal structures of great subtlety, and contemporary with them was the free-standing Lady Chapel at Ely, completed just before the devastation of the Black Death. This is another rectangular building, but is perhaps the greatest architectural and sculptural celebration of the life of the Virgin ever created in England. Let us look at each of these splendid buildings in turn.

In January 1307 the Wells chapter had announced that so much money had been spent on completing the cathedral, and in particular on the fine two-storeyed chapter house, that nothing was left for other work. Yet only a decade later a large central tower and spire was starting to go up, and a brand new eastern arm and Lady Chapel were planned. The tower, extensively remodelled after a fire which destroyed the spire in 1438–9, still survives, though from the outside it now looks more like fifteenth-century than fourteenth-century work. All that remains of the spire are the corbels inside the top of the tower that supported its base. Of the eastern arm we can still see the Lady Chapel, retrochoir and four other projecting chapels, as well as the higher presbytery with its fine flying buttresses that went up between about 1323 and 1340.

The first stage of the work was to lay out the plan of the flattened irregular octagonal Lady Chapel on the ground to the east of the existing east end. Its position was very carefully measured in relation to the then existing cathedral as it was always intended to join the two buildings. The plan is, in fact, based on two equal overlapping circles within a larger circle, the radius of which exactly equals the square root of twice the square of the radius of the smaller circles. If the larger circle were to be stood vertically on the main east-west axis of the chapel it would exactly fit the section of the vault, which is a perfect semi-circle in this plane. The vault itself is the most beautiful star vault, with concentric circles of bosses having on them stylised vines, acanthus leaves, oak leaves and roses. It seems likely that the whole of this work went up rapidly between 1323 and 1326 so that the next stage, closely modelled on the east end of Salisbury cathedral, could be built. This involved demolishing the old eastern Lady Chapel and replacing it with a new space for a shrine to William de Marcia (Bishop of Bath and Wells, 1293–1302) between the Lady Chapel and a new high altar. De

The star vault over the Lady Chapel at Wells cathedral.

Marcia was a highly controversial figure who, as Edward I's treasurer, had helped raise money for the Anglo-Scottish wars, but miracles were supposed to have happened at his tomb, and it is clear that Wells was trying to emulate the success of Hereford in obtaining the canonisation of a recent bishop, Thomas de Cantelupe, in 1320 (Canterbury was also trying to get a recent archbishop, Thomas of Winchelsea (1294–1313) canonised at this time). The attempt was not successful, and the new retrochoir at Wells was to take many more years to complete.

As Dr John Harvey has shown, the many similarities between this work and that at Exeter (see below) make it likely that the two main master masons for both were Thomas Witney and William Joy: both men are documented as having worked at the two places. It is in the beauty of the slender shafts and the vault-patterns in the retrochoir area, giving the impression of a wood full of trees, that the similarities with Exeter are most clearly seen. Above this retrochoir,

104

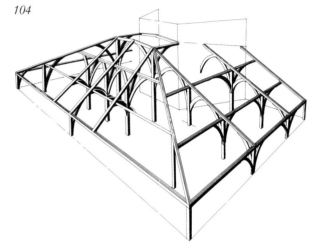

The retrochoir roof at Wells cathedral.

as Cecil Hewitt has pointed out, the original roof survives. This is most unusual, as it consists literally of a forest of vertical posts with a mass of curved braces at their tops. The main posts actually stand on the vaults showing without doubt that the vaults were constructed first. Dendrochronological dating of this and the other fine roofs in this part of the cathedral have yet to be carried out. The Lady Chapel roof, a separate structure at a higher level, is a very ingenious piece of carpentry, while the choir aisle roofs are roughly similar to the retrochoir roof and also have posts actually standing on the vaults. The most complicated of the roofs, however, is that over the chapter house. Yet again there are intermediate posts standing on the vaults, and in this case, it is apparent – as Linzee Colchester has recently pointed out – that the carpenter who framed the roof did not understand where the ridge of the vaults would lie. Consequently, when erected *in situ*, the roof timbers had to be turned round one-sixteenth. As well as all these shallow-pitched roofs, there are fourteenth-century steep-pitched roofs over the north and south projecting chapels and over the choir high vaults, which also still await detailed dendrochronological analysis.

To turn now to the second of the cathedrals under review, Lichfield. Here we are hampered by the great destructive work of the Civil War, for the cathedral virtually became a keep within a castle and was extensively battered in three separate sieges. This means that none of the mediaeval roofs have survived and that many broken vaults had to be replaced. The masonry, despite much skilful restoration in the late seventeenth century and later, does all the same have much to tell us about the building activities of the early fourteenth century. Like Wells, the east end of the new Lady Chapel was polygonal. In every other way, however, it is a very different building, though it was again planned as the eastern end of an enlarged presbytery based around a shrine, not of a new saint in this case, but to provide a more grandiose setting for the existing shrines to the Virgin and St Chad, the first Anglo-Saxon bishop of the diocese, to whom the cathedral was jointly dedicated. The most striking thing about the Lichfield Lady Chapel is the very tall traceried windows which have a continuous internal wall passage at their base with a marvellous decorated arcade below. In the restorations of the seventeenth century most of the windows of the Lady Chapel, the presbytery and the choir aisles were 'perverted' to Perpendicular, as one nineteenth-century commentator put it, but decorated tracery was in many cases restored at the end of the nineteenth century, particularly in the Lady Chapel. The original form of the tracery in these windows is therefore difficult to reconstruct, though it does seem likely that the tracery of the Lady Chapel windows (which have ogee heads) was then, as now, quite different from the slightly higher presbytery windows (which do not have ogee heads).

The sequence of building work at Lichfield cathedral between the end of the eleventh century and the Black Death is extremely complicated, and has yet to be fully worked out. However, Professor Robert Willis recorded various Romanesque archaeological remains found under the choir and presbytery floor during the cutting of trenches for a new heating system in the mid-nineteenth century, and in recent years much detail, particularly in the choir area, has been filled in by Dr Warwick Rodwell, who has found further remains of the twelfth-century cathedral preserved in a vertical sandwich between the south side of the choir and the St Chad's Head chapel. Broadly, the sequence of building followed a pattern in general similar to that at York minster (see chapter 5).

A late eleventh-century church with an apsidal east end and radiating chapels replaced the Anglo-Saxon cathedral in the time of Bishop Robert de Lymesey (1087–1117). The foundation of the curved ambulatory wall, which was uncovered in 1856, now lies under the magnificent Minton tile floor in the presbytery. In the mid-twelfth century a small rectangular chapel, probably a Lady Chapel, (the foundations of which were also discovered in 1856) was added, but well before the end of the century a large new rectangular choir and presbytery had started to replace the Romanesque eastern arm. There was then a large scale reconstruction during the first half of the thirteenth century. This was mostly replaced a century later by the Lady Chapel and presbytery just described, and only in the three western bays of the choir, in the side walls and arcades, has the early-thirteenth-century work survived above ground. Willis's and Rodwell's brilliant analyses of the 1856, 1860 and recent discoveries was, however, able to show the reconstructed plan of the earlier square east end with an ambulatory and four eastern chapels. This plan was soon to be used at Glasgow cathedral.

The re-building of Lichfield then continued in stages. First the south and then the north transepts were rebuilt, followed by a splendid new vestibule and elongated octagonal chapter house, the plan of which was perhaps the inspiration for the later polygonal east end of the Lady Chapel. All this work was completed by the middle of the thirteenth century: surviving licences of 1235 and 1238 grant the Chapter permission to dig Hopwas stone for 'the new fabric of the church at Lichfield'. In the second half of the century, the nave was rebuilt in a particularly splendid form with very striking spherical triangles containing three circles, each filled with trefoils, in the clerestory – it is not difficult to see why the later thirteenth century is often called the 'Geometric' period of English architecture. We have already encountered its use at Wells in the Lady Chapel, and it is clear that the study of 'sacred geometry' is today very important if we are to understand how these remarkable buildings and their decorative elements were conceived. Above the nave is a beautiful tierceron high vault, a forerunner of the quite exceptional vaulting at Exeter cathedral to be discussed later on.

The cathedral at Lichfield culminates in yet another fine west front, which despite much later work (including the complete alteration of the tracery patterns in the great west window in two separate 'restorations') is still a very splendid sight. The west front was built in three separate horizontal stages in the late thirteenth and early fourteenth centuries, and by the time the stone spires were being completed Bishop Walter de Langton (1296–1321) had started to build the new Lady Chapel. He is known to have left money in his will for its completion, though this was confiscated by Edward II in 1322 to help pay for the Scottish wars. Despite this, records show that work continued from 1322–36 under the master mason William de Eyton, and that in 1337 the king's master mason William Ramsey was engaged to help complete the work on the presbytery and the choir. From this period we know much more about the work of itinerant master masons and how they and other craftsmen travelled around. Ramsey was one of the greatest of the early-fourteenth-century masons and his hand can almost certainly be traced in the more 'Perpendicular' work in the presbytery. As Dr John Harvey has suggested, he more than any other master mason was responsible for the introduction of the Perpendicular style. In the 1330s Ramsey was supervising the building of the new cloister and chapter house at St Paul's in London, as well as working for the king at the Tower of London. For each journey to Lichfield, which took four days, he was paid a fee of 20 shillings with 6 shillings and 8 pence for travelling expenses. A major problem facing him at Lichfield was how to link up the presbytery with the 'old work' of the choir. The completed Lady Chapel was not on exactly the same axis as the old work because of a natural ridge of sandstone which had been used for its foundations. In linking the two, the axis was modified as each bay westwards was built. At the point where the new and old work met, Ramsey joined the two together with quite remarkable skill, despite a 2–foot difference between the width of the choir

and the eastern width of the presbytery. It seems that William Ramsey was a victim of the Black Death, but the work must have been virtually complete by the time of his death, and only minor works were carried out after this.

The large cathedral priory of Ely, standing on its island above the surrounding fenlands, was by the beginning of the fourteenth century one of the richest foundations in the east of England. In 1321 the foundations for a vast new Lady Chapel (46 by 100 feet in internal dimensions) were laid out as a freestanding building north of the presbytery, joined on to the north-east corner of the north transept only at the south-west corner of the new chapel. At first sight the building looks more like a large monastic chapter house, similar to the one recently completed at Canterbury cathedral priory, and the resemblance continues inside the building, for all around the walls was a series of exquisitely beautiful canopied monks' seats. Here the parallel ends, however. If we look more closely at the canopies in particular we see that amongst the profuse decoration the sculpture (now alas terribly smashed) was a great celebration of the life and cult of the Blessed Virgin Mary, and the raised dais at the east end had an altar on it rather than the bishop's or prior's seat. Luckily the Lady Chapel became a parish church after the Reformation, and so we are still able to see its complete architectural form today, but its rich decoration was brutally smashed by the Reformers and is only a shadow of its former glory. Not only were the windows filled with coloured glass, but all the decoration and sculpture would have been painted so that the whole must have had a feeling of brightness and warmth; in fact, a miniature paradise.

Work on the Lady Chapel probably went ahead rapidly at first but the fall of the crossing tower in 1322 must have brought an inevitable delay while the new octagon and western bays of the presbytery were being built. Once again the Black Death called a halt to the major work when the monk in charge, John of Wisbech, died of the plague in 1349. But it seems likely that the Lady Chapel had already been completed by then, for we know that Bishop Montacute was buried before its altar in 1345. The large east and west windows, which have a distinctly more 'Perpendicular' feel to them, are much later though; we know that the particularly unusual seven-light east window was paid for by Bishop Barnet and inserted between 1371 and 1375.

Despite the destruction done to it in the sixteenth century, the interior of the Lady Chapel, with its incredibly intricately carved 'nodding ogee' canopies all round the walls, is still an extraordinary sight. The carving is done in clunch, a slightly harder form of chalk, and it must have required scores of highly skilled sculptors to cut both the decorative work and the very large numbers of statues and figured scenes. In the projecting shafts on either side of the canopied seats Purbeck marble is used, while much of the upper walls between the windows contains decorated niches for statues that make the shell of the building appear to be in incessant movement. The whole structure is completed with a magnificent vault, which is not only beautiful but a great technical achievement. The vault spans 46 feet, and between the heads of the side windows and the central ridge it only rises about 18 inches. In the centre of the vault are beautiful star-patterns of liernes with many small bosses, but the overall effect anticipates that of fan-vaulting introduced over a century later. In fact, in other ways too Ely's Lady Chapel appears a sort of forerunner to the nearby King's College Chapel at Cambridge, and it seems more than possible that Reginald of Ely, the first master mason of the latter building, got his inspiration from the Lady Chapel in the city from which he took his name.

The collapse of the great Norman crossing tower on to the monks' choir on 12 February 1322 must have been a terrible catastrophe. We can imagine the bishop, prior and monks of Ely surveying the scene of utter devastation in the centre of their great church the next day. However, as at Canterbury after the devastating fire of 1174, there was a determination to rebuild on an even more splendid scale. The driving force behind this was the sacrist, Alan of Walsingham, but he was undoubtedly fully supported by the bishop, John de Hotham (1316–36) and the prior, John de Crauden (1321–41). It was in fact the bishop who paid for the rebuilding of the three western bays of the presbytery, which were also destroyed by the fall of the tower, and it was in the centre of the new work that he was to be buried, immediately behind the choir altar with Prior Crauden's tomb just to the east (see plan on p.16).

A contemporary chronicle tells us that Alan of Walsingham, the sacrist, was so overwhelmed by the fall of the tower that he did not know at first 'where to turn and what to do'. However, he soon composed himself and had the rubble and smashed timber cleared away and then, in a moment of inspired genius, decided not to build a new tower but to demolish the four crossing piers to ground level and to lay out new foundations for an irregular octagon within the greater space. The chronicle goes on to say that, 'he had the place excavated where the new tower was to be constructed, measuring it out with architectural skill in eight parts, in which eight stone columns were to be erected to support the whole building,' and there is therefore no doubt that the originator of the whole project was Alan of Walsingham himself (who is known to have been a goldsmith before he became a monk in 1314). The Sacrist was a senior monk who was in charge of all the furnishings and fittings of the church as well as being responsible for the fabric, and the Sacrists' Rolls tell us that in 1323 someone was brought in from London to give advice on the design for the 'new work', and later we learn that two Ely masons, John Cementarius (i.e. mason) and John Attegrene were given charge of the work.

Once massive new foundations had been constructed, the new stone octagon began to go up over the next five years. The first stage was relatively simple. Eight great piers were built with diagonal walls on each of the short sides with an arch underneath leading into the aisles. In the angles above each arch to the right and left were two extremely elaborate triple-niches for statues (now gone) which clasp the shafts running up the angles. At the base of each niche are marvellous corbel capitals carved with scenes from the life of St Etheldreda, the foundress of the monastery in 673. In the blank walls above are three oddly-shaped trefoiled niches with canopied ogee tops, and above this are the diagonal traceried windows which flood the crossing area with light. As in the Lady Chapel, this whole area was originally full of colour and richly carved and painted imagery, and it was here that the monks' stalls were originally situated, a glorious place in which to spend much of one's day as a monk chanting the Benedictine offices (see p.70).

The octagon itself was completed by immensely tall arches into the nave transepts and presbytery, and above this by an upper wall at roof level which was pierced by a wall passage and by a row of windows (six in the four main sides and three in the diagonals). Pinnacles were then placed over the angles. By this time, in the 1330s, Alan of Walsingham must have been trying to work out how the whole vast space was to be covered. Luckily a genius called William Hurley was at hand, working with William Ramsey as the master carpenter on the roof of St Stephen's chapel in Westminster palace. From 1334 he was advising Alan for a fee of £8 a year, a considerable sum of money at the time. To span the distance of over 72 feet across the octagon, William Hurley conceived the idea of an inner ring of eight timbers supported in the first instance by 'hammerbeam-like' trusses from the angles (i.e. large horizontal brackets). The basic concept was not new, however, and had been used at Exeter in 1321–2 for the timber vaults in the towers as we shall see below (p.118). What was new was the sheer scale of the work. The lower timbers of these huge trusses at Ely (as at Exeter) were to be the carved principal ribs. How this first part was erected is unknown, but some sort of scaffold must have been used. Once the initial ring was in place other diagonal ribs (tierceron ribs) could be added. These were carved while a 'floor' was completed above. Once all eleven ribs to each of the eight sides were in place, the effect from below must have been spectacular, and all that was now needed was to fill in the spaces with boarding.

The next stage was to hoist up the eight vertical posts for the sides of the lantern. These were made of joined timbers 64 feet long which tapered from 3ft 4in by 2ft 8in at the base to about 1 foot square at the top. These huge posts were then placed on the inner angles of the newly erected 'floor' and supported by pairs of raking shores (very long braces) from each of the outer angles. Another octagon of timbers with cross timbers held the posts at the top and from this a central post was suspended which held the large central boss for the upper star vault. In the space between the top of the star vault and the upper octagonal timbers a bell chamber was conceived, and between the great vertical posts eight windows were created with lovely decorated tracery in their tops. The result of all this very sophisticated carpentry was a miraculous vault and lantern which only needed a lead covering on the outside and painted decoration on the inside. All of this was probably done by the time of the Black Death.

Standing on the crossing floor below and looking up at the lantern, none of the technical details of its building are of course visible. Only when an ascent is made to the inside of the lantern above the vault does the mass of timber that makes up the structure become clear. To confuse matters, much of this timber is now of eighteenth or nineteenth-century date, put there during the restorations of James Essex and Sir George Gilbert Scott. Cecil Hewitt's pioneering investigations, however, have revealed the original method of construction and also shown which mediaeval timbers have been removed. A full structural analysis (with dendrochronology) is now required.

Before the timber lantern was completed, work on the three new bays of the presbytery must have been well in hand. Although not as visually spectacular as the octagon, this area has, nevertheless, some exceptionally fine work, and the bishop got good value for his money. The triforium and clerestory openings are filled with superb decorated tracery, with more fine windows in the aisles as well as the original beautiful doorway that lead to the passage to the Lady Chapel.

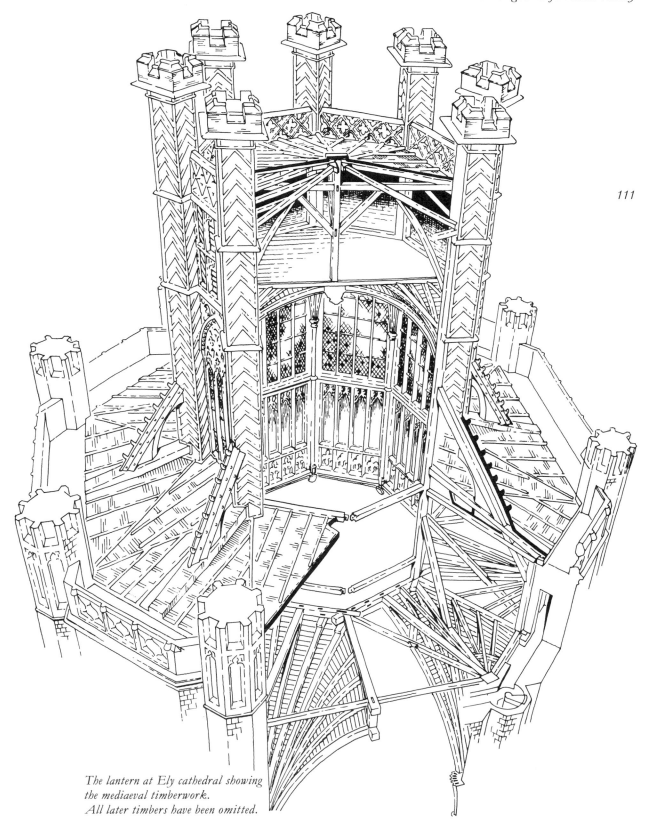

The lantern at Ely cathedral showing
the mediaeval timberwork.
All later timbers have been omitted.

Particularly striking are the polished Purbeck marble drums for the arcade; at either end these have extraordinary keels, almost like knife blades. It is noticeable that two different masons were at work in this area; the later one's style is very much in the 'Perpendicular' idiom, with octagonal tops to the columns and octagonal sub-bases. The high vault over this new work, as well as over the north aisle (and over the roughly contemporary Lady Chapel), contains liernes in addition to tiercerons, an early example of their use. (Tiercerons are the secondary ribs which run from the main springers to the ridge-rib (as over the octagon), while liernes are the smaller tertiary ribs which run between the principal ribs to form the characteristic star patterns on later fourteenth- and fifteenth-century vaults.) Where the ribs meet or intersect carved bosses were contrived.

William Hurley was not only a great structural carpenter, he was also a great worker in wood, and his designs for choir stalls were famous in his own time. Sadly, his two greatest works in this idiom, which we know of through contemporary accounts, the stalls for the royal chapels at Windsor castle and Westminster, have been destroyed. However, the splendid new stalls for the monks at Ely, placed under the octagon as soon as the structural work was complete, have survived, despite being moved into the eastern arm of the cathedral in the later eighteenth century and back to their present position in the nineteenth century. There are still 47 magnificent back stalls with their original misericords and canopies (with cusped arches and ogee detailing), as well as 37 front stalls, a third of which still have original misericords. These stalls are very likely to have been made by carpenters from Hurley's workshop and to his design.

Forty-eight fine thirteenth-century misericords also survive at Exeter cathedral (the oldest set in England), but by far the finest piece of carpentry at Exeter is the 60-foot-high bishop's throne. This splendid structure was completed in 1312 by a carpenter called Robert Gampton. It was drawn and examined in detail in 1982 by the archaeologist John Allen, and it is this sort of study which allows us to see how such a complicated structure came to be put together: Allen's findings revealed that a change of design took place during the construction. The niches, canopies and miniature spire which decorate the throne are all highly ornamented and were originally covered in paint. They show that carpenters, as well as masons, had by the early fourteenth century (a date confirmed by dendrochronology) reached a peak in terms of the use of carved figures and ornaments never to be attained again.

Exeter cathedral itself is undoubtedly the finest and the most complete cathedral of the 'Decorated' period in Britain. Apart from its Romanesque transept towers, it was completely rebuilt, starting at the east end, in the hundred years after 1275. The eastern arm up to the first bay of the nave was rebuilt between c.1275 and 1328, and by this date the newly appointed bishop, John

Grandisson (1327–69), could write in a letter to Pope John XXII, whose chaplain he had been: 'The cathedral of Exeter, now finished up to the nave, is marvellous in beauty and when completed will surpass every church of its kind in England and France.' Grandisson then went on to complete the nave and to start the construction of the beautiful image screen which is built on to the west front. Remarkably, a chantry chapel containing Bishop Grandisson's tomb was built into the gap between the two, with entry from the south side of the west door. This tiny chapel, often missed by the visitor, originally contained Bishop Grandisson's effigy, the eyes of which were intently fixed on the figure of the Trinity carved in marvellous relief on the pointed barrel vault above. This latter still survives. It is interesting to note that the splendid gilt bronze effigy of the Black Prince in Canterbury cathedral also has its eyes fixed on the Trinity above, only in this case as a beautiful painted scene on the tester (board ceiling) above the tomb.

After entering the great west porch of Exeter cathedral, and pausing briefly to look into Bishop Grandisson's chantry, you go through the principal doorway into the nave. Ahead is one of the most sumptuous sights to greet the visitor to any British cathedral. A mass of vertical shafts leads the eye upwards to an extraordinary patterned vault made up entirely of tiercerons of exceptional beauty. Only on the ridge-ribs in the centre is the flow interrupted by richly carved bosses. The whole effect of the architecture is of walking down an avenue of huge palm-like trees in a great stylised forest. There could be no better setting for the elaborate liturgy which Bishop Grandisson in particular wanted to be performed in the building, and if you keep your eyes well up, you will notice the amazing little minstrels' gallery which makes such a striking break in the uniformity of the upper levels on the north side halfway down. On the front there are still the painted figures of an angel band playing twelve different fourteenth-century musical instruments. At the end of the nave is a magnificent pulpitum (or choir) screen which marked the dividing line between the part of the cathedral where lay people could walk and stand, and the canons' choir, and which until the 1870s gave a view into the east end through the central doorway only. On the miniature vaults beneath the screen, liernes as well as tiercerons can be seen, rare for Exeter. Moving further eastwards through the choir and past the splendid bishop's throne, you are in the presbytery before the high altar. Here is perhaps the best place to begin an examination of the 'Decorated' rebuilding of the cathedral.

As usual, the construction of a new Lady Chapel was the earliest part of the rebuilding, and took place between c.1275 and 1287 after the apsidal east end of the Norman cathedral had been demolished. This was just as Salisbury cathedral was being completed, and if the inside of the two cathedrals are contrasted it can

be seen how rapidly English Gothic architecture had developed during the middle of the thirteenth century. The Lady Chapel at Exeter, which already has the striking tierceron vault shafts over it, is flanked by two smaller chapels, but there is no space for an eastern shrine (Exeter had no major saint or relic). After a short ambulatory cross-passage, which has later chantry chapels at each end, the presbytery proper is reached, and it is this part of the cathedral that was nearing completion at the opening of the fourteenth century. At Exeter we are exceptionally lucky in having a great body of surviving documents – (the Fabric Rolls) – which allow us to date closely much of the work after 1279 (though there are some big gaps in the accounts), but a systematic analysis of the whole fabric and its relationship to the documents has yet to be undertaken.

In 1982–3, when the choir was scaffolded right up to the high vaults for cleaning and conservation, the opportunity was taken to make detailed measured drawings of the vaults which not only revealed the way they had been painted, but showed very clearly the different materials that had been used, and how they had changed during the course of the fourteenth century. In the high vault at the east end above the high altar (completed by 1303), all the ribs were of Salcombe stone. A little later on, stone from Caen in Normandy and from Beer in south-east Devon (a hard chalk) were used, while in the nave vaults Beer stone only is found. The great bosses along the ridge-ribs in the presbytery, carved with some particularly fine figures, are of the fairly coarse Ham Hill stone from south Somerset. Later, Portland stone and Caen stone are used for the bosses, and once again, when we reach the nave, Beer stone only is used. These observations allow us to identify much more closely some of the sets of bosses in the presbytery with the accounts in the Fabric Rolls which specify the type and cost of stone used. A Ham Hill stone boss, for example, cost 5 shillings (25p).

The main shafts at Exeter were mostly made of Purbeck marble, and particularly striking are the small monolithic shafts in the miniature arcades below the large clerestory windows. The Fabric Rolls for 1316–7 record:

For thirty-eight columns of marble … for the galleries between the high altar and choir £10 9s. at 5s. 6d. a column brought from Corfe [where the marblers from the Isle of Purbeck were based].

This is long after the main work was finished, and a close look at these arcades in the presbytery reveals that they only become proper 'galleries' after the fourth bay (i.e. in the choir proper). The earliest work (in the presbytery) had been finished without arcades in about 1300, and only seventeen years later, for the sake of uniformity, were these arcades inserted. The very accurate stone-by-stone elevation drawings recently made by the Exeter Museum Archaeological Field Unit show this modification clearly (see over).

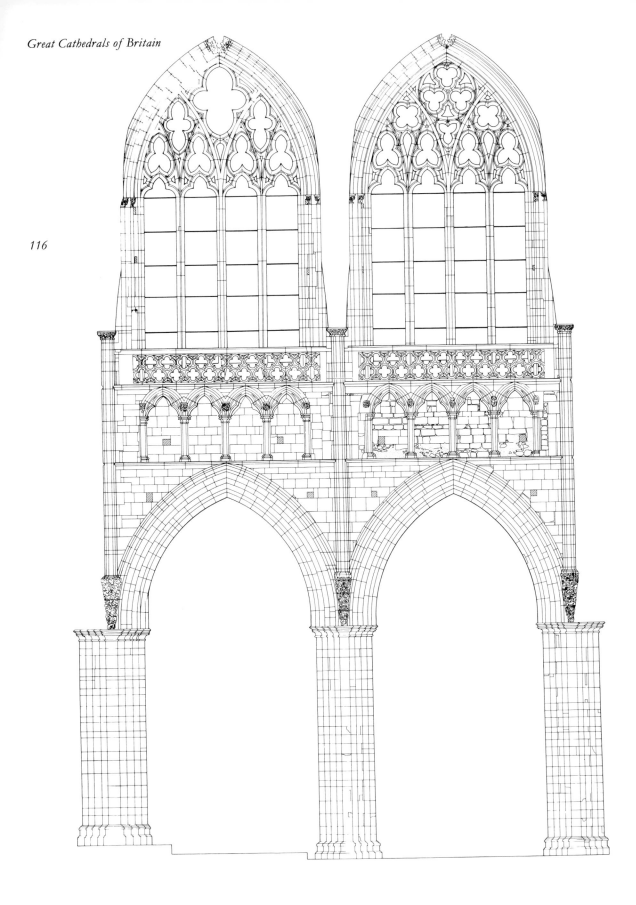

It is also clear that the great nine-light east window was first made in the Decorated style, and only in 1389–90 was changed to a perpendicular window. The original late-thirteenth-century mullions and jambs in Salcombe stone survive up to the springing of the head of the window. The tracery above is of Beer stone which, as we have already seen, was the common material of the later fourteenth century at Exeter. A close look at the window from the scaffolding revealed that very small Beer stone capitals had been inserted at the tops of the Salcombe stone mullions.

Although the transept towers were never rebuilt, their insides were reclothed in the early fourteenth century. The high-up projecting galleries in place of the triforium passages are particularly striking. The vaults over the transepts (built in 1321–2) are identical to all the other high vaults except that they are in timber. The carpentry details were carefully studied in 1981, when the south transept was fully scaffolded, and it can be seen from the diagrams that in form they are small scale 'prototypes' of the Ely octagon vaults. The hole in the centre was for raising the bells through, and was plugged with a detachable boss and rib structure, All the tierceron ribs are hung from the floor timbers.

The use of dendrochronology has added another new dimension to our knowledge of Exeter cathedral. In 1984 work started on examining and dating the great high roofs over the building. When this work is complete, the various phases of roofing should be identifiable and these can then be compared with the written accounts. All in all, a great deal of important new information about the rebuilding of Exeter cathedral has come to light as a by-product of the large-scale restoration campaign which was started at the beginning of the 1980s.

From about 1298 the bishop, dean and chapter agreed between themselves to contribute quite large fixed sums from their stipends each year to allow the rebuilding campaign to be planned for several years ahead. When Walter Stapledon became bishop in 1308 this was continued. Stapledon was the king's treasurer, and was a very rich man indeed. After 1325 he increased his share to 1000 marks (£666 13s. 4d.), a huge sum for the time. Unfortunately for Exeter, he was murdered in London the following year, not long before Edward II himself suffered the same fate at Berkeley castle. Stapledon's short-lived successor, James Berkeley, was not a wealthy man, but with the advent of John Grandisson as bishop in 1328, money and help in kind were again forthcoming to complete rebuilding of the nave. The master masons continued the wonderful vaulting unchanged, and only in the smaller details and the window tracery is it possible to see how the architecture was developing. The nave window tracery, with its spherical triangles, is very striking and is certainly an advance on the more regular geometric tracery of the eastern end. In 1329 work on the new west front was started, but not long after that it was decided to add a splendid new image screen

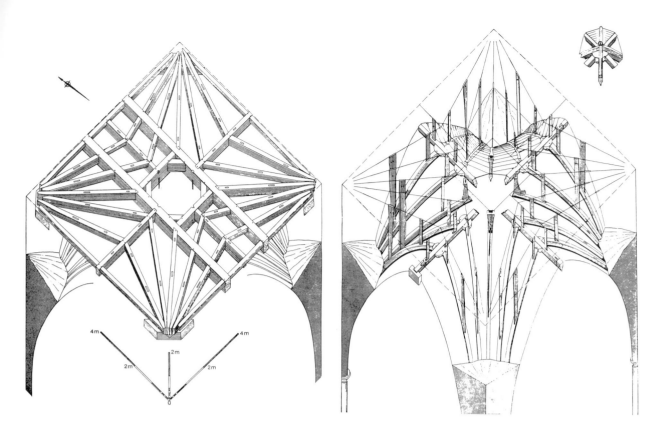

to the outside of the west front, and this, and the great west window were still being completed in the 1340s.

A detailed archaeological survey of this great image screen during the conservation and restoration campaign of the early 1980s has allowed many new facts about its construction to be understood. The lowest two tiers of the screen, which still contain some wonderful figured sculptures, were built in Bishop Grandisson's time (with his chantry behind the screen as we have seen). At this stage, the screen was finished off above this level with a parapet on either side (allowing the aisle windows to be fully seen), and perhaps a gabled top in the centre above the west door. In the 1370s a new north doorway was inserted, but it was not until the mid-fifteenth century that the screen was heightened, with the addition of a whole new upper tier of figures, and an elaborate crenellated parapet above. The archaeological survey has revealed all the many restorations that were later carried out, including a hitherto unknown replacement of the canopies above most of the upper tier of figures in the early sixteenth century. Despite all the later work and restoration, Exeter's western screen still remains a magnificent counterpart to the great west front sculptures of Wells cathedral.

It was in the summer of 1348 that the Black Death first reached England from the continent. Within the next year or so perhaps one third to one half of the population had died. It must have been a truly terrible time to live through – no wonder that many people thought the world was coming to an end. At Exeter, about ten out of the twenty-five canons died, as well as many of the minor clergy. In the longer term, it was these more junior clergy who proved impossible to replace. As more and more chantry chapels were endowed by rich laymen and clerics in the first half of the fourteenth century, large numbers of extra priests were needed to say the required masses for the souls of the founders. Until the Black Death, these priests were easily recruited, but afterwards, it became much more difficult to find men to serve the smaller chantries, and in quite a few of them masses ceased to be said, as was the case in the chapel of St Edmund at the north-west corner of Exeter cathedral.

When the Black Death struck Exeter, most of the main rebuilding of the cathedral had been completed and the nave was fully roofed. Whether the nave vaulting or all the window tracery was in place is uncertain, but we can be sure that much finishing and decoration had still to be done. Work stopped for four years and only in 1353 is the '*novum opus*' (new work) mentioned again, indicating that a new project was in hand (perhaps the completion of the vaults or west front). By the time of Grandisson's death in 1369 all major fabric work must have been finished.

Elsewhere in England, it is not easy to say what effect the Black Death had on cathedral building. Nowhere do we have a permanent monument like the very famous unfinished arm of Siena cathedral in Italy to remind us of the plague's devastating effects on economic and social life. At Worcester cathedral, where documentary evidence is scarce, Professor Robert Willis's analysis of the cathedral fabric carried out in 1863 led him to the conclusion that the work of rebuilding the nave was halted by the Black Death, and that this pause accounts for the difference between the more decorated style of the architecture on the north side, and the more perpendicular style on the south. For years Willis's dating has been accepted, and with good reason, for Robert Willis was possibly the greatest architectural historian and cathedral archaeologist who has yet lived in England. However, recent detailed analysis of the mouldings by Dr Richard Morris suggests that much more was built before the Black Death than Willis thought, and we should now perhaps reconsider the evidence.

Worcester cathedral was a very different place from Exeter. It was an ancient monastic cathedral, and the whole eastern arm had been rebuilt in the thirteenth century as a setting for the shrines of the Virgin and the cathedral's two great Anglo-Saxon bishops, St Oswald and St Wulfstan. Wulfstan had been canonised as recently as 1203, and probably as a result of this King John chose to be buried here in 1216. This rebuilding started in 1224 and was complete by the middle of the century. The central tower had collapsed in 1176 and, though it had been repaired, a proposed later thirteenth-century rebuilding seems never to have been carried out. By the beginning of the fourteenth century the contrast between the splendid new eastern arm with its shrines and the rather out of date nave and crossing where the monks' choir was situated would have been very marked.

The north and south sides of the nave at
Worcester cathedral showing the stages of
rebuilding between c.1320 and 1350.

At Worcester, sadly, the Fabric Rolls seem to have disappeared, though extracts from some of them were copied out by a canon at the end of the seventeenth century, giving us a few dates. We also have one other reliable source which tells us that 'Thomas Cobham, Bishop of Worcester, made the vault of the north aisle in the nave of the church.' Cobham became bishop in 1317 and was buried in 1327 in the north aisle of the nave opposite the Jesus Chapel, which was apparently his chantry chapel. It is very clear that the first three piers at the east end of the north aisle are earlier than the rest. The higher, cruder bases are particularly noticeable. It is also obvious that the webbing between the vault ribs of the two eastern bays behind the arcade (as well as in the Jesus Chapel) is different from the rest, using roughly laid red tufa. All the other vault webbing in the north aisle is done in a more regularly laid sandstone. We can therefore be certain that the first stage of the rebuilding of the nave took place in the 1320s. The study of the mouldings by Dr Richard Morris confirms this, and suggests that work then continued fairly rapidly during the 1330s on the rest of the north aisle, at least as far as the porch.

To study the mouldings carefully a large engineer's template former is needed. This instrument, which looks like a large comb, is placed against the mouldings that are to be recorded and all its sliding slats (the teeth of the comb) are pushed firmly in to provide the precise shape of the mouldings, which is then drawn, full size, on to a pad of paper. A computer programme enables the profiles of hundreds of mouldings to be compared, and Dr Morris has shown that those in the north aisle of the nave at Worcester are very similar indeed to the mouldings used in the remodelling of the east end of Tewkesbury abbey, started in about 1318. The similarities are so striking that he even suggests that

Dr Richard Morris using the template former.

some of the masons working at Tewkesbury subsequently moved to Worcester.

If you look carefully at the whole of the north side of the nave, as Professor Willis first did in 1863, it is clear that the two westernmost bays are of late-twelfth-century date, while the rest is of the fourteenth century. A closer examination, however, shows that there is a distinct change in style between the upper parts of the third and fourth bays from the west (the triforium and clerestory) and the rest of the fourteenth-century work on the north side (bays five to nine). By contrast, the whole of the southern side of the nave is of uniform work, but quite different from the north, except in the upper parts of the western two bays (three and four). Willis's diagram of the comparative elevations makes this quite clear. The southern side of the nave is certainly stylistically of a later date, and it was this work (as well as the small portions of the upper parts of bays three and four on the north) that Professor Willis suggested was not carried out until after the Black Death, i.e. not before the later 1350s. However, Dr Morris's analysis of the mouldings suggests to him that all the work dates to the 1340s, and that only the high vaulting perhaps remained uncompleted before the Black Death. He makes the interesting suggestion that the long-reigning prior of Worcester, Wulfstan de Braunsford (1317–49), who had employed his own masons to build the Guesten hall on the south side of the cathedral (sadly now only a ruin), transferred these same men to work on the nave when he became bishop in 1339, and this would account for the sudden change in style. Bishop Wulfstan de Braunsford died of the Black Death in 1349.

After the Black Death there seems to have been an interval of about eight years before work started on recasing the four large crossing piers in about 1357. This was in preparation for the rebuilding of the great crossing tower, the lowest stage of which was complete by 1374, having taken seventeen years to build. The following year Henry Wakefield became bishop, and he is credited, during his twenty-year reign (1375–94), with completing all the work on the rebuilding of the cathedral, including the stone vaults under the western transepts and crossing in 1375–6 and over the nave in 1377–8. We are also told that the new choir stalls for the monks (at the east end of the nave) were made in 1379 and that the great west window was finished in 1380. Finally the north porch (probably the last part of the cathedral to be rebuilt), was completed in 1386 at the same time that the rebuilding and vaulting of the cloisters was taking place, followed by the conversion of the round Norman chapter house to a ten-sided structure.

Worcester cathedral has, unfortunately, suffered very greatly from unsympathetic restoration and rebuilding in the eighteenth and nineteenth centuries, and so the majority of the windows and the window tracery that is visible today is not mediaeval. The great west window of 1380, for example, has twice been totally reconstructed (in 1789 and 1865) and bears no resemblance to the Perpendicular original. The outside of the cathedral has also suffered greatly from 'scraping' and the constant removing and adding of pinnacles, buttresses and windows. If we look at the vaults inside, however, we are, on the whole, on safer ground, and we will conclude our brief survey of the rebuilding of Worcester in the fourteenth century here.

The thirteenth-century eastern arm of the cathedral is covered in typical sexpartite high vaults, with quadripartite aisle vaults. When the work on the nave started in the north aisle in about 1320 octopartite vaults (i.e. quadripartite vaults with ribs along the ridges) were used. It is clear that during the rebuilding of the clerestory levels on the north side of the nave similar rib-patterns were to be used for the high vaults, and the springing blocks at the base were constructed accordingly. These springing blocks, which are a solid part of the wall-masonry, are the first five courses of stone above the capitals and clerestory string course. They were built for five radiating ribs only (i.e., one transverse rib and pairs of wall ribs and diagonal ribs). When the vaults actually came to be constructed half a century later, they were built with tiercerons as well, and as there was no base from which these tiercerons could spring, small ogee arches were introduced between the diagonal and wall ribs to act as a support. The ogee arches can clearly be seen all the way along the north side of the fourteenth-century nave. On the south side, however, there are no ogee arches and it is evident that when the southern nave clerestory was built (probably in the 1340s as shown above), there had already been a change of plan to a tierceron vault, even though it was not to be erected until 1377, thirty years later. In the vault under the central crossing tower we find lierne vaults being introduced for the first time, and there are also small liernes in the cloister vault, which in some ways appear to be an afterthought. The cloister vaulting also contains some fine carved bosses. The vaulting in Worcester cathedral is very conservative, and though of interest from an archaeological point of view, it has nothing of the beauty of the vaulting at Wells and Exeter, which we have already examined, or of the great Perpendicular nave vaults of Canterbury and Winchester, which we will be discussing in the next chapter.

Perhaps the most beautiful vault in Worcester cathedral is the remarkable flat miniature vault over the chantry chapel of Prince Arthur, Henry VIII's elder brother who died at Ludlow castle in 1502. The chapel, which stands near the tomb of King John and in close proximity to the now vanished shrine of St Wulfstan, was built in 1504 during the final flowering of chantry chapel building before the Reformation. Another place where two royal tombs are close to an important shrine is in the Trinity Chapel at the east end of Canterbury cathedral. Here the great shrine of St Thomas Becket was flanked by the tombs of Edward, the Black Prince, and King Henry IV. Ironically, Henry IV had usurped the throne from the Black Prince's son, Richard II, and the Black Prince had never wished to be buried here, but rather in the crypt chapel of Our Lady close to his own chantry chapel. This chantry had been built in the crypt thirteen years before the Black Prince died in 1376.

At Canterbury cathedral no major building work had taken place for about 200 years (i.e. since the rebuilding of the choir and Trinity Chapel in 1175–84), but interestingly it was the Black Prince who could be said to have laid the ground for the remarkable rebuilding of the nave, which started in the 1370s, to

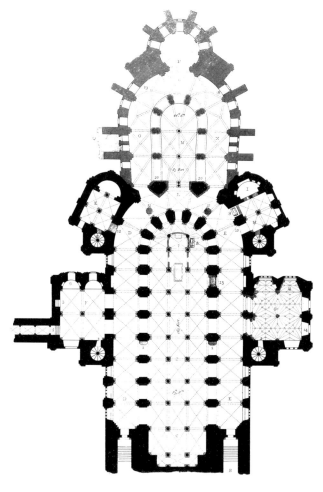

Plan of the huge Romanesque crypts of Canterbury cathedral showing the Black Prince's chantry chapels in the south transept and the later screen walls for the chapel of Our Lady in the undercroft.

be discussed in the next chapter. In 1361 he had married his father's cousin, Joan, the 'fair maid of Kent'. Because it was within the proscribed degrees of marriage, the Pope, Innocent VI, allowed it to go ahead only on condition that Edward founded and endowed two chantries. This he did in the south transept of the huge late-eleventh-century crypt of Canterbury cathedral, and in 1363 the Romanesque shell of this area was cut back and replaced with an exceptionally beautiful fourteenth-century interior. (The chantries are now used as the French Protestant or Huguenot church.) To fit in a vault system, with tiercerons and liernes, the small capitals on colonnettes were set at a very low level. Consequently, the exceptionally fine vault with its superbly carved bosses can be examined close to. The original twin apses have been sharply cut into to produce small polygonal sanctuaries in which stood the new altars to the Virgin and the Trinity. Here the mass-priests were to spend many hours each day saying all the different services as laid down in the foundation deed.

Ten years later, in 1373, in failing health, the Black Prince came on a pilgrimage to the shrine of St Thomas. At about this time the chapel of Our Lady in the undercroft, which was close to the Black Prince's chantry chapels, was being refurbished, and it was probably now that the Black Prince chose it as his burial place. This beautiful chapel, immediately below the cathedral's high altar, has been very battered since the Reformation, but it is still possible to see the exceptionally fine stone screens that were inserted into the two easternmost bays of the crypt for the chapel. On the groin vault above the sanctuary are the remains of a magnificent painted dark sky with gold painted suns with rays and stars on it. At the centre of each sun was formerly placed a convex mirror to reflect the candlelight, and below the vault in the middle of the eastern screen is a large niche which held a statue of the Virgin Mary. This was once again a sumptuous setting for the cult of the Virgin.

When the Black Prince died in 1376, for some unknown reason his wishes were ignored and he was buried beside the shrine of St Thomas in almost the holiest spot in the cathedral. Twenty years later, another of the great financial benefactors of the cathedral, Lady Joan de Mohun, was allowed to use the chapel of the Virgin as her chantry, and she was buried on the south side of the chapel in 1404. A century later, in 1500, the immensely wealthy archbishop, Cardinal John Morton, was buried before the altar in the place originally chosen by the Black Prince. This powerful man, who was also chancellor of England (and famous as the wielder of 'Morton's fork', by which he raised taxation for Henry VII), was, as we shall see in the next chapter, the builder of the great crossing tower. He too founded a chantry in the chapel of the Virgin so that two of the monks could pray for his soul for twenty years after his death as well as for the souls of his parents, benefactors and friends, as stated in his will.

All this is evidence of a great change that had taken place in the motives of those engaged in building the great cathedrals. A desire to build cathedrals simply for the glory of God had given way to the desire to build rich new settings for the cult of the Virgin, and to establish lavish memorials in honour of the rich and famous incorporating chapels in which their souls could be prayed for in perpetuity. Very often these chantries would be endowed while the founder was still alive, as a powerful reminder of his or her worldly wealth and influence. All the great cathedrals, and indeed all other sacred buildings, where reconstruction work was undertaken between the fourteenth and early sixteenth centuries include associated chantries of great men. Over a third of these were founded by bishops in their own cathedrals, and we have surviving evidence for nearly eighty such chantries. The architecture most associated with them is Perpendicular, and it is to this final flowering of cathedral architecture that we must now turn.

Later mediaeval dioceses in England and Wales.

DURHAM

TO YORK

CARLISLE

YORK

BANGOR

ST. ASAPH

COVENTRY
AND
LICHFIELD

BANGOR

HEREFORD

ST. DAVIDS

WORCESTER

LINCOLN

ELY

NORWICH

LLANDAFF

SALISBURY

LONDON

ROCHESTER

BATH AND
WELLS

WINCHESTER

CANTERBURY

CHICHESTER

EXETER

0   50   100

miles

5

THE FINAL FLOWERING OF ENGLISH GOTHIC

The Perpendicular cathedrals

Despite the terrible mortality of the Black Death, which must undoubtedly have included hundreds of masons amongst its victims, the middle years of the fourteenth century saw the evolution and the perfecting of what is perhaps the most uniquely English style of mediaeval architecture – Perpendicular.

More than anything else, Perpendicular architecture is the architecture of vertical lines, particularly in windows. It is a much purer form of architecture than the Gothic from which it evolved in the 1330s, with most decorative elements disappearing. No doubt the sudden dearth of masons meant that it was no longer practical to spend hours of time carving thousands of decorative details like ballflowers and foliated capitals. The piers in Perpendicular work are always long and thin with tall semi-shafts, shallow mouldings and small capitals. Above them, some of the finest vaults ever built were contrived. Initially these were lierne vaults, but in the fifteenth century the extraordinary fan vault was evolved (made of inverted trumpet-shaped concave half-cones), and finally the so-called pendant vaults in which long bosses hang down, as if defying gravity.

Another characteristic of Perpendicular architecture is the use of very thin walls with huge windows full of many rectilinear panels. One of the earliest and greatest of these was the stupendous east window of Gloucester abbey, the largest ever built. The introduction of light into buildings must have dramatically transformed them, and large windows were the rage everywhere – they were frequently put into great churches even where a Perpendicular rebuilding was not being carried out. Particularly common are large windows in the north and south transept walls and at the west end of the nave. Examples of the former can be found at Chichester and Durham, while great west windows can be found at the ends of the Romanesque naves at Rochester, Norwich, and Worcester.

In 1370 the monks had decided that the very ancient nave of Canterbury cathedral (built 300 years earlier) should be rebuilt, and a subscription list was opened. Not very much money was raised, and it was not until after the state funeral of the Black Prince in 1376 (mentioned in the last chapter) that the new archbishop Simon of Sudbury (1375–81) paid for the demolition of the whole of the nave between the Norman west towers and the transepts. This work started early in 1377 and over the next six years much archiepiscopal money was spent on it. The man responsible for its design was almost certainly the royal master mason, Henry Yeveley. One modern writer has called him 'the Wren of the fourteenth century', for Yeveley, who died in 1400, was also the master mason of the new western arm of the nave at Westminster abbey as well as of the rebuilt Westminster Hall and many lesser buildings. He was a contemporary (and probably a friend) of the poet, Geoffrey Chaucer, who was also clerk of the royal works in the 1390s. Earlier Yeveley had been the Black Prince's master mason, as we have seen.

128

Archbishop Sudbury became Chancellor of England in 1380 and his munificence to Canterbury (he paid for the rebuilding of the still-surviving west gate as well) was overshadowed by the anger that was felt for him as the man behind the hated poll-tax, one of the targets of the Peasants' Revolt. On 14 June 1381 Sudbury was summarily executed by the rebels on Tower Hill at the height of the revolt. A year later, on 21 May 1382, a severe earthquake struck south-east England and badly damaged many buildings in the cathedral priory at Canterbury, causing work on the new nave to cease for about nine years. The accounts tell us that between 1377 and 1383 about £400 was spent by the priory on the 'new work of the nave of the church'; Sudbury is credited with having spent over £2000 on the work, and having built the 'two aisles' of the cathedral.

If one looks at the nave of Canterbury cathedral today, undoubtedly one of the great masterpieces of English architecture, several clues can be seen to suggest the extent of Yeveley's earlier work in the aisles. The aisle walls are made of a mixture of Caen and Merstham stone, a soft greenish limestone from Surrey, used on the inside, with Kentish ragstone for the external buttresses. It is clear that some of the smaller Caen stonework in the lower walls has been reused. Particularly noticeable is the use of Purbeck marble for all the bases and mid-shaft rings of the south aisle, while in the north aisle only some of them are of Purbeck. This suggests that the south aisle was started first. The main arcades do not have any Purbeck, and all the bases, shaft rings, shafts and capitals, as well as all the ashlar masonry, are of new Caen stone. Purbeck marble, and the use of shaft rings, which had been so popular throughout southern England in the previous two centuries, were now out of fashion

Robert Willis's drawing of one compartment in the perpendicular nave of Canterbury cathedral.

elsewhere. Only at Canterbury and in the continuation of the nave at Westminster abbey, another Yeveley design, are they still found at this time.

In 1391 a man called Thomas Chillenden became prior at Canterbury cathedral, and immediately a fresh start was made on the work. Over £3000 was spent in the first seven years (a huge sum of money at the time, amounting to many million pounds today) and by the time of Henry Yeveley's death in 1400 we are told that the high vaults were being built. It was in this year that Henry IV usurped the throne from the deposed Richard II. He would later be buried at Canterbury, the only king to be interred there, and we know that he and Archbishop Thomas Arundel were generous benefactors of the new work. Arundel in fact gave 1000 marks (£666 13s. 4d.) immediately after his arrival back in Canterbury from exile in 1400 for the 'building of the vault'. In 1397 Arundel had been impeached and exiled by Richard II, but he returned at the end of 1399 to witness Richard II's abdication speech and crown Henry IV.

A survey of the heraldic shields to be found in the bays of the nave vaults reveals a second group of clues to their dating. Quite a lot of the shields were repainted with new arms in the early nineteenth century, but sufficient of the originals survive to give some helpful indications: for example, on the south side of the south aisle many shields of Archbishop Sudbury alternate with the shields of the see and the priory. In one bay, however, are the royal arms of before 1405, and its neighbour contains a unique central boss with four shields on it: those of the priory, the see, Courtney and the see impaling Courtney. William Courtney succeeded Sudbury as archbishop from 1381 to 1396; and the royal arms next door perhaps commemorate a gift from Richard II who is known to have made various contributions to the work.

However, all the ancient arms in the high vaults relate to the later phase of the work from 1400 to 1405. They include the arms of Archbishop Thomas Arundel and of Bishop John Buckingham who, on resigning the see of Lincoln in 1396, came to live at the priory. He died a year later and his executors paid 1200 marks in 1399 to the prior and convent to endow a chantry for him in the north side of the nave, situated under his arms. It was destroyed at the Reformation. In the final shorter western bay between the two western Norman towers (and perhaps the last vault to be built) are the arms of St Edward the Confessor and Henry IV. On a special group of bosses in this vault are the arms of Henry's two sons, Henry of Monmouth (later Henry V) and John, Duke of Bedford, as well as the shields of Sir Humphrey Stafford and Ralph and Henry Percy; the latter well known from Shakespeare as 'Hotspur'.

So much for the details of the nave. As a whole, it is one of the finest and most beautiful spaces ever created in England. It is miraculous that so great a building could be created during these years of turmoil, paid for by so many of the principal characters involved. In plan, the nave is identical to that of Archbishop Lanfranc three centuries earlier. The genius of the work is in its verticality: its shafts reach to a remarkable height, and above them springs a magnificent vault 80 feet above the floor. The extremely large transomed windows in the aisles of the nave fill it with light, and there are more windows high up in the clerestory. The vaults themselves have many liernes with small bosses at the highest points, making star-shaped patterns; those in the aisles are slightly simpler than those of the high vaults.

When Archbishop Arundel died in 1414 he was buried between two of the piers on the north side of the nave, well to the east of Bishop Buckingham's chantry, in a small chantry chapel that had already been created for him before his death. Like Buckingham's, this chantry was totally removed soon after the Reformation, and all that remains today are the repaired scars on the piers made by its lower walls.

At Winchester cathedral, by contrast, the chantries of the two bishops who created the fine, much longer nave there remain to remind us of their munificence. William Eddington (1345–66) began the process of rebuilding the vast Norman nave, and his work can be seen at the west end of the nave and in the west front which replaced the Norman western towers. Two aisle bays on the north and

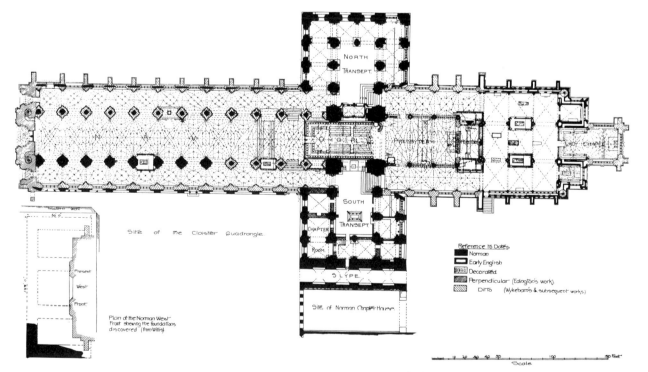

Phased plan of Winchester cathedral.

one on the south are also his work. This can be clearly distinguished as the aisle windows are much wider and lower than those of the later period. After Eddington's death there was a pause in the work similar to the one that occurred at Canterbury: Eddington's successor, William of Wykeham (1367–1404) did not return to rebuilding the nave for over twenty-five years. Before his appointment as bishop, Wykeham had been Edward III's chief warden and surveyor of the castles of Windsor, Leeds, Dover and elsewhere. His experience of building work was therefore considerable, and as bishop he went on to found and endow colleges at Winchester (now the public school) and Oxford (New College). In 1393 he held an official visitation to his cathedral and ordered the prior to recommence work on the nave. Shortly afterwards he agreed to pay for the whole of the work himself and in 1394 the master mason, William Wynford, second only in stature to Henry Yeveley, and a large group of masons and carpenters were engaged to build a structure to rival that at Canterbury, a task that would take them at least the next decade.

William of Wykeham died in 1404. His will, written a year before, reads:

Item. I desire that my body be buried in the middle of a certain chapel newly erected on the south side of the nave of the cathedral church of Winchester.

Item. I will and ordain that my executors shall cause to be reconstructed the body or middle part of the aforesaid church, between the north and south aisles, from the west door of the choir downwards as far as the west end, in its walls, windows, and vault, handsomely and well, according to the form and manner of the new work of the aforesaid aisles now begun, and they shall also complete the said aisles through the same extent in length. And they shall expend upon the work as much as 2,500 marks, if so much be required for its completion in the form and manner above defined. It being premised, however, that the prior and convent of the church shall provide all the scaffold necessary and convenient for the work; also, that they shall freely and without charge permit lime and sand to be taken by the workmen sent by myself or my executors, from any part of the lands of the convent or of their tenants, where it is of the best quality; also that the stones, lead, iron-work, timber, glass, or any other of the materials which the old building may yield entire, shall remain, and be employed in the new work.

And I will and ordain that the arrangement and conduct of the new work shall be entrusted to Master William Winford, and such others discreet, sufficient, and approved in their art, as may be chosen, if necessary by my executors . . .

Item. I bequeath five hundred marks for the glazing of windows both above and below [i.e. clerestory and aisle] of the south side of the aforesaid church by me repaired, to be done handsomely and well, according to the directions of my executors. And I desire that the glazing shall be begun at the west end of the church, with the new work there made by me, and carried on seriatim and in order, to the completing of all the windows of the south side of the said new work. And if then any portion of the sum remains, I will that it be expended upon the windows of the north aisle, beginning at the west end, with the first window of the new work by me made [i.e. the third bay from the west], and so going, on eastward as I have already ordained, from the south side, etc. . . .

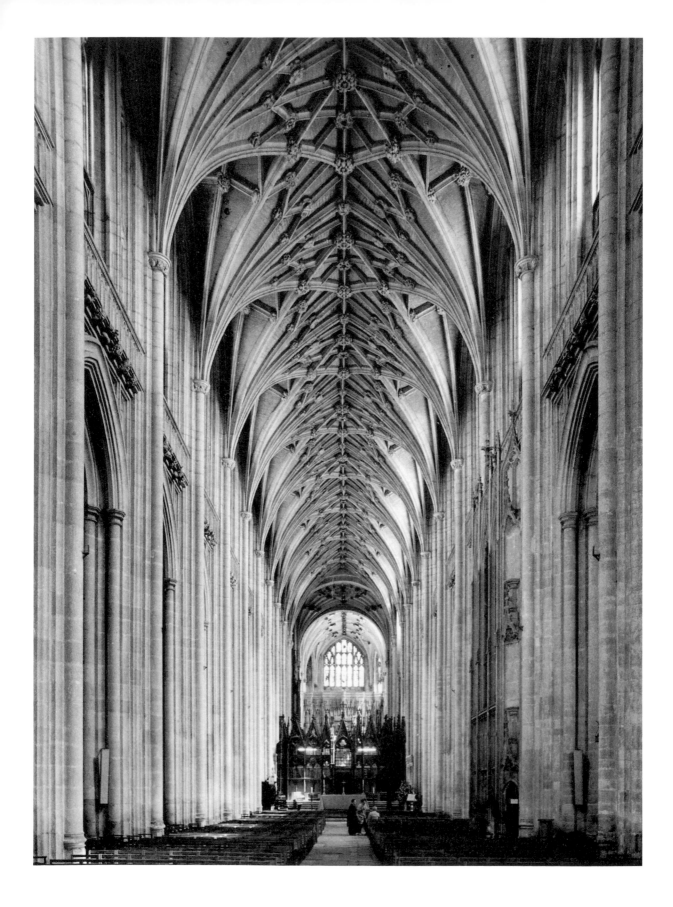

Here is a splendid account of how far the work had progressed at this time, and also an explanation of the mechanics of how it was being carried out. As Professor Willis showed in 1846, the will implies that the south side of the nave was almost complete by 1404, and that work was now in hand on the north aisle, leaving only the north clerestory wall and the high vault to be finished by Wykeham's executors. 'This view', Willis says, 'is perfectly borne out by the building itself.' As at Canterbury, the shields in the nave vault confirm this. Here we find the arms of Wykeham's two successors as bishop, Cardinal Beaufort (1405–47) and William Waynflete (1447–86), mixed with Wykeham's own arms. These imply that the high vaults may not have been finished for nearly half a century.

Unlike Canterbury, the huge nave at Winchester was not demolished and rebuilt but transformed bay by bay from Norman to Perpendicular. The evidence for this is to be seen in many hidden areas under the triforium roofs above the high vaults and on the outside of the clerestory walls, as well as in the eastern bays of the nave where Norman shafts and capitals still survive at the bases of several main piers – they were left unaltered because they were covered by the now-vanished rood and pulpitum screens. Willis's classic study of the cathedral showed exactly how this transformation was carried out. The massive Norman piers were cut back to the core on the nave side leaving only the inner triforium arch in place. At the base of the piers the original ashlar work was initially kept, in the first eight piers in the south side of the nave at the west end, and the new mouldings of the Perpendicular piers just cut into the Norman work. In the last four piers and for the whole of the north side, however, the piers were cut right back to the core and new ashlar work was inserted. The difference between the small Norman blockwork and the large Perpendicular blocks is still clear.

The work at Winchester was able to proceed in this way because the original Norman walls and piers were so massive that there was no danger of the building collapsing when they were being cut back. So strong, in fact, are the walls that no flying buttresses were needed to support the high vault, though it should be said that this vault springs from a much lower level than at Canterbury, and then has very steeply rising ribs which thrust the load downwards. The crown of the vault at Winchester is only 2 feet below that at Canterbury but because of its great length and lower arcades, it appears to be considerably less. With its much greater width (about 100 feet), the aisles at Winchester also appear not to be nearly so tall. Both works are masterpieces. While in terms of proportion and sheer beauty, Canterbury is perhaps pre-eminent, from the point of view of its construction Winchester is far more interesting.

To return to the two chantries in the nave: Bishop Eddington's is a simple affair, just consisting of two stone screens between two piers immediately south of the rood screen. William of Wykeham's, five bays further west, is, however,

INTERMEDIATE
STATE

PRESENT STATE.

ORIGINAL STATE.

*Robert Willis's elevation drawing of the Norman
nave at Winchester showing how the piers were
cut back to receive the Perpendicular masonry.*

a miniature chapel in its own right, reaching up the full height of the nave arch
and with its own beautiful miniature vault. The tomb inside the chapel contains
a fine effigy of the bishop with three of his monks at his feet. It faces an altar at
the east end of the chapel above which is a miniature reredos. All in all, it is a
most sumptuous affair, tempting almost every one of Wykeham's successors over
the next century and a half to try and go one better. Cardinal Beaufort's and
William Waynflete's magnificent chantries are in the retrochoir, flanking the
shrine of St Swithin on the north and south sides, while Thomas Langton (1493–
1500) chose to convert a small thirteenth-century chapel to the south-east. It has
a fine new vault and is filled with the most exquisite carved woodwork. Finally
the tombs of Richard Fox (1500–28) and Stephen Gardiner (1531–55) are in large
chantries just behind the high altar on each side of the presbytery. Each chantry
shows a new development in ceiling vaults, and perhaps the most interesting
(but not the most beautiful) of the seven chantries is the last. Bishop Gardiner
uniquely managed to remain bishop from Henry VIII's reign through the very
'Protestant' reign of Edward VI and on into the reign of Queen Mary. His
chantry, which was built after all other chantries in England had been abolished,
is architecturally a mixture of the latest Gothic and the early Renaissance style.
There are even a few high Renaissance elements in it, reflecting in stone the
religious uncertainties of the time. John Britton, writing in the early nineteenth
century, calls it 'a compound mixture of bad Italian and bad English', but this
only reflects the prejudices of his time.

In the late fifteenth century the Lady Chapel at the east end of Winchester
was lengthened and remodelled, bringing the total length of the cathedral to 554
feet. Canterbury was already 540 feet long and, with the exception of the now-
vanished Old St Paul's (quite exceptionally about 600 feet long), they were the
longest cathedrals in Britain. York minster, at 524 feet, was not much shorter;
however, in overall size it was by far the largest cathedral in Britain. The
transformation of that vast building from the Norman structure we examined in
chapter 2 is a remarkable story which we shall now consider.

Whereas the architectural history of York minster up to the end of the
twelfth century has only very recently been unravelled, the various stages of the
building of the present structure from the early thirteenth century to 1472 have
long been known, in outline at least. Again Robert Willis's article of 1848 is the
modern starting point for any detailed analysis. In his studies, particularly of the
earlier phases (mostly below ground), he was greatly helped by the work of John
Browne, who after his excavations in the choir following the fire of 1829, went
on to examine and draw other areas of the building. His two-volume *History of
the Metropolitan Church of St Peter, York*, published in 1847, contained many
splendid drawings.

The rebuilding of York minster may have been planned at the very beginning of the thirteenth century, but it was not until after the last chaotic years of King John's reign, and the appointment of Walter de Gray as archbishop (1216–55), that work started. A plan probably existed by 1220 at the latest to rebuild the Norman north and south transepts on a very large scale by adding aisles to each side. Work must have started first on the west side of the south transept, but it seems likely that both transepts were being built at roughly the same time by two quite separate teams of masons. The detailed architectural studies in recent years of Dr Eric Gee have shown, among other things, that the masons' marks in each area were different. This confirms that two different teams were at work.

The south transept was certainly under the patronage of the archbishop himself, inspired no doubt by the canonisation of St William, a mid-twelfth-century archbishop, in 1227. A shrine and altar to the new saint were erected in 1230 on the north-east side of the transept, and it was close to this that Archbishop de Gray was himself buried in 1255. His is perhaps the finest tomb to survive in the minster. The north transept at York was largely the work of a rich canon, John le Romeyn (his name indicating that he came from Rome) who was successively precentor (or 'chaunter'), sub-dean and treasurer. He died in the same year as de Gray.

The north transept is today perhaps the finest of the two. Almost the whole of the north wall is taken up with the famous 'five sisters' lancet windows (still with much of their original grisaille – that is grey – glass). Each of them is 53 feet high, but just 5 feet wide. The south transept, on the other hand, has a great rose window in the top of the gable (severely damaged in the 1984 fire); a close look at it shows that it is out of line with the double lancet below. Dr Gee has shown that it was inserted at a later date, and in fact the whole of the south wall of the transept seems to have been remodelled in the middle years of the thirteenth century in a much more French style, perhaps as a result of the shrine of St William that was being created within. But the remodelling did not produce a really grand south door, with sculpture all around it, in the French way, and the south front of the minster is in many ways a disappointment.

When the transepts were built they consisted of three full bays each, projecting out from the aisleless Norman nave and the narrower presbytery of c.1160. With the building of the new aisled nave and wide choir, the transepts were shortened. The archaeological evidence for this is still visible in the upper triforium walls at the south end of the north transept, where the remains of the earlier arches can still be seen above the shortened bays.

As well as rebuilding the transepts, Archbishop de Gray and the treasurer John le Romeyn rebuilt the tower over the central crossing. This collapsed a century and a half later, in 1407, but documentary evidence exists to tell us that it contained a lantern and a bell-chamber and that later it had a spire on top (called a *broche* in 1370). The tower must therefore have been taller than the 212–foot lantern which replaced it, and with its timber and lead spire must have been well over 300 feet high. All of this work was almost certainly finished by 6 July 1253 when King Alexander III of Scotland married Margaret, daughter of Henry III, in the minster. We can imagine the pride of the archbishop and the treasurer, now elderly men, as they watched the couple walk in state through 'their' new transepts and crossing. Walter de Gray actually performed the marriage, and the hospitality for the wedding cost him the enormous sum of 4000 marks.

About a decade or so later work started on what was to be the largest octagonal chapter house in England. This magnificent structure, which could seat the archbishop and all thirty-six canons easily under beautiful stone-canopied stalls, was originally designed to have a stone vault. Before it was completed, however, a superb wooden vault spanning 58 feet had been erected instead, and the veritable forest of timber above it (and under the lead roof) is another of the great marvels of mediaeval carpentry. It was probably complete by about 1285, and therefore just predates the spire scaffolding at Salisbury and the Ely octagon.

Connecting the chapter house and the north east corner of the north transept is a splendid L-shaped passageway which also contains some magnificent windows, arcading and sculpture. Both of these areas must have been in constant use almost immediately after they were finished, not just by the canons but also by the crown and parliament. With the start of Edward I's Scottish wars in 1297, York became the administrative centre of the kingdom and remained as such until his death in 1304.

By the end of the 1280s plans were clearly in hand to start the next stage of the rebuilding of the minster. Buildings were removed from either side of the Norman nave, including the old school, and trenches 200 feet long were dug westwards from two-thirds of the way along the west walls of the transepts. Then, on 6 April 1291, Archbishop John le Romeyn laid the foundation stone at the east end of the southern foundation trench. John le Romeyn, one of the great scholars of the age (he had taught Theology at the University of Paris), was the illegitimate son of the canon treasurer who had built the north transept.

Adding the new outer walls to the exceptionally wide Norman nave gave the cathedral an internal width of over 100 feet. The base of the Norman walls acted as foundations for the new arcades and careful examination of the aisle walls shows that they were each to be capped with a series of eight large triangular gables. This almost certainly indicates that the first plan was to have a series of small transverse roofs, as in the outer aisles (chapels) at Chichester. It is also clear that the early plan was for the west end of the aisles to clasp the existing western towers and for there to be a great façade covered in statues, as at Wells. By about

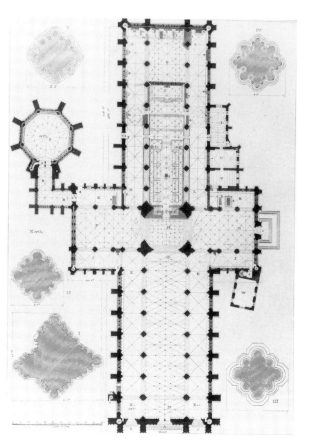

*Plan of York minster made in 1819
with enlarged plans of different piers (above) and
the west front of York minster (opposite).*

1310, however, this scheme was modified. The gables were joined together with a continuous parapet, the western towers were demolished, and the south-west and north-west corners of the new work were strengthened with larger buttresses for new towers. This change of plan can be clearly seen inside because the wider piers for the towers against the walls cover parts of the elegant blind arcading that had been built earlier. Work on the lower stages of the western towers continued for a decade or so and was then abandoned. Still visible are the springings only for the unfinished vaults under the towers.

Between about 1335 and 1338 a new master mason was brought in. This was probably a man named Ivo de Raghton who seems to have built the great east window at Carlisle cathedral and had undertaken various projects for Archbishop William of Melton (1317–40). He built the upper part of the great west window in a totally different style with remarkable curvilinear tracery in the head. It is also clear how he introduced nodding ogee canopies (instead of the earlier plain ones) in the upper arcading on either side of the window, inside and outside, as well as a fine curvilinear gable over it.

Early in the fourteenth century the nave aisles were given stone vaults, and it was certainly intended to build the high nave vault in stone as well: heavy pinnacles on the clerestory and aisle walls on the south side were built, but no flying buttresses. These were only added in 1905–7. By the time of the Black Death, however, a stone vault had not been achieved (the span was nearly 50 feet), and in 1353 the carpenter Philip of Lincoln was given the job of building a timber one. Details of the original wooden ribs can be clearly seen in the watercolour drawing by Joseph Halfpenny made in 1796 when the webs were being replaced. Sadly the whole roof and vault were totally destroyed in the fire of 1840. The present vault is a replica of the early 1840s.

The western towers of the minster were not completed in their present form for over a century. The southern tower had its upper stage built in c.1433–46 (it

Watercolour by J. Halfpenny of the nave vault of York minster being repaired in 1796.

became the belfry in 1446), while the northern one was apparently not built until after 1456. This finally made the west façade of York minster 'the most French of all English façades' in the words of Sir Nikolaus Pevsner, albeit two centuries after the type had evolved in France.

When the Black Death struck York in the summer of 1349, the nave was complete, except for the high vault. The next stage in the transformation of the minster was to rebuild the eastern arm on as grand a scale as the nave. In plan, it was to cover almost exactly the same area as the nave: as completed, the minster had an almost symmetrical rectilinear plan about a north-south axis through the centre of the transepts, but a closer look shows that the eastern arm is in fact slightly narrower (exactly 100 feet wide internally) but longer (220 feet internally) than the nave. Rising to a height of 100 feet it is the largest and loftiest choir and presbytery in Britain. Its walls are less thick than the nave not only because technology was improving, but because it seems that from the start, after the failure to vault the nave in stone, the high vaults were planned to be in timber only. The consequences of this would be felt very greatly 500 years later when the roofs and vaults of the eastern arm and the nave were totally destroyed in the terrible fires of 1829 and 1840. With the very recent destruction of the south transept roof and vault in 1984, only the crossing tower and the northern arm remain unscathed today, though the latter was heavily repaired in 1934–5, and the central tower was re-roofed in 1970 using reinforced concrete.

It seems likely that Archbishop William de la Zouche (1342–52) had started work on the eastern arm just before the Black Death, having had the plan marked out on the ground around the late twelfth-century presbytery. He started in 1350 to build his own chantry chapel, dedicated to St Mary Magdalene and St Martha, on the south side of this: a request to the dean and chapter, dated 11 April, 1350, in which he asks to be allowed to build the chapel, which he states would not offend the main structure and would provide extra ministers, still survives. In it, de la Zouche also says that he would like the master of the masons and his own men to erect it. The archaeological evidence makes it clear that the chapel formed an integral part of the south aisle wall of the new eastern arm, and that parts of it were put up after the lower part of the south aisle wall had been built. This in turn strongly suggests that some parts of the main aisle walls were built before the Black Death.

To build the Zouche chapel, it would have been necessary to demolish the south-east transept of the twelfth-century presbytery. There is some evidence for this in the two vestries built at the same time immediately to the west of the chapel, the vaults of which re-use late twelfth-century ribs. Over the vestries is a loft with a fine original timber roof and a gypsum plaster floor. This was almost certainly the fourteenth-century carpenters' lodge. An even more remarkable survival, however, is the L-shaped room above the chapter house vestibule. This, too, was added in the mid-fourteenth century and was provided with its own fireplace and garde-robe (WC). The floor is again made of gypsum plaster and lines can still be seen in it matching the tracery elements in the building, including the full-size setting out of the tracery for the windows in the aisles of the eastern arm. Only one other similar floor is known in England, namely the one over the north porch at Wells. Still hanging on racks in the room today are later templates for use by the masons, showing that it continued as a drawing office for a long time. There is a very fine fourteenth-century scissor-braced roof above it, and it seems very likely that both the masons' drawing office and the carpenters' lodge were specially constructed in the 1340s for the work on the new eastern arm. Dendrochronological dating of the roof timbers may one day confirm this.

As with the nave, the first stage of the new work was the building of the aisles, and the walls from the transepts to the east corners may mostly have been constructed before Archbishop de la Zouche's death in 1352. The Black Death

142

John Harvey's plan of the mid-fourteenth-century lines on the plaster floor in the drawing office at York minster and detail (inset) of the floor itself.

obviously caused much disruption: no further work on the eastern arm seems to have been carried out until 1361 when the new archbishop, John de Thoresby (1352–73), formally laid a new foundation stone on 29 July. He also donated £200 a year and stone from the demolished hall of his manor at Sherburn-in-Elmet to the work, and during the next decade the easternmost four bays (the Lady Chapel) of the minster were rapidly built. After 1365 the church of St Mary *ad valvas* (i.e. at the gates), immediately east of the minster, was pulled down so that the east front could be built (the great east window would not be created for another thirty years, however). In 1369, the master mason William Hoton was replaced by a man called Robert de Patrington (both men received a salary of £10 a year and a house nearby), and it was probably Patrington who first introduced fully Perpendicular architecture to the minster.

In the nave the clerestory wall-passage had been placed outside the window. This revolutionary new idea allowed the internal panelling of the clerestory windows to continue down into the triforium, unifying the whole design. In the Lady Chapel clerestory a similar, but more developed, form of this idea was adapted, and outside the windows an elaborate form of panelling was added. In the eastern bay this panelling had simple arched heads; in the next three bays the head was considerably refined with beautiful tracery of cusps and mouchettes. At the same time splendid Perpendicular tracery was being put into the clerestory windows, and not long afterwards fine painted glass.

When Archbishop Thoresby died on 6 November 1373 he was buried in the Lady Chapel in front of the altar. By this date the four eastern bays must have been roofed but not vaulted. Work then came to a halt for twelve years, following a quarrel between his successor, Alexander Neville, and the chapter. (All three deans between 1342 and 1385 were Roman cardinals who never came near York.) Neville was deposed in 1388 after being found guilty of treason. He was translated to St Andrews and replaced by Thomas Arundel, later Archbishop of Canterbury. Despite the political difficulties of the time, in which Arundel was heavily involved, the building work got underway again and demolition of the final parts of the twelfth-century choir were carried out. The vaults of the crypt were removed and it was filled in, only to be rediscovered in the excavations after the fire of 1829. A new small crypt was constructed, re-using twelfth-century sculptured capitals and bases, under the new high altar and shrine of St William. This would be removed at the Reformation in 1541, but the high altar remained in its mediaeval position until 1726 when it was moved one bay further east to its present site, just beyond where St William's shrine had been. In its original position the high altar would have been brilliantly lit by the exceptionally tall windows in the two eastern transepts. These transepts, and the rest of the choir arcade between the central crossing and the high altar, were built in the later 1390s.

Work started in earnest early in 1395 with a gift of 100 marks (£66 13s. 4d.) from Richard II (choir services had been temporarily transferred to a vestry to the south). Later in the same year the king visited the minster and made another gift of a relic enclosed in a silver and gilt shrine. This visit was perhaps marked by the carving of the king's badge (a chained white hart) on a capital on the south-east crossing pier where it faces the south choir aisle. For these final bays of the eastern arm, the clerestory windows were once again put on the outside of the wall-passage so that there was now an abrupt break between the window tracery and the panelling below, over the triforium. These were turbulent years in the history of England, yet despite the translation of Archbishop Arundel to Canterbury in 1396 (the first archbishop to be so translated) and the deposition of Richard II in 1399, work seems to have continued uninterrupted. By about 1405 the whole eastern arm was roofed but not vaulted. In that year Archbishop Richard de Scrope (1398–1405) was executed under the city walls as a traitor to the new king, Henry IV. He was buried in the new chapel of St Stephen in the extreme north-east corner of the new work, and his tomb soon became the object of popular devotion.

143

In October 1405, the great east window was finally complete. An agreement had been drawn up between the dean and chapter and John Thornton of Coventry for the latter

to make a great window at the East end of the quire, according to the best of his skill and cunning... And to finish the same within three years... and... with his own hands to portraiture the said window with Historical Images and other painted work, in the best manner and form that he possibly could. And likewise paynt the same where need required according to the ordination of the Dean and Chapter.

(James Torre's 1688 transcript of the original contract.)

Thornton was to be paid 4 shillings a week, plus £5 per annum, plus £10 on completion 'if he performed his work well and truly'. This marvellous window still contains Thornton's glass. It is the largest area of mediaeval painted glass surviving anywhere in Europe, being 78 feet high and 32 feet wide. York is, of course, uniquely lucky in having very large numbers of its original windows surviving and, with the heraldry, these tell us much about the dates of the final completion of the new work. For example, the vaults of the north and south aisles of the new choir (some of them using brick webbing) were not finished until about 1420, and only about this time were most of the aisle windows glazed by members of John Thornton's workshops.

At the bottom of the great east window, in the middle, is a small painted panel of Bishop Skirlaw of Durham kneeling at an altar. He it was, who paid for the window, and he was probably hoping to become archbishop. Sadly, though, he died in 1406 in the middle of what was to be a two and a half year vacancy in the see while the king and the pope argued over who should fill it.

In 1407 came a great setback. The central tower collapsed – 'by the carelessness of the masons', as an appeal sent to King Henry IV puts it. Unlike many other tower collapses, however, only the upper masonry appears to have fallen; the crossing piers remained intact. The re-building work here was to put in hand the final stage of the transformation of the minster.

Even before this, the great crossing piers had already been enlarged and encased in new masonry – we have seen how the visit of Richard II (with his chained whitehart) was commemorated on the south-east pier, and it seems likely that the upper stages of de Gray's thirteenth-century tower were perhaps already being demolished before 1407. Following the collapse, Henry IV sent his own master mason from Westminster, a man called William Colchester, to supervise the building of a new tower. Over the next few years the crossing piers were further strengthened, and two ingenious stone screen-arches were inserted at the west ends of the choir aisles. They were designed to be bonded into the aisle walls but to be able to slide against the shafts of the eastern crossing piers, thus allowing for subsidence in the piers when a heavy upper stage was placed on them. A magnificent pulpitum screen was also built under the eastern side of the crossing. Reference is made in the accounts of 1419 to the great hoisting wheel in the 'campanile', and there is no doubt that the intention at this time was to make a large new bell-tower above the lantern over the crossing. If completed, this would have been a stupendous structure, rivalling the 'Bell Harry' tower at Canterbury (see p.147). In the event, however, the masons must have realised that the ground under the tower was unstable (this would be remedied over 500 years later in the restoration work of 1967–72), and the lantern tower only was built, work being completed on it by the middle of the fifteenth century. By this time the bells were already installed in the south-west tower.

To this day, the lantern looks unfinished. It has no pinnacles, and is only fractionally higher than the two western towers. In almost every other way, however, the rebuilding of York minster was nearly complete. The last stage was to build another timber vault above the lantern. This vault, which is 190 feet above the floor, is the only complete mediaeval vault surviving in the minster. The fabric accounts for 1471 tells us of 17s. 4d. being paid to David the Carver 'for the carving of certain bosses, according to the agreement'. These bosses can be inspected from the crossing floor with binoculars; the great central one, which is 5 feet across, shows the two patron saints of the minster – St Paul with his letters and sword, and St Peter with his church and keys. Among other details, the accounts tell us that the painting of the inside of the central tower was not carried out until 1473. Brought specially from London for this were:

3,100 leaves of beaten gold [gold leaf], two cakes of linseed oil, 12 lbs of verdigris, 2 lbs of dark blue, 2 lbs of vermillion, 6 lbs of red lead, bleacher leather, 2 lbs of ochre, fat oil, 2 stones for the grinding of colours, 1 box for keeping the painter's tools, white feathers [used for painting], varnish, 4 lbs of gum mastic, 319 lbs of white lead.

A great service of re-dedication was held in the minster on 3 July 1472. The York minster of that date was almost the minster we still admire so greatly today, over 500 years later. It had taken almost exactly 400 years to build from the day when the great Norman prelate, Thomas of Bayeux, set the work in hand. Only by understanding how the final building was evolved can we fully appreciate what a stupendous achievement it is. In scale at least, it must be rated as the greatest of all the British cathedrals.

Elsewhere, tower building – usually without spires – had become fashionable at many other cathedrals. At Wells, for example, western towers were added to the top of the great west front, completely transforming it. Work started on the south-west tower in about 1385 under the master mason William of Wynford (already encountered at Winchester), but the almost identical north-west tower was apparently not built until c.1424.

The upper stages of the western towers of Durham cathedral had been completed in the early thirteenth century, and some time after that they each acquired a beautiful slender spire. The central tower had been struck by lightning in 1429, and as a result the timber belfry inside caught fire and very badly damaged the masonry. Not until 1455, however, was work put in hand on the lower stage (the lantern). This was complete by 1474 and, unlike York, there were no foundation problems, so that a new upper stage (the belfry) could be built once the money had been found. When complete, in about 1490, the tower was 218 feet high, only 5 feet taller than the lantern at York, showing the enormous scale of the latter. Remarkably, there were even later plans to add a spire on top, and work apparently began on this some time around 1510 under the master mason, Christopher Scune. It was, however, never finished.

At about the same time – c.1509–22 – an upper stage was being added to the exceptionally plain central tower at St David's cathedral in Wales. Bangor cathedral also received a new nave and western tower at this time. However, the finest of the Welsh cathedral towers (all, it must be said, on a very small scale compared to those in England) was the north-west tower at Llandaff, built between about 1485 and 1500 and capped by a splendid pinnacled 'coronet'. The south-west tower at Llandaff, with its spire, is an addition of the 1860s.

At Canterbury, after the completion of the nave in the early fifteenth century, and the rebuilding of the chapter house and cloister, work was put in hand to rebuild the south-west tower and the western transepts, all part of the early Norman cathedral. Building accounts survive which show that the south-west tower was reconstructed between 1423 and 1434, and, just as at York, it then became the bell-tower. Early in the 1430s the central crossing piers were being re-cased and strengthened, and on 4 August 1433 'the first stone of the new work of the Angel Steeple' was laid. This was the very ancient name for the central tower, on top of the spire of which had been a golden angel. However, this work was soon abandoned and, as we shall see, it was over seventy years before the tower was completed. In the meantime, the south-west transept was rebuilt with a fine new chantry chapel of St Michael to the east, dedicated in 1439. Next, attention turned to the north-west transept. This was one of the most sacred areas in the whole cathedral; it was here that Thomas Becket had been murdered. East of this transept a very beautiful new Lady Chapel was built in 1448–55 with an early fan vault and (yet again like at York) a splendid new pulpitum screen was erected to glorify the House of Lancaster.

At various points in the middle of the century, and particularly from about 1460–70, the masons had to be 'put away' – as a contemporary letter calls it – and work ceased. The political upheavals of the Wars of the Roses often involved the patrons of building work both at York and at Canterbury.

In 1472 a new prior called William Sellinge was elected. After becoming a monk he had been to Oxford and had then gone on to get a doctorate of divinity in Bologna and to study in Venice. Sellinge returned to Canterbury priory in 1470, bringing with him a number of new books including a copy of Cicero's *De Republica*. He was soon able to show that not only was he a great scholar, but also that he could be a very careful administrator. His twenty-two years as prior coincided with the final building phase at the cathedral when much was achieved. He also sometimes acted in his later years as an ambassador abroad for King Henry VII.

Prior Sellinge's first task was the completion of the north-west transept. A fine timber roof was erected (which still survives), and beneath it a stone lierne vault was put up which followed the design of the high vault in the nave of three-quarters of a century earlier (it also contains heraldic shields of its principal subscribers). The transept was not finished until 1482 when King Edward IV gave the glass for a magnificent great north window. Sadly, much of this was smashed by a Puritan fanatic in 1642, but some remains, including the figures of Edward IV and his whole family at prayer in a line of central lights.

In 1485 the civil wars between Lancaster and York finally came to an end after the battle of Bosworth. The victor, Henry Tudor, was crowned Henry VII by the very elderly Archbishop of Canterbury, Cardinal Thomas Bourchier. When he died in the following year (he had been at Canterbury for thirty-one years), Henry VII was able to secure the election of his friend and adviser John Morton as archbishop. The following year Morton became Chancellor of England, and as such he became famous as the user of the proverbial fork in raising money for the king. It was Morton who finally completed the building of the great central tower of Canterbury cathedral.

Known as 'Bell Harry' tower since the seventeenth century (after the one bell which hung there), it is one of the finest and most beautiful cathedral towers in Britain. It is 235 feet high to the top of the large pinnacles, and over 100 feet of this is clear of the apexes of the surrounding roofs. Its superb unity of design is a perfect culmination to the cathedral, linking the early Gothic choir to the marvellously rebuilt nave. The designer of the tower was John Wastell, a master mason from East Anglia. He had already built Morton's brick gatehouse at Lambeth Palace, and no doubt was brought in by the archbishop. In due course he would put the finishing touches to King's College chapel at Cambridge, including its famous fan vaults.

A set of accounts tell us that between Easter 1494 and Michelmas 1497 the top 50 feet of the Bell Harry tower (i.e. the bell chamber) were built, and that wages cost just under £400. Much of this money was provided by the archbishop. After 1495 large sums were paid to bricklayers and, in 1496-7, £46 14s. 4d.

was paid for 440,000 'redde bryks'. An inspection of the inside of the bell-chamber shows that the whole of the upper stage is indeed made of fine red brick; stone is used only for quoins and for the outside facing. Unfortunately the accounts for the lower stage of the tower are missing, and it is not known if the lantern was built immediately before the top stage, or if it was built earlier. All we know for certain is that work started on the base of the lantern in 1433 and then stopped for a time when it had reached the level of the tops of the roofs. It seems probable, though, that the rest was not built until after Morton became archbishop in 1486. Remarkably, however, a letter survives which testifies that some time before 1494 pinnacles were being planned for the lantern. It was only in that year that the plan changed, and the extraordinarily bold decision was made to increase the height of the tower by another 50 feet. This letter (known from a draft kept in the cathedral archives) was sent to Archbishop Morton by Prior Sellinge, and it is of much interest, showing as it does the involvement of the patron, and his relationship with the master mason:

Most Reverent father in God, and my most singler gode Lorde, after all due recommendation and humble obediens please it the same to understande that Master Surveyor and I have communed with John Wastell your mason, berer hereof [ie. of this letter] to perceyve of hym what forme and shappe he will kepe in resying [raising] of the pynacles of your new towre here: he drew unto us ij [two] patrons [patterns] of hem. The one was with doble fineall withowte crocketts, and the other was with croketts and single fineall. Thys ij patrons please yt your gode Grace to commande the syd Jo Wastell to draw and shew hem unto you, and upon the sycht, your good Grace shew him your advise and pleasure whyche of them ij, or of any other to be devised, shall contente your gode Lordshyp to be appoynted. And furthermore if your gode Grace wolde require the seyd Jo Wastell so to do, I think that he might provide that these pynacles may be finished and accomplyshed this next somer folowing, the whiche if it mytt be so then your tour outwarde should appere a werke perfite.

As we have seen the pinnacles were not built, and work continued on the building of the new brick upper chamber. However, the pinnacles which do cap the tower (and no doubt went up in 1497–8) are similar to those on the south-west tower and have no crockets (i.e. the leafy knobs on the sloping edge of the pinnacle). The finial is the decorated topmost feature or capstone, but the meaning of a 'double finial' remains uncertain.

In 1493 Archbishop Morton eventually obtained his cardinal's cap from the Borgia pope Alexander VI. In building an extra stage on the central tower at Canterbury, he was literally 'capping' his cathedral in a magnificent way, and it is surely no accident that the angle buttresses of Bell Harry tower are covered with Morton's rebuses and cardinal's caps.

John Wastell's work on Bell Harry tower was finally finished in about 1503 when a magnificent fan vault was put into the tower at the top of the lantern. The pattern of this is almost identical to that at King's College chapel. The rebuilding of Canterbury cathedral was virtually finished, except the north-west tower. This early Norman structure, which had a tall lead and timber spire on it until 1703, was not finally demolished and replaced with a copy of the south-west tower until 1832. To do this the dean and chapter obtained an Act of Parliament empowering them to raise £20,000 by mortgage on their estates with power to raise a further £5000 if required; the money to be paid off by annual instalments in forty years. In the event it cost £24,515 (including £733 for getting the Act of Parliament), and now a century and half later we can only regret this rebuilding, even if it did 'finish' the rebuilding at Canterbury and give it a perfectly symmetrical west front as at York minster.

Apart from tower-building, perhaps the most splendid piece of later-fifteenth-century work in any English cathedral was the project to put high vaults into the nave and presbytery of Norwich cathedral. The nave vault went in first, in c.1464–72, to be followed soon after by the presbytery vault which was helped financially by a bequest of 2000 marks in 1472 from Bishop William Lyhart. The designer for this work was the local master mason Robert Everard. His flying buttresses to support the presbytery vault on the outside are particularly striking. In 1463 the tower had been struck by lightning and this appears to have set alight the timber ceiling and roof (perhaps the original, dating from the twelfth century) of the nave. The vault is still of the tierceron and lierne type, but in its overall effect is moving towards fan-vaulting. It is interesting to compare Norwich with Winchester. Both were monastic cathedrals with immensely long Norman naves, and with their monks' choirs at the east end of the nave under the crossing. At Winchester, the whole of the nave was to be reclothed and a new vault put in. At Norwich, by contrast, only a new vault was installed, but this fits perfectly with the much earlier work below. It is helped by the extra light thrown into the nave by the large windows at triforium level and by the great west window.

At Norwich the lofty wooden spire had crashed down onto the presbytery during a storm in 1362. The tower was patched up and the presbytery rebuilt with fine large early Perpendicular windows in the clerestory. Only a century later, after the lightning strike of 1463, was a new spire built. This graceful stone structure, now the second highest in England at 315 feet, is covered in crockets and buttressed at the bottom. It is surrounded by four separate spirelets, which sit on the corner turrets. It is of particular interest that a note of 1478–80 (made by William of Worcester) exists to inquire of Robert Everard of Norwich 'How many inches doth the spere of Trinite chyrch of Norwich [the cathedral] bater yn. vj feete [batter in 6 feet]'. This is a rare insight into the passing of ideas between master masons.

One cathedral, often not thought of as having cathedral status, is Bath abbey. Even though the bishop of Bath and Wells had his principal seat at Wells after 1218, he still remained the titular abbot of the great Norman abbey at Bath. Of later mediaeval rebuildings at Bath we know almost nothing until the final complete rebuilding of the early sixteenth century.

In 1495 Bishop Oliver King was translated from Exeter to Bath and Wells. He was Henry VII's secretary and was one of the trio of bishops (with Morton of Canterbury and Fox of Winchester) who were at the very centre of the king's circle of advisers. In 1499 King visited Bath for the first time and found it in a very ruinous state. At that time he is said to have had a vision of the Holy Trinity in a dream, with angels ascending and descending a ladder (like Jacob's in the Old Testament). He also heard a voice which said 'Let an Olive establish the Crown, and a King restore the church'. As a supporter of Henry Tudor before the battle of Bosworth, he had helped establish him on the throne, and now as bishop he had to restore and rebuild his cathedral in Bath. For this task he brought in the two brothers Robert and William Vertue, the master masons, who were working for the king in London, and at St Augustine's Abbey in Canterbury.

At Bath they demolished the whole of the Norman nave and started to erect a totally new building in its place. This was to have its own miniature transepts. The structure was to be more like a Chapel Royal than a monastic church, and it involved abandoning the old eastern apsidal arm (the Norman presbytery). A man called Thomas Lynne was recommended as resident mason, and the Vertue brothers wrote to Bishop King that 'of the vawte devised for the chancelle... there shall be noone so goodely neither in England nor in France.'

Bishop King died in 1503 (his successor was the Roman Cardinal Hadrian di Costello) and was buried at St George's Chapel, Windsor Castle, another marvellous building that the Vertue brothers were transforming at this time. Three years later Robert Vertue died. He was buried at St Augustine's Abbey in Canterbury where he seems to have been building a great crossing tower for the monks to match Bell Harry tower on the cathedral (this was sadly demolished only just over thirty years later). William Vertue carried on the work at Bath for many years, but at his death in 1537 it was still not finished, though the last two priors of Bath did much to push it on. Prior William Birde, who died in 1525, also built himself an exceptionally beautiful chantry chapel on the south side of the choir. Work started on this in 1515, by which time the Vertue brothers had given fan vaults to the whole of the new chancel and its aisles. Fan-vaults are a magnificent peculiarity of the final stage of English Perpendicular architecture. Ribs are dispensed with, and halved concave cones are built up until they meet at the centre of the vault. On the surface of the cones is carved decorative blind tracery which, in the centre of the vaults at Bath, is mostly of a quatrefoil form. In the aisles the Vertues went one stage further and introduced pendants, that is hanging bosses, into the central lozenge-shaped panels. At Henry VII's chantry in Westminster abbey the master masons took this motif to the limits of virtuosity by creating pendants in the main fans, as well as in the central panels.

By the early 1530s it seems likely that the whole of the shell of the new abbey at Bath was complete and roofed in timber and lead. Fan-vaults had been built in the choir, choir aisles and transepts, but not in the nave. A new east window was being erected at the east end of the choir, and the whole of the Norman eastern arm was being systematically demolished, no doubt to supply some of the materials needed for the new work. At this time Henry VIII's antiquary, John Leland, visited Bath and saw the tomb of the first Norman bishop, John de Villula, in the ruins of the presbytery, 'at which tyme al the church that he made lay to wast, and was onrofid, and wedes grew about this John of Tours sepulchre'. The old and the new must have made quite a contrast, and within a few years the buildings of both were to be in ruins.

By the 1530s, however, abbeys and priories all over the country were being dissolved, and Bath did not have long to wait. The abbey was surrendered to the Commissioners of King Henry VIII on 27 January 1539 and the monks were pensioned off. At the same time, the church was offered to the city for 500 marks, but they turned it down. Soon the lead had been stripped off the roof and sold, along with the glass, iron and bells, and the nave was left open to the weather. The ruined abbey was purchased in 1548 by the local MP, Matthew Colthurst, and it was his son, Edmund, succeeding to his father's estates in 1559, who started to restore it. The north aisle was re-roofed, and in 1572 Colthurst gave the abbey to the mayor and citizens of Bath. Two years later Elizabeth I visited Bath and encouraged the city to restore the whole church by ordering collections to be made throughout her kingdom for it for the next seven years. Divine service was resumed in the choir in 1576, but it was not until early in the seventeenth century that Bishop James Montague (1608–15) finally re-roofed the nave at his own expense. This roof still survives and can be compared with the choir roof of a century earlier. The fine plaster ceiling that Montague had put in under it survived until 1869 when Gilbert Scott eventually supplied the missing fan-vault to the nave and its aisles. Only the plaster ceiling in the early-seventeenth-century vestry on the east side of the south transept remains to give an impression of what it was like. Montague himself went on to become bishop at Winchester, but at his death in 1618, and on his own request, his body was brought back for burial in the nave at Bath, and his splendid tomb still records his fine benefaction.

Bath abbey may be regarded as bridging two different ages for not only is it the last Gothic cathedral to be built in Britain, but it also looks ahead to the buildings of the Renaissance, particularly in its use of thin walls and vast areas of glass (the triforium has vanished to be replaced by huge clerestory windows)

Bath abbey as it might have appeared in 1530. Note the unfinished vaults and flying buttresses in the nave.

which puts it in the same world as the private chapels belonging to Tudor palaces and university colleges. Ultimately, perhaps, it may even be held to look forward to the Crystal Palace and railway architecture of the nineteenth century, for it is an astonishing fact that there is a proportion of 6 to 1 in the window to masonry area ratio of the walls. Externally, the building is not quite so impressive, though the representation of Bishop King's vision (angels ascending and descending on ladders on the buttresses) on the west façade is another Renaissance detail comparable with the cardinal's caps which decorate Morton's Bell Harry tower at Canterbury, or with the ornamental conceits that enrich the façades of Tudor palaces. The rectangular central tower can never have been entirely happy, but it was certainly not helped by the restoration and constant alteration of its pinnacles in the last century.

At Bath, just as at every other cathedral, archaeology still has much to tell us. A detailed survey of the whole of the surviving fabric is needed, as well as the complete excavation of the destroyed eastern arm, before we shall be able to understand how a great Romanesque church, built during the high point of English Benedictine monasticism, was transformed, first into a Renaissance 'chapel', and then into the great parish church of the most fashionable spa in eighteenth-century Britain. For, it is paradoxical that Bath abbey, without an official bishop's see for over 400 years, should mark the final flowering of the previous four centuries or so of English cathedral building. Let us now look at the story in Scotland.

6

RUINS AND KIRKS

Scottish cathedrals 1070–1560

In August 1072, just a few months after Archbishop Lanfranc had won the primacy dispute for Canterbury, William the Conqueror invaded Scotland and was soon able to get the Scottish King, Malcolm III (Canmore), to do homage to him at Abernethy, an important royal and ecclesiastical centre on the Tay (not far from the modern Perth). At Abernethy today, there is still a splendid round tower in the modern graveyard, which was probably first built not long before William's visit. The upper part of the tower, which is slightly later in date and has belfry windows of a Norman type, was perhaps completed about 25 years after the Conqueror's visit. Only two of these round towers now survive in Scotland (the other is built into the later Brechin cathedral), and they reflect very well the Irish Celtic tradition that existed in much of Scotland at the time.

Until the beginning of the twelfth century, Scotland was virtually a country without cathedrals, the only exceptions being St Andrews and the Anglo-Saxon cathedrals in Whithorn and Abercorn, built during the late seventh century when southern Scotland was part of Northumbria. The whole of the rest of the country had an ecclesiastical organisation which was still basically Celtic, in which the bishops were missionaries without permanent sees. At one time Abernethy was the centre of the principal, indeed only, bishopric in Scotland, but this was merely because it was the principal royal residence. Then, in 908, the see was transferred twenty miles eastwards to St Andrews on the coast of east Fife, and it is here that we should seek the earliest Scottish cathedral. No archaeology below ground has yet been carried out to look for the tenth-century cathedral. When and if it is found, it may well turn out to be an early eighth-century Northumbrian church. The legendary history of St Andrews says that relics of St Andrew were brought there from Patras in Greece by St Regulus in the mid-fourth century, but this is most unlikely, and it is more probable that St Andrews was founded in the reign of Angus I (731–761), with the help of the exiled Bishop Acca of Hexham, St Wilfrid's successor and a well-known venerator of St Andrew, who brought the relics here in about 732. It is even possible that there may be a crypt like that at Ripon or Hexham waiting to be discovered.

King Malcolm III came to the Scottish throne in 1057 after defeating the well-known usurper Macbeth. In his youth he had spent fourteen years in exile at the court of the last Anglo-Saxon king, Edward the Confessor, and in about 1070 he married Margaret, a devout member of the English royal line. It was her influence which saw Norman ecclesiastical institutions starting to be introduced in Scotland soon after the marriage; in particular she built a Benedictine abbey at Dunfermline in the 1070s to which Archbishop Lanfranc of Canterbury sent some monks. The prior of Durham cathedral priory, Turgot, was chosen as her spiritual director (Lanfranc was her spiritual father), and after the death of Malcolm and Margaret it was Turgot who became the first 'Norman' bishop of St Andrews in 1107.

154

The ruins of a very complicated ecclesiastical site are still to be seen in St Andrews today. At the eastern end of the city there were three churches: the huge cathedral started in about 1160 which will be described later in the chapter, the church of St Regulus and, outside the precinct walls, the Culdee church of St Mary of the Rock. The Culdees were the priests of the later Celtic Church who, until 1147, nominally had the power to elect the bishop. They were married men who lived in a loose community, and during the twelfth century they gradually lost all their powers to the Augustinians who were established at St Andrews in about 1127. The Culdees survived until at least the thirteenth century, and the ruins of their cruciform church can still be seen on the cliff top to the east of the priory.

The church of St Regulus is today a strange structure consisting of a 108–foot tower with the complete shell of the chancel to the east. It is built of exceptionally fine, well-dressed ashlar masonry and is obviously an early structure. A close examination of the masonry shows that it has two main phases; the tower and chancel were built first, followed by the insertion of two large arches into the east wall of the chancel and the west wall of the tower. The former led into a sanctuary of which only the broken off wall-ends survive, while the large western arch under the tower clearly led to an enlarged nave, though this, too, was later completely demolished. Both the inserted arches have very distinct features which are closely paralleled in the little church of Wharram-le-Street in Yorkshire. John Bilson pointed out over sixty years ago that Wharram church was given in the early Norman period to Nostell Priory, and it was from Nostell that six canons were sent in about 1120 to found the first Augustinian priory in Scotland at Scone. Four years later, Robert, the prior of Scone, was elected bishop of St Andrews in succession to Turgot and shortly after his consecration in 1126 he

St Rule's church at St Andrews from the north-west.

established Augustinian canons at St Andrews. It was almost certainly Bishop Robert who brought up masons from Nostell in Yorkshire (in the 1120s) to enlarge the existing church for his canons with a new nave and sanctuary. These masons had probably a few years earlier rebuilt Nostell's parish church at Wharram-le-Street.

What is completely unknown, however, is who built the original church of St Regulus, and when. All that can be suggested, without an archaeological excavation, is that it was probably built by English masons (the masonry and original windows all suggest this). The most likely date is sometime in the eleventh century, possibly after 1070 and the introduction of English priests to Scotland under Queen Margaret, though an earlier date in the eleventh century is not impossible.

It was, however, during the reigns of Malcolm and Margaret's third and fourth sons, Alexander I (1107–24) and David I (1124–53), that the church in Scotland had its real beginnings. Both kings were, like many members of their family, noted for their piety, and it is they who founded the many new abbeys and priories that were created in Scotland during the first half of the twelfth century. They also reorganised the church in Scotland, and distinct dioceses were created for the first time. There were dioceses of some sort at an earlier date but their history is obscure. Apart from St Andrews, which was always the most important see, new dioceses were created based on Glasgow, Dunblane, Dunkeld, Brechin and Aberdeen. In the south-west, the diocese based on Whithorn was revived, and in the northern Highlands there were three new dioceses covering Caithness and Sutherland, Ross, and Moray. The diocese of Argyll was only divided off from Dunkeld and given a cathedral on the island of Lismore in about 1200. In these northern dioceses there was initially no obvious place for the bishop to be based, and only later were cathedrals built at Dornoch, Fortrose and Elgin. The earliest bishop in Ross had been based at Rosemarkie, and the move to Fortrose was not made till 1256, while in Moray Birnie, with its handsome twelfth-century church, appears to have been the bishop's earliest centre. In 1187 he moved his seat to Kinnedar, and then in 1203 to Spynie. All these places, which were quite close together, were old Culdee centres and none of them had a 'cathedral church' in anything other than name. A new cathedral was started at Spynie in 1207, the foundations of which have apparently been located, but soon afterwards the bishop, Bricius Douglas (1203–23), petitioned the pope with the king's agreement to have his cathedral transferred to the church of the Holy Trinity *'juxta Elgyn'* ('outside Elgin'). We shall consider later the splendid thirteenth-century cathedral that was eventually built there.

By this time there were, therefore, eleven dioceses in mainland Scotland: St Andrews, Dunkeld, Elgin, Glasgow, Lismore, Fortrose, Whithorn, Brechin,

155

Dornoch, Dunblane and Aberdeen. Towards the end of the twelfth century the pope had granted them independence from England, through there was not as yet a metropolitan see in Scotland. Only in 1472 did St Andrews eventually become an archbishopric, with Glasgow following twenty years later in 1492. Earlier, in the twelfth century, there had been an unseemly squabble between Canterbury and York over who should command the obedience of the Scottish dioceses, which was part of the rivalry between the two English metropolitan sees which had broken out again in 1114.

It is also of interest to note that the Northern Isles (the Orkneys and Shetlands) and the Western (or Southern) Isles (the Isle of Man and the Outer and Inner Hebrides) were at this time dioceses under the archbishop of Trondheim in Norway. They only became Scottish dioceses in the later fifteenth century. The Norwegian connection went back to the Norse conquests of the west coast and islands of Scotland in the ninth century. The western of these two dioceses, later called 'Sodor and Man', covered the Norse kingdom of Man and the Western Isles, and extended from the Isle of Man to the Butt of Lewis. The last Norse king of Man died in 1266, and the islands became part of Scotland under Alexander III, but the ecclesiastical link with Norway continued. In 1507 a new diocese was apparently created which took in the Western Isles, based on Iona abbey (the see had been moved from nearby Lismore Island), while the Isle of Man, with its cathedral of St German, was formally joined to the Province of York in 1542. The diocese is still known as Sodor and Man to this day, and derives from the Norse *Sudreyjar* (meaning Southern Isles) and the Isle of Man.

During the last decades of Norse rule on the Isle of Man, Bishop Simon of the Southern Isles (c.1227–47) started to build a new cathedral church of St German on St Patrick's Isle at Peel, just off the west coast of Man. This cathedral has sadly been a ruined shell since the eighteenth century, but the building (about the size of a large parish church) begun by Bishop Simon in about 1230 can still be seen. To the west of this cathedral is the ruined church of St Patrick (with a nearby round tower). The lowest courses of this building may have been part of the earlier cathedral, but recent excavations north of the thirteenth-century cathedral have found a large early Christian and Viking period cemetery which may have surrounded an early church and cathedral. Bishop Simon only completed the chancel, transepts and crossing tower of his cathedral, leaving his successor, Richard (died 1275), to build the nave.

By far the most splendid building in the whole of the remote area of the Western and Northern Isles is the exceptionally fine cathedral of St Magnus at Kirkwall in the Orkneys, in the Northern Isles, built during the twelfth and thirteenth centuries. In the year 1116 Earl Magnus of Orkney had been murdered on the small island of Egilsay by his cousin Haakon who had seized possession of the earldom after Magnus had taken refuge with Malcolm III of Scotland following an invasion of Orkney by the King of Norway. Shortly afterwards a fine church with a round western tower (all now unroofed) was put up to mark the spot where the murder took place. Magnus was buried in Christ Church, Birsay which was the first cathedral of the Northern Isles. Magnus was much noted for his piety, and within years of his death an incipient cult was starting to blossom. After Earl Rognvald, Magnus's nephew, had regained the earldom of Orkney in 1137 he began to build a large new cathedral church dedicated to St Magnus at Kirkwall. This fine structure is very much in the Anglo-Norman tradition, and masons were perhaps brought in to help from northern England or from Lowland Scotland where Anglo-Norman masons were already enlarging buildings like Dunfermline abbey. Ultimately the influence on all the new Scottish Romanesque buildings can be traced back to Durham cathedral.

Kirkwall cathedral originally had a three-bay eastern arm ending in three apses, and this was probably built by about 1142. The proportions of this eastern arm are exceptionally fine, but very plain. There is, however, an interesting use in the aisles of alternating courses of red and white ashlar (so-called polychrome masonry), which is reminiscent of the green and white stone at Worcester. The crossing area followed on quickly and by 1151, when Earl Rognvald and his bishop William went on crusade, three bays of the nave had also been built. No dedication date is known but by this time St Magnus's remains had probably been placed in the main eastern apse of the cathedral. Earl Rognvald was himself murdered in Caithness in 1158, and after his burial in the cathedral, and canonisation in 1192, his tomb became a secondary shrine. Bishop William 'the Old', who was bishop for over sixty-six years, was buried in the cathedral in about 1168. When the new enlarged presbytery was built in the thirteenth century, the bishop's tomb was moved to the centre bay of the new north arcade, and it was re-discovered here in 1848 complete with an inscribed lead plate describing him as 'William the Old of happy memory, first bishop'. This tomb was no doubt immediately north of the new thirteenth-century shrine of St Magnus. Building work on the nave continued during the later twelfth and early thirteenth century, and by the time of the Norwegian withdrawal from Orkney after the death of King Haakon there in December 1263, the cathedral was probably complete except for the two western bays, which were not built until the fifteenth century.

Let us now return from the fringes of Scotland to the very heart of the country at St Andrews cathedral. We have seen how Augustinian canons were brought to St Andrews in the later 1120s by Bishop Robert, and how he enlarged the church of St Regulus for them. Bishop Robert also tried, but with only partial success, to persuade the Culdee priests to become canons. He did, however, get the pope to remove their right of electing the bishop, and at the same time decree

that as the Culdees died their places were to be filled by canons regular. This persistent suppression of the old Culdee priests continued, but the Culdee order did not finally die out until the fourteenth century although the Culdees were effectively gone by the thirteenth century.

In 1144 the first prior of the Augustinian house was appointed, and it is clear that the enlarged church was almost complete. It seems likely that the priory buildings at this time were only temporary structures, for the thirteenth-century 'Legend of St Andrew' tells us that the canons were intended to be 'men of moderate and contented minds who would wait with patience till better accommodation were provided'. Bishop Robert died in 1159 and his successor Arnold, abbot of Kelso, immediately started to plan a new cathedral on a really monumental scale. With the encouragement of King Malcolm IV, he began work in about 1160 on a completely new building well to the north-west of the existing church of St Regulus. This new cathedral was to be over 400 feet long with an extended rectangular presbytery, followed by an aisled choir of five bays, a large crossing with deep transepts on either side, and finally a huge aisled nave of fourteen bays. Here for the first time in Scotland was a cathedral to match the greatest churches in England.

The new bishop, Arnold, had already carried out extensive building works at Kelso abbey, which were in the so-called 'transitional' style of northern England. Part of his nave at Kelso can be compared with the new work at St Andrews. Round arches are still the order of the day, but new piers, which in the St Andrews choir are bundles of eight shafts, have been introduced. We also find that the old Norman scalloped capital is being replaced by the water-leaf capital, a much more elegant affair.

St Andrews was terribly damaged in the years after 1559 when it was at the centre of the Reformation in Scotland, but some remarkable ruined parts of the cathedral still tell the story of how it was built. The earliest part of the building, which has survived almost complete, is the great east front. It is over 60 feet high and originally had three tiers of three round-headed windows (the upper two tiers were replaced by a single large perpendicular window in the early fifteenth century). Below this on the inside was 'blind' interlaced arcading which surrounded the shrine of St Andrew; it, too, was removed in the fifteenth century, but the bases of the arcading are still visible. In the west wall of the south transept, however, the blind arcading survives and this wall still has its three original high windows (looking out over the cloister roof) which are in turn linked by blind arcading. Almost the whole of the rest of the eastern arm has disappeared but the stub-ends on the east front show clearly where the original triforium and clerestory passages were situated. They also show that a vault was later built over the choir and sanctuary, and that the eastern clerestory was the first place where pointed arches were introduced. Of the crossing and north-transept area only the lowest courses have survived, giving little more than the plan. Both transepts had three chapels in an eastern aisle, and there was no doubt a large central crossing tower, probably capped later by a spire.

Of the very long nave, only the south wall of the south aisle survives, but this does at least show us that before the end of the twelfth century ten of the fourteen planned bays were under construction. In the tenth bay was a pro-cessional door (now blocked) leading into the west walk of the cloister. This was narrowed in the later Middle Ages. The south aisle wall also still contains its original round-headed windows in the first four bays with the rest being replaced by pointed windows (containing simple Y-tracery) in the later thirteenth century. By looking closely at the two types of windows (side by side in the fourth and fifth bays), it is easy to see how the new windows were inserted. Above them are the scars for a quadripartite vault.

The west end of the cathedral, which still has one tall turret surviving to its full height, is another area of very great archaeological interest where several changes of plan can be seen. During the time of Bishop Wishart (1273–9) we are told that the original west front was thrown down in a great tempest and then rebuilt on the present site two bays in. The original west front may have contained two towers, but the surviving remains tell us nothing and we have no idea how much of the west end of the cathedral was completed before the storm. Excavations of the foundations may throw new light on this. The earliest work that is visible now, the northern and southern side walls, though of later-thirteenth-century date, suggest that the first plan was to rebuild on the original line. This work can best be seen on the south side where it clearly runs on behind the present west front (some stones have been removed to show the shafting buried beneath the later masonry). At some stage in the 1270s it was decided to shorten the cathedral and the present west front was built. Soon after this it was decided to utilise the new redundant longer side walls by making a vaulted porch, sometimes called a Galilee porch, across the west front of the cathedral. The wall-shafts for the vaulting and the lines of this vault are still clearly visible, particularly in the south-east corner of the porch.

In 1378 the cathedral, which was still largely without high stone vaults, was badly damaged in a fire and very extensive rebuilding followed. In the west front there is plenty of evidence for this rebuilding in the upper levels. The Galilee porch vaulting was removed and the area above the west door was completely rebuilt. New blind arcading was constructed on the outside with above it two tiers of pairs of large three-light windows. Yet further up there was probably a round window in the gable. These new windows appear, from the broken ends of the tracery, to have had Geometric tracery patterns.

Reconstruction bird's-eye view of St Andrews cathedral
before its destruction in the sixteenth century.

Much other rebuilding work in the cathedral no doubt took place after the fire of 1378 (particularly the nave arcades), but most of the evidence for this has disappeared. We are told, for example, that the south transept gable was thrown down in a storm in 1409, causing much damage. Also that the nave was unfinished until Prior James Haldenston (1419–43) provided it with glass windows, altars, images and furnishings. By the time that St Andrews became the seat of an archbishop in 1472, it was past its peak and the corruption which was to destroy the church, as well as many of its buildings, was already endemic. Our final view of the cathedral comes from a 'bird's eye view' map of St Andrews made in about 1580. This seems to show the cathedral already unroofed, but with a forest of towers around it. Apart from the detached tower of St Regulus's church, there are pairs of turrets on the north and south transept fronts as well as those partially surviving at the east and west ends.

The next cathedral in Scotland after St Andrews where major building work took place was Glasgow. This splendid building, albeit still today covered in industrial soot, is the only cathedral to survive intact in mainland Scotland, though sadly its western towers were demolished as late as the 1840s. The legendary figure of St Kentigern (popularly known as St Mungo) is supposed to have founded a church here early in the seventh century, and he certainly appears to have been an important missionary figure of the Irish Celtic Church in the area. The beginnings of the diocese of Glasgow, however, go back no earlier

than about 1114 when John was appointed the first bishop. He had been tutor
to David, brother of Alexander I (later to become king himself), and was
appointed bishop of the Strathclyde area by him. In about 1118 John started to
build a small church which was consecrated in 1136, but the site of this building
has yet to be located. During the middle years of the twelfth century the diocese
of Glasgow was trying to throw off the yoke of the archbishopric of York, but
it was not until 1192, under Bishop Jocelin (1174–99), that the pope made
Glasgow independent of the province of York. The neighbouring south-west
Scottish diocese of Whithorn, however, remained under the control of York

Plan of Glasgow cathedral.

until the mid-fourteenth century.

The Chronicle of Melrose abbey tells us that in 1181 Bishop Jocelin 'gloriously enlarged the cathedral'. Jocelin was very keen to promote the cult of St Kentigern (he had no doubt heard of what was happening in Canterbury) and commissioned a new written life of the saint. He also seems to have started to build a new presbytery at his cathedral, and small fragments of late-twelfth-century work survive in the south-western bay of the later crypt. A small stump of an eastern cross-wall can be seen here with the earliest base and engaged column (the capital is perhaps a little later) visible in the cathedral. This phase of work seems to have been complete by 1197, but not long afterwards, perhaps during the time of Bishop Walter (1207–32), there was a change of plan and the work here was modified. The architectural history of these early phases of building is very complicated, and as only small fragments survive it is not possible without excavation to get any idea of the size of the cathedral at this time. However, it appears that in the 1220s and 1230s the whole of the lower part of the walls of the nave was built. A distinctive plinth can be followed round the outside of the nave from the south-western bay of the crypt to the north side of the crossing, the form and mouldings of which visibly contrast with the later plinth around the choir. By about 1240 the nave was perhaps complete as far as the base of the windows only, and the bishop at this time, William Bondington (1223–58), seems suddenly to have decided that work must stop while a large new choir and presbytery were constructed. Again the documentary evidence is poor, but in about 1242 the faithful in every parish were urged to contribute towards the building throughout Lent. During the next two decades a work of genius was evolved.

In plan, the new choir was just a simple rectangle exactly balancing the plan of the nave, a most unusual arrangement. In detail, however, it is a much more complicated design, as the eastern part of the cathedral ran steeply downhill to a stream, the Molendinar burn, and a large crypt had to be incorporated from the beginning. The plan was also to include an ambulatory for pilgrims, and four eastern chapels at both levels. All in all it was to be a quite remarkable 'double' eastern arm with the canons' choir, high altar, and principal shrine of St Kentigern in the upper level, and a secondary tomb-shrine of St Kentigern and a Lady Chapel in the lower level. There was nothing quite like this anywhere else in Britain, though the general arrangement, in a far less compact form, could be found at Canterbury cathedral where the huge Romanesque crypt also contained a Lady Chapel and the secondary shrine of St Thomas Becket.

At Glasgow the crypt is a design of extraordinary subtlety with the shafts and vault pattern at the centre forming an incredibly complex spatial arrangement. The central focus on the west was the tomb of St Kentigern, and the shafts and

vaults are formed in such a way as to make them appear to be a canopy for the tomb. The carving on the capitals and bosses in this area is of the highest quality, with marvellous stiff-leaf and figured work. Further east the central pier is removed in the Lady Chapel area, and we have another very complex space. Unfortunately, with the removal of the altar from here at the Reformation and the later construction of steps (originally there were only steps down in the north and south aisles), it is much more difficult today to understand the original form of the chapel. In the extreme east end of the crypt, at the lowest level, there were four chapels beyond the eastern ambulatory and these now contain some important loose architectural fragments including some large parts of the thirteenth-century shrine of St Kentigern.

Above the crypt was an equally glorious choir. This contained the canons' stalls at the west end, the high altar in the middle, and (probably in the main eastern bay below the tall east windows), the large shrine of St Kentigern. Beyond this was the eastern ambulatory and four more subsidiary chapels. The design for this upper eastern arm of the church, which (like so many Scottish buildings) probably had its origins in northern England, is another masterpiece with finely proportioned arcades surmounted by an equally fine triforium and very tall clerestory. There was never any intention to have a high vault in stone, and this made possible the four exceedingly tall and compact lancets in the east wall, as well as the high clerestory. Again, there is splendid stiff-leafed decoration on the capitals. The side aisles, which were covered with vaults, have a fascinating sequence of windows containing a series of variants on early plate tracery (this is the name given to the earliest form of window-tracery when the thin plate of stone between the tops of the lancet windows is pierced by additional Geometric openings). Soon after the choir was finished (with a wooden high vault under the timber roofs), work started on the crypt of a very long (four-bay) south transept. Work on this was, however, discontinued in the later thirteenth century, before even the crypt could be vaulted, and was not taken up again for over two centuries. The crypt vault was finally built by Archbishop Blackadder (1492–1508), but the upper storey has never been built. A square, two-storied chapter house was also built on the north-east side of the presbytery, though the upper part of this had to be extensively rebuilt after it was damaged during an early-fifteenth-century fire.

At the end of the thirteenth century, the masons continued work on the nave and inner transepts, though clearly with a new master mason, whom Richard Fawcett suggests may have come from western Britain. When work resumed on the nave in the 1280s and 1290s the western towers probably already stood much higher than the rest of the work, and what was required were the aisle windows, arcades, triforia and clerestories. On the south only, the aisle windows contain some fine Decorated tracery (the less visible north side only has simple Y-tracery), and this ties in with the fine tracery in the nave triforium. The latter is unique in having its arches set back within very tall super-arches which also contain the clerestory windows. Again the nave was never intended to have a high stone vault, but a timber ceiling. Sadly, the last traces of this and the mediaeval high roof where almost completely removed in the extensive restoration of 1911.

When the disastrous wars with England started after the death of Alexander III in 1286, it is likely that the presbytery and nave of Glasgow cathedral were pretty well complete. The bishop at this time, Robert Wishart (1271–1316) was deeply involved in the wars (he was taken prisoner in 1306 at Cupar still wearing his coat of mail, and released after the battle of Bannockburn in 1314), and spent much of his money on secular rather than spiritual needs. At one stage he was accused of making siege engines from timbers which had been supplied for building work! It is unlikely, therefore, that any major building work was undertaken for at least another century after c.1290, and it was only after lightning struck the cathedral and caused much damage during Bishop Matthew de Glendinning's time (1387–1408), that major new works were, of necessity, started. The strike was actually in about the year 1406 and the central tower was perhaps the main casualty, though the chapter house was also badly damaged. There may have been a tall lead-covered timber spire, but no evidence survives for this except that when bishops William de Lauder (1408–26) and John Cameron (1426–46) came to rebuild it they chose, unusually for the time, to have a tower and spire, rather than a large crossing tower only.

The fifteenth-century work was slow and small-scale (except for the tower and stone spire), and seems also to have included a refurbishing of the presbytery with a sumptuous new shrine to St Kentigern in about 1420. At the same time a fine new pulpitum screen was built at the west end of the canons' choir. The final piece of building work was by Robert Blackadder, who became bishop in 1483 and the first archbishop in 1492. He vaulted over the uncompleted aisle projecting from the south transept, and presumably intended to build the principal floor as well. By the time of his death in 1508, on pilgrimage in the Holy Land, however, the work had been abandoned.

It is something of a miracle that after the Reformation, when such widespread destruction was taking place, Glasgow cathedral was taken over by no less than three presbyterian communities and therefore saved for posterity. The Inner High Kirk took possession of the choir in 1567, followed by the Outer High Kirk in the five western bays of the nave in 1587, and finally the Barony Kirk which took over the crypt in 1595. During this time, it is strange to account that archbishops were still being appointed until the General Assembly, meeting in the cathedral in 1638, abolished the episcopacy (Parliament was soon to follow suit in England). There was a brief revival of the episcopacy from 1661 to 1690, but after this all bishops were finally abolished in Scotland and the cathedrals technically became crown property.

Only in the early nineteenth century, however, did the crown start to look after some of the ruined cathedrals of Scotland. One of the finest they had to contend with was the great cathedral at Elgin in Morayshire, 'the Lantern of the North', which had suffered the most dreadful depredations since the Privy Council ordered the lead to be stripped off the roofs in 1567. The central crossing tower was allowed to fall in 1711, and throughout this period the ruins were used as a stone quarry. In 1825, however, the first keeper was appointed, and the ruins that survived to the early nineteenth century are still intact today. In fact in 1988 a fine new lead roof was put on the chapter house once again by the office of the Secretary of State for Scotland, a really splendid new investment!

Despite its very ruined state, at Elgin cathedral like St Andrews there is much to see. The bishop of Moray only officially moved his seat to Elgin in 1224, but there is little doubt that building work had already been in hand there for many years. The ruined end wall of the south transept still has round-headed windows (as well as lancets) which suggest a date of before 1200, and it is highly likely that work on the present building started under Bishop Richard (1187–1203) whose see was nominally based at the nearby church of Kinnedar. Richard no doubt started at the east, and the foundations of his east end presumably await excavation under the present choir. Bishop Richard was a close friend of King

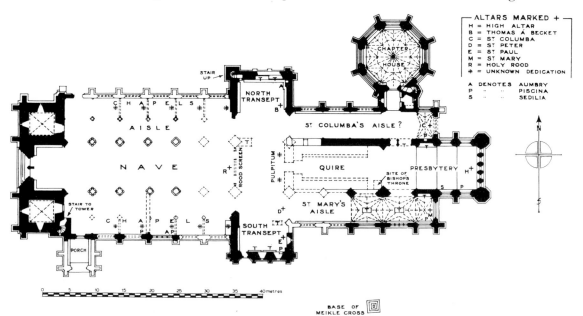

Plan of Elgin cathedral.

View of the south side of the ruins of Elgin cathedral.

William the Lion (1165–1214), who is known to have made many grants of land to the see. It was he who probably helped the bishop to build a large new cathedral just outside the town of Elgin on the east. William the Lion also encouraged trade in the area and gave the burgesses in Moray the right of 'free hanse', that is freedom from royal tolls.

For some unknown reason, Richard's successor Bricius Douglas (bishop 1203–23) applied to Pope Innocent III to have his cathedral see fixed at 'Sancte Trinitatis de Spyny', and this was agreed in 1207, perhaps because the principal castle of the bishop was there. Bricius Douglas quickly changed his mind, however, and as noted earlier, we soon find him writing to the Pope again to ask for the transference of his see from Spynie to the Church of the Holy Trinity *'juxta Elgyn'*. This was not, however, agreed until 1224 when Bishop Andrew (1224–42) had just been appointed, and we know that in July 1224 a large service of consecration took place at Elgin under the bishop of Caithness. By now a new college of eight canons had been founded (replacing the old Culdee monks) and the cathedral had a new constitution based on that at Lincoln where Bishop Andrew had lived.

The cathedral at this date consisted of the two transepts, an aisled nave, and the two fine surviving western towers (added slightly later) with a magnificent great west doorway between them. The northern altar in the north transept was, significantly, dedicated to St Thomas Becket (whose translation had just taken place in Canterbury cathedral in 1220). Although all traces of the nave and aisle walls of the first cathedral (except a few nave bases) have disappeared above ground, it is possible to get some idea of their size and extent by looking at the south and east walls of the south-west tower. It can be seen clearly that the porch and outer aisle have been added later, covering the early-thirteenth-century arcading. The upper (clerestory) passage end can also be seen. The finest of the thirteenth-century work visible is in the beautiful double west doorway of c.1270 which was covered with a mass of decoration (now very worn) and surmounted by three decorated gables. This doorway had to be considerably rebuilt after the destruction of 1390 (see below), but it is fairly easy to see which is thirteenth-century and which fifteenth-century work, the inner doorways most obviously being later work.

Soon after the dedication of 1224, Bishop Andrew must have decided that he needed a much larger choir and presbytery (he had increased the number of canons from eight to twenty-three), and with the support and patronage of King Alexander II (1214–49), and many of the powerful families of Moray, a splendid new eastern arm was started. The east front, with its two large tiers of five windows surmounted by a great round window and clasped by two large octagonal buttress-turrets, is the high point of this work. It shows the influence of St Andrews and, from further south, the great cathedral of Lincoln in England which Bishop Andrew had seen as a young man.

Work on the presbytery no doubt continued well into the later thirteenth century and was presumably finished in Bishop Archibald's time (1253–98). The high vaults were in timber, as at Glasgow, but parts of the thirteenth-century stone vaults still survive in the aisles. In 1270 there was a bad fire, and much repair work had to be done, but despite this the great church must have been complete before the onset of the Anglo-Scottish wars at the end of the century. As well as the choir and presbytery, a fine octagonal chapter house had been built, and in the nave area, outer aisles for a whole series of chapels were added. These outer aisles, unique in Scotland, are very similar to those which had recently been built at Chichester cathedral. Unfortunately the destruction of the early records, in the sack of 1390, and of the cathedral itself, give us little to go on, but it seems likely that Chichester rather than a French or Flemish source was the inspiration here. In the west part of the south aisle enough survives to show that the chapels had transverse gables, and although these were restored in the fifteenth century, the basic form must be of thirteenth-century date, and hence very similar to Chichester.

As in other dioceses in Scotland, the bishop of Elgin in the early fourteenth century was much embroiled in the Anglo-Scottish wars. David de Moravia (1299–1325) came from an important local Moray family and was one of the chief war leaders in the north. After Edward I's victory he was excommunicated and had to flee to Norway, and the cathedral no doubt went through a lean period. The lowest point in Elgin's fortunes in the fourteenth century, however, came at the very end of the century when Alexander Stewart, Earl of Buchan (nicknamed the 'Wolf of Badenoch') was excommunicated by the elderly bishop, Alexander Bur (1362–97). In June 1390 he left his stronghold at Lochindorb intent on revenge, and with his 'wyld Wykked Heland-men' he burned:

> the whole town of Elgin, eighteen noble and beautiful manses of canons and chaplains and what was further still more cursed and lamentable the noble and highly adored church of Moray with all the books charters and other valuable things of the country therein kept.

The evidence for this destruction is visible in several places in the ruins, but it is perhaps most apparent at the west end: the two western towers in particular show very clearly all the repair work that had to be undertaken, as well as heavy calcining from the fire. The great west window had to be completely rebuilt, and this was not done till Bishop Columba de Dunbar's time (1422–36). The tracery has unfortunately disappeared, but the broken-off 'tusks' show it had seven lights at the base and a large round panel above. There is also an interesting parapet walk above the window (just below the gable), and this can be seen close to from the towers, which are now open to the public. It is also possible to look along the first parts of the clerestory and parapet-walk passages of the nave from the towers. In the chapter house, the burning was so intense that the interior had to be completely refaced and new windows and a new vault with a central column provided. Just outside the chapter house, next to the vestibule, a fascinating 'lavatorium' (washing place) was added, and this still contains its decorated washbasin. Next to it a new stair-tower was created which leads on to the roof.

Chapter houses on the north side of the choir were a very common feature in Scotland's secular cathedrals, and they survive at many places, though only Elgin's was octagonal. We have already noted that Glasgow's chapter house was square in plan and of two storeys. At Dunblane, Dunkeld and Fortrose, rectangular buildings of various sizes still survive in part attached to the north side of the choir, and to these smaller Scottish cathedral churches we now turn.

Dunblane, in central Scotland, is today a fine, completely roofed, but heavily restored church. After the Reformation only the choir was retained for parochial use, but at the end of the nineteenth century the nave was once again reroofed and brought back into use. Bishops of Menteith and Strathearn are first documented in the mid-twelfth century (though a Celtic church had been here for much longer than that), and they seem to have had two centres, at Muthill (in Strathearn) and at Dunblane. As it happens, both these churches still retain early- to mid-twelfth-century tall towers (probably for bells), which were presumably erected soon after the diocese was first created. They were originally built as free-standing structures (the associated churches have not yet been found), and only later was the tower at Dunblane incorporated awkwardly into the south aisle of the

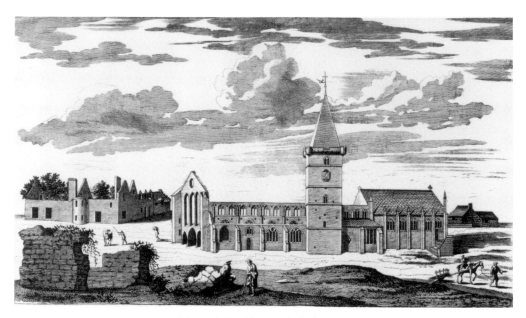

View of Dunblane cathedral in 1690.

cathedral. Building work on Dunblane cathedral started soon after 1237 when the new bishop, Clement (1233–58), reorganised the diocese and acquired a papal mandate to fix the see at Dunblane. As at Elgin, a new chapter of secular canons was created and building work on a new church was started. Compared to St Andrews, Glasgow and Elgin this was a modest building, but even so it was to be large compared to most other non-monastic churches in Scotland at the time.

The basic plan was probably agreed early on, with an unaisled chancel 81 feet long and an eight-bayed aisled nave 129 feet long (the total overall length was about 230 feet). The long chapter house and sacristy on the north side were also part of the original plan. A careful study of the rest of the upstanding fabric by Richard Fawcett has suggested that the north side of the choir (with the chapter house) was finished first, followed, oddly, by the nave and then by the rest of the choir. Perhaps there was an earlier existing choir still in use elsewhere on the site. The nave here is of particular interest as it shows several changes of design during the course of building work. Initially it was planned with low arcades, triforia and clerestories, and evidence at the east end of the south aisle shows that it was also to include stone vaults over the aisles. In the event this plan was not proceeded with and tall arcades with a clerestory only were built. This did not allow for vaulted aisles so shed-roofs were built instead. The clerestory also shows a change of design, with a simple row of lancets giving way to wider windows of two lights with bar-tracery decoration at the top. The inner arcade, beyond a wall passage, also has the same thing. Bar-tracery (the next stage in the evolution of proper tracery after plate-tracery, which we saw in the Glasgow choir aisles) consists of decorated bars of stone being used to create small geometrical lights at the top of the windows.

The west front of Dunblane cathedral was probably completed in the third quarter of the thirteenth century and has a fine triplet of traceried windows above an elaborately moulded processional entrance. The choir has much larger windows which, although they are heavily restored, reflect the larger amount of light (and no doubt stained glass) that the canons wanted in their part of the building. Dunblane is also one place (rare in Scotland since so much was destroyed in the Reformation) where one can still see some very fine fifteenth-century carved wooden choir stalls. The canopies over the largest of the stalls, which were probably used by the canons, are particularly finely carved, with various fabulous creatures moving through a profusion of foliage.

North-east of Dunblane, and at the entrance to probably the most important route into the Highlands, is Dunkeld. This was initially the seat of a huge diocese stretching westwards to the Argyll coast and south-west to the Mull of Kintyre. Early in the thirteenth century, however, Argyll was separated off to have its own small cathedral on Lismore island (this moved to Iona in the early sixteenth century. The cathedral at Dunkeld, which is very similar in plan to that at Dunblane, was also probably started during the middle years of the thirteenth century. The choir and presbytery contain some mid-thirteenth-century and early-fourteenth-century work, including a fine blind arcade along the inside of the north wall. As at Dunblane, this part of the cathedral was rebuilt for parish use after the Reformation, and was reroofed in 1600, and again in 1691 after further destruction. It has consequently been fairly heavily restored. Only the still-unroofed nave remains as an 'archaeological' monument, dating entirely from the fifteenth century. It is not clear whether there was an earlier (thirteenth- and fourteenth-century) nave on the site, or whether the nave had only been planned but never been built during this difficult time.

In 1398 Robert de Cardeny was appointed to the see of Dunkeld and it is recorded that, starting in 1406, he built the nave of the church to the level of the blind storey. His work was continued by his successor Bishop Thomas Lauder who consecrated the completed building in 1464. Lauder is also recorded as having built the porch, the chapter house (placed as usual on the north side of the choir), and having started work on the new north-west tower. The nave is in many ways an unusual structure. It has massive round pillars, which hark back to Romanesque buildings, that are quite short and have pointed arches above. Over these are strange semi-circular openings at the triforium level which contain smaller traceried openings. At first glance the nave appears symmetrical, but on closer inspection it can be seen that the mouldings on either side are different and that only the south aisle was vaulted. There are therefore more buttresses on the south than on the north. This presumably means that one side, the north, was probably completed first. The aisle and clerestory windows are of two main types, which must be early and mid-fifteenth century in date. This last date is confirmed by the arms of Bishop Lauder which appear on a shield between the fourth and fifth windows in the south clerestory. The three finely traceried windows at the east end of the south aisle, and all those in the north aisle (except the westernmost), are of the early type, and were probably in place before Bishop Cardeny's death in 1420. It can also be seen that the eastern three bays of the south aisle are earlier than the western bays, and it is here that Bishop Cardeny was buried. His now very worn tomb and effigy is set into the south aisle wall (originally the chapel of St Ninian), and is a good example of early-fifteenth-century Scottish carving. Inside the choir, but not *in situ*, is another fine effigy. This is of a recumbent figure in full armour on a sarcophagus decorated with small sculptured figures in armour set into canopied niches. The tomb is supposed to be that of the infamous 'Wolf of Badenoch' who burnt Elgin cathedral in 1390. He later did penance and received absolution from the Bishop of St Andrews, and died in about 1406.

The west front of the cathedral was also rebuilt by Bishop Lauder in the mid-fifteenth century, and the large west window still contains a few fragments of tracery in a late flamboyant style. Whereas in the twelfth and thirteenth centuries English architectural influence was paramount, after the wars with England, continental influences (particularly from France and the Low Countries) were of more importance, though by this time Scotland had evolved its own style of late Gothic. The idiosyncratic nave of Dunkeld is a good example.

The last thing to be built at Dunkeld was the north-west tower. This went up in the last quarter of the fifteenth century, and is another fine late mediaeval structure. The ground floor of the tower was the bishop's court and still contains two fine wall-paintings of Biblical judgement scenes, very rare survivals which must have been overlooked by the Reformers, for in 1560 a letter was received at Dunkeld which ran thus:

To our Traist friendis, the Lairds of Arntilly and Kinvaid, Traist friendis after maist harty commendacion, we pray you faill not to pass incontinent to the kyrk of Dunkeld, and tak doun the faill images thereof, and bring furth to the kyrkzayrd, and burn thaym oppinly. And siclyk cast down the the altaris, and purge the kyrk of all kynd of monuments of idolatrye. And this fail not to do, as ze will do us singular empleseur; and so committis you to the protection of God. From Edinburgh, the XII of August, 1560. Faill not, but ze tak giud heyd that neither the dasks, windocks, nor durris, be ony ways hurt or broken – either glassin wark or iron wark.
(Signed) AR. ERGYLL.
JAMES STEWART
RUTHVEN

It is interesting that the first phase was only to cleanse the church of papistical things (altars, images and so forth), and not to 'hurt' the doors, windows, and ironwork, or by implication take off the roof. This must, however, have followed soon afterwards, though we are lucky that, being fairly remote, Dunkeld cathedral did not become a quarry like St Andrews and Elgin. The worst destruction here came as late as 1689 when almost the whole town was destroyed during fighting between Jacobites and Covenanters.

Many of the middle rank of Scottish cathedrals were partly reused as kirks after the Reformation and, as we have seen, it was the eastern arm at Dunblane and Dunkeld (as well as Lismore) that was used. At Aberdeen and Brechin, on the other hand, the nave was used, and the chancel was allowed to become ruined. Let us finish our survey of Scottish cathedrals by looking at St Machar's cathedral, Aberdeen, another building where only late mediaeval work survives above ground.

Like many of the cathedral sites in Scotland, the area around the old building is covered by masses of large post-Reformation tombstones. Starting at the east end of the present building, it soon becomes apparent that only the lower parts of the walls of the two transepts survive, though these still contain the battered remains of the tombs of late mediaeval bishops, that of Bishop Dunbar in the south transept being particularly fine. It was he who carried out the final building work in the cathedral, including the south transept itself (in 1522), the western spires and the truly magnificent nave ceiling made between 1518 and 1531. The eastern arm of the cathedral has completely vanished, and even the foundations must have been heavily cut into by the forest of graves. Late-seventeenth-century views of the city do, however, give us some idea of the vanished parts. The earliest work still surviving today are the columns of the west side of the cathedral crossing which are partly masked by the post-Reformation east wall. These were built in Bishop Alexander Kinninmond's time (in the 1370s), and stand out as being made of sandstone. Most of the rest of the cathedral is made of the exceptionally hard Aberdeen granite which is such a feature of the more recent buildings of the city.

The nave and west front were built by Bishop Henry Lichtoun between 1422 and 1440 (he also built the north transept and was buried there), and are therefore roughly contemporary with the nave of Dunkeld and the rebuilt west front of Elgin. Both Aberdeen and Dunkeld have cylindrical piers in the nave, but the upper walls at Aberdeen (without a triforium) are very simple compared to those at Dunkeld, and the eye is led straight away to the magnificent heraldic timber ceiling.

Probably the most unusual and interesting surviving feature of Aberdeen cathedral is the fortress-like west front with its two western towers and steeples (the latter only completed in the early sixteenth century). The towers contain only thin slit-windows and at the top are massive oversailing parapets on deep triple corbels. The whole thing is much more like a castle and is in many ways unique in Britain. Ironically, when the towers were built in the early fifteenth century, Scotland was going through a relatively peaceful period. When the three stone spires (the central spire has now gone) were completed in the sixteenth century, Aberdeen must have looked an extremely fine and tough-looking structure, both from a distance and close to. The exceptionally hard granite adds to this impression, and we must regret the disappearance of the eastern parts.

In less than four hundred years, between the twelfth and sixteenth centuries, Scotland had acquired an exceptionally interesting group of cathedrals, and it is a tragedy that, compared to England, so much destruction had taken place at the Reformation and since. All that is possible now is to try to imagine, in the mind's eye, what it would have been like to have walked into the nave and choir of the completed cathedrals at St Andrews or Elgin, or even the small cathedrals at Dornoch and Fortrose in their final sixteenth-century form. The total rebuilding of the former in 1835–7, and the almost complete destruction of the main parts of the latter have left gaps that may be small compared to St Andrews, but are nevertheless significant. However, we must also not forget that at Kirkwall and at Glasgow we still have almost intact, two exceptionally fine cathedrals.

The Scottish episcopacy was not totally abolished until 1689, but after the Reformation, though bishops continued to be appointed, they had little connection with their cathedrals, and of course no new building work was undertaken in this period. Bishop James Wedderburn (1585–1639) of Dunblane, for example, was also Dean of the Chapel Royal in Scotland and Professor of Divinity at St Andrews university. When he died he was buried in the Dean's Chapel in Canterbury cathedral. Oddly enough one further cathedral can be added to the list in the seventeenth century, and this is the High Kirk of St Giles in Edinburgh. This is, of course, still a splendid building but it was only nominally a cathedral, having been elevated to this status in 1633 when King Charles I came to Scotland (with William Laud, his new archbishop of Canterbury) to be crowned there. Only five years later all bishops in Scotland were deposed.

In 1587 King James VI's Act of Annexation allowed the crown to claim ownership of ecclesiastical estates on the grounds that it was the crown who had made the original endowments. Two centuries later this allowed the Barons of the Exchequer (the Treasury in Scotland) to spend money on looking after the ruins when a new age of enlightenment dawned. In St Regulus's church at St Andrews a stone dated 1789 records the repair work carried out by the Barons of the Exchequer there exactly two hundred years ago. Since then, and the passing of the Ancient Monuments Acts in 1882 and 1900, excellent work has been done by the State in looking after Scottish cathedrals. In Scotland, some cathedrals now fully in use again, like Glasgow and Dunblane, are cared for and maintained by the State. Maybe one day the same will happen in England and Wales.

7

DISSOLUTION AND RESURRECTION

Henry VIII's new foundations

In the year 1514 Thomas Wolsey became, in quick succession, Bishop of Lincoln and Archbishop of York. He then went on to add Bath and Wells, Durham, and finally Winchester to his roll of sees. He was also Bishop of Tournai, in modern Belgium, from 1514 to 1518 and 'farmed' the sees of Salisbury, Worcester and Llandaff, keeping the non-resident Italian bishops of these dioceses on fixed stipends. In addition, he held many other positions in the English church, including Dean of York, and Abbot of St Albans, and within a short time he was a cardinal also. As such, he had agents in every diocese who advised him on vacancies which he filled without consulting the local bishops. Even the Archbishop of Canterbury, William Warham (1503–32), was overawed and made to resign the lord chancellorship in his favour. In short, Wolsey had complete control over the English church, and was soon to have control of the state as well. To foreign observers he was the real ruler of England. Wolsey's power, however, was short lived. It was his monarch, Henry VIII, who soon wrested it from him, in particular his unique hold over the English church.

Despite his huge wealth and vast income, Cardinal Wolsey never spent àny money on building work at any of his cathedrals. Indeed, it appears that during his tenure of the see of Bath and Wells (1518–23) work on the new cathedral ground to a halt while he used the money for other things. Just before the Reformation in England (the same is true in Scotland as well) bishops were concentrating increasingly their new building schemes on their secular palaces rather than their cathedrals. Certainly, men like Archbishop Morton or Bishop Fox of Winchester a generation before had built themselves large palaces, but they also initiated some new projects in their cathedrals. Not so their successors. It was the vast palace built by Archbishop Warham at Otford in Kent, and even more so that of Cardinal Wolsey at Hampton Court that prompted the king to acquire them, and then to go on and build even more remarkable palaces like Nonsuch in Surrey (1538–44). By the time of Wolsey's fall in 1529, therefore, all cathedral building work had effectively come to an end. It is ironic that Wolsey's most grandiose scheme, Cardinal College – later Christ Church – in Oxford would shortly house one of Henry's new cathedrals.

In 1535, in order to facilitate his divorce from Catherine of Aragon and marriage to Ann Boleyn, Henry VIII had thrown off the yoke of Rome and had declared himself head of the Church in England. Shortly afterwards the process of dissolving the monasteries began. Commissioners were sent throughout the country to inquire into the state of the monasteries, starting with the smaller ones, and then, from 1538, the rest. If they failed to satisfy the commission's scrutiny (which of course they did) they were ordered to be suppressed, and their revenues and lands taken over by the king. Events moved quickly. By the spring of 1540 the last one of all, the great archiepiscopal monastery of Christ Church, Canterbury, had been dissolved by royal commission.

Although Thomas Cromwell, as Henry VIII's vicar-general, is often credited with the dissolution of the monasteries, he had taken the idea over from Wosley, whose great power he had also assumed. Some years earlier Wolsey had already started to suppress some of the smallest monasteries, ostensibly because they were corrupt, and he apparently had the scheme at the back of his mind of turning many of them into new cathedrals, and of creating thirteen new dioceses, roughly approximating to counties. None of these plans were carried out at the time, but they had been revived by 1540, and Henry himself was to write that it was 'most expedient and necessary that more bishoprics, collegiate and cathedral churches' should be created from the resources of the dissolved houses. There is even a list, in the king's own hand, headed 'Bishoprics to be made', and reading:

Essex	Waltham
Hertford	S. Albans
Bedfordshire & Berks	Dunstable, Newenham, Elnestowe
Oxford & Hunts	Oseney & Thame
Northants & Hunts	Peterborough
Middlesex	Westminster
Leicester & Rutland	Leicester
Gloucestershire	S. Peter's, Gloucester
Lancashire	Fountains & Richmond
Suffolk	Bury S. Edmunds
Staffordshire & Salop	Shrewsbury
Notts & Derby	Welbeck, Worksop & Thurgarten
Cornwall	Launceston, Bodmin with another

In the event only six new cathedrals were created: Chester, Gloucester, Bristol, Peterborough, Oxford and Westminster. Of the dissolved cathedral monasteries, only Bath and Coventry were no longer retained as episcopal sees. I have already given a brief account (in chapter 5) of Bath's survival as a parish church. Nothing remains today, of the mediaeval cathedral of Coventry, except for some small fragments of its west front: it quickly became a stone quarry after its suppression in 1539. The 'cathedral' of Coventry, which was destroyed by bombing in the last war, was only a parish church and did not acquire a cathedra until 1918.

The first of the new foundations, Chester, had already had a brief period as a cathedral city between 1075 and c.1095, when the bishop's seat was located in

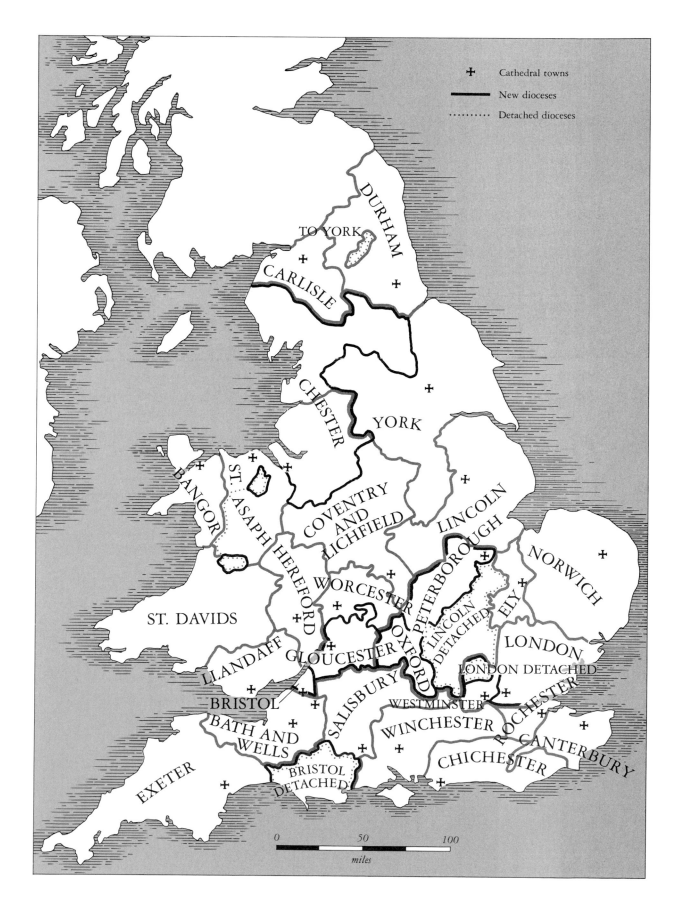

Cathedral towns

New dioceses

Detached dioceses

DURHAM

TO YORK

CARLISLE

CHESTER

YORK

BANGOR

ST. ASAPH

COVENTRY
AND
LICHFIELD

LINCOLN

NORWICH

HEREFORD

WORCESTER

PETERBOROUGH

ST. DAVIDS

LINCOLN
DETACHED

ELY

LONDON

LLANDAFF

GLOUCESTER

OXFORD

LONDON DETACHED

BRISTOL

SALISBURY

WESTMINSTER

ROCHESTER

BATH AND
WELLS

WINCHESTER

CANTERBURY

EXETER

BRISTOL
DETACHED

CHICHESTER

0   50   100

miles

St John's church: the fine monastery church of St Werburgh had been built after the see had moved on to Coventry. Initially, as the list shows, Henry had considered creating a new bishopric and diocese centred on Shrewsbury, but in the event it was established in 1541 at Chester, the diocese being carved out of the western part of the mediaeval diocese of York and the northern part of Coventry and Lichfield.

Chester cathedral is today a fine building, but it suffers from having been over-restored in the nineteenth century. It has a complicated, totally asymmetrical plan; the very large aisled south transept is particularly out of proportion to the rest of the building. On the north side of the cathedral many of the principal buildings of the old Benedictine abbey were allowed to survive around the cloister – particularly striking is the beautiful Early English vestibule to the chapter house, with shafts that turn straight into vault ribs. Inside the cathedral itself the exceptionally fine stalls of the monks, with forty-eight magnificently carved misericords, are still to be found within the choir. Most of the vaults, with the exception of the Lady Chapel, are of wood only, as at York minster. Much building work had been undertaken by the monks of Chester in the half century before their dissolution, so when the abbey church became a cathedral, it was in many ways new, the nave, north arcade, central tower, south porch and part of the south transept having all been built between about 1490 and 1537. Work had started on a new south-west tower, and the fine central lantern tower is almost contemporary with (and has echoes of) Canterbury's Bell Harry tower, though it was never given an upper stage, but has large corner turrets only.

Another great Benedictine abbey – that of St Peter at Gloucester – had been the place of burial of King Edward II after his murder at nearby Berkeley castle on 27 September 1327. The Act of Parliament which created the new see of Gloucester on 3 September 1541 says 'considering the site of the late monastery in which many famous monuments of our renowned ancestors, Kings of England, are erected is a very fit and proper place ... we have decreed that the said monastery be an episcopal see.' The abbot's fine lodging consequently quickly became the bishop's palace, and the prior's lodging on the west side of the cloister the dean's house. The dormitory and refectory were rapidly demolished, but the glorious cloisters, with their very early fan vaults, were saved. The other buildings were adapted as new canons' houses.

The original abbey church at Gloucester was a large, early Norman structure, with an apsidal east end, built at the end of the eleventh century. After Edward II's burial there, large sums of money were contributed by the young Edward III, as well as by 'pilgrims' to the King's tomb, which allowed the whole of the eastern arm of the abbey to be reclothed in early Perpendicular style. The master mason for this was almost certainly William Ramsey, the royal master mason, who was then working on the new chapter house and cloister at St Paul's cathedral. Unfortunately, there is no documentary evidence to confirm this, but we know that Ramsey was working at Gloucester castle from 1336 onwards, and it seems more than likely that Edward III would have sent him to help transform the dark Romanesque eastern arm into the superb 'chantry chapel' we see today, in memory of his murdered father.

The rebuilt presbytery and choir at Gloucester end in an east window that is nothing but a wall of glass. Both artistically and technologically it is a masterpiece. It is larger than the great east window at York minster, and the way it is constructed – not all in one plane, and built across the outer wall of the Norman apse – makes it one of the most daring works of architecture in the whole of the Middle Ages. Behind it runs a tunnel which connects the Norman galleries on either side. The window was glazed in the 1350s, half a century before York's east window. Above the presbytery is a superb vault with three longitudinal ridge-ribs and a mass of liernes and tiercerons, and to the east of it a magnificent new Lady Chapel had been erected at the end of the fifteenth century. It is no wonder, therefore, that Gloucester abbey was considered 'a very fit and proper place' for a new cathedral by Henry VIII.

181

Not far from Gloucester, a second new cathedral was created the following year within the abbey of Augustinian canons at Bristol. This was founded in the mid-twelfth century, as the splendid chapter house testifies – the blind-arcading and early rib-vaults to be seen here, as well as the exceptionally fine chevron and zig-zag decoration, make it a remarkable structure. Even more important, however, is the quite exceptional choir and presbytery of the abbey church, built during that extraordinary period in the early fourteenth century that also saw the creation of the exquisite Lady Chapel at nearby Wells cathedral.

The new eastern arm at Bristol was built in the time of Abbot Knowle and is unique in Britain in many ways (sadly we do not know the master mason). First, it is a hall-church – that is, a building with all three aisles of the same height, without triforium and clerestory. Next, the vaults are totally different from

John Carter's elevation drawing of the presbytery at Gloucester abbey, with the tomb of Edward II behind the screen.

*The choir aisle vaults in
Bristol cathedral.*

anything ever constructed before or since. In the side aisles are a series of open cross arches which hold up amazing double-vaults set sideways. At the end of the south aisle, in the entrance to the Berkeley chapel, is an even more remarkable vault with flying-ribs and huge decorated bosses, slightly like a sexpartite vault but without the webbing. The central vault, equally unusual, has tiercerons and very early lierne ribs. All this work was probably done between c.1306 and c.1320. In Sir Nikolaus Pevsner's view, St Augustine's abbey church 'is superior to anything else built in England, or indeed Europe, at the same time', and he goes on to say that 'it proves incontrovertibly that English design surpassed that of all other countries in the first third of the fourteenth century.' This architectural brilliance was to continue in Bristol with the construction soon afterwards of the glorious parish church of St Mary Redcliffe nearby.

This extraordinary work at St Augustine's had all been completed by the time of the Black Death. It was to be more than a century before anything new was begun, under Abbots Hunt (1473–81) and Newland (1481–1515), when the twelfth-century crossing and transepts were reclothed in the Perpendicular style, and a large tower was built above. Early in the sixteenth century the original nave was demolished and Abbot Newland began to rebuild it 'to the soiles [sills] of the wyndos of the north side and the west end'. On his death in 1515, however, the work seems to have been discontinued, and when St Augustine's became Bristol's cathedral twenty-seven years later, on 4 June 1542, it had only a partially built nave. The new walls, 'up to the sills'. were demolished soon afterwards, and work was started on reordering the eastern arm to compensate for the lack of nave. The mediaeval high altar, reredos and rood screen were removed, making the altar of the eastern Lady Chapel the principal altar. The pulpitum screen was also removed, but another fine screen, acquired from the dissolved White Friars church in Bristol, was placed in the second bay east of the crossing, with the canons' stalls, built in 1520, and the new bishop's stall, to the east of it. The area west of the screen was furnished with an early-seventeenth-century pulpit and pews, and it was here that the citizens of Bristol would be admonished with sermons, an important aspect of the reformed church in England.

Sadly, almost all was swept away at various dates in the nineteenth century, to be replaced after 1868 by a brand new nave. The bishop's palace was burnt in 1831 during the riots in support of the Reform Bill, and the demolition of the deanery and many canons' houses followed later in the century. There is, therefore, little that survives today to tell us about Bristol's early history as a cathedral. Luckily, however, its great mediaeval architectural glories have mostly survived.

The diocese of Bristol, as created in 1542, was drawn up on completely irrational lines. Geographically it consisted of the city and county of Bristol, cut out of the new Gloucester diocese and part of Bath and Wells, and the county of Dorset, from Salisbury diocese. This last was, of course, completely detached from the rest. Bristol did not even feature in Henry's original list of putative dioceses – it is too close to Gloucester to make logical sense – and in creating it, it seems likely that Henry was bowing to a strong political lobby from Bristol's powerful governing class.

The new diocese of Peterborough, created on 3 September 1541 at the same time as Gloucester and Oxford, covered the counties of Northamptonshire and Rutland and the soke of Peterborough. It thus bisected the huge ancient diocese of Lincoln, leaving Buckinghamshire, Bedfordshire, Huntingdonshire and parts of Herefordshire as a detached part of Lincoln diocese. The diocese of Oxford was also cut out of south-west corner of the Lincoln diocese.

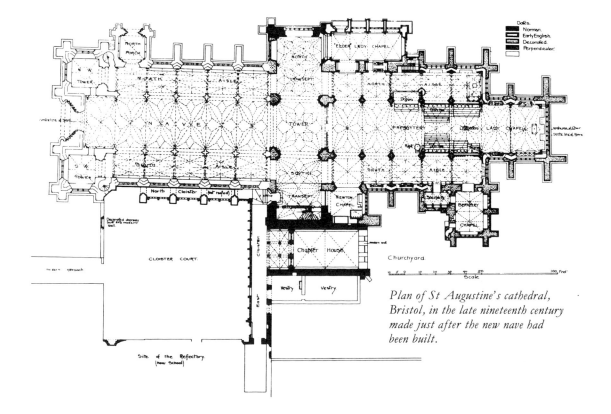

Plan of St Augustine's cathedral, Bristol, in the late nineteenth century made just after the new nave had been built.

At Peterborough, formerly the great Anglo-Saxon Benedictine abbey of Medeshamstede, the transition to cathedral church went very smoothly. The last abbot, John Chambers, who had been appointed by Cardinal Wolsey, was made the first bishop and therefore did not even have to move out of his large house to the south-west of the cathedral. The first dean came from the Cluniac priory of St Andrew in Northampton, where he had been prior, and four of the abbey's monks became canons; the rest were retired with pensions. The abbey church consequently remained little changed, except for the removal of shrines, until the mid-seventeenth century, when the cathedral suffered greatly during the Civil War. Much decoration was needlessly destroyed by parliamentary troops in 1643.

The abbey church at Peterborough, started in 1118, was another of those very long Romanesque buildings like Ely and Norwich cathedrals. Unusually, the twelfth-century apsidal end to the sanctuary has survived. It was only at the very end of the monastic period that an exceptionally beautiful new ambulatory was built around the outside of this, put up between about 1496 and 1508, and almost certainly designed by the master mason, John Wastell, who built the central crossing tower at Canterbury. Its extremely beautiful fan-vaults bear comparison with those at King's College Chapel, Cambridge, built by Wastell soon afterwards. This whole area was called the 'new building', and it still retains that title nearly 500 years later (see p. 206).

Two queens were buried later in the century just to the west of the 'new building': Catherine of Aragon (died 1536), whose body still lies there, and Mary, Queen of Scots who was executed in 1587 in nearby Fotheringay castle. Her body was later moved to Westminster abbey by her son, James I.

On the north side of Peterborough abbey a fine detached Lady Chapel had been built between 1272 and 1290, and was probably the inspiration for the beautiful Lady Chapel at Ely, described in chapter 4. Unfortunately it was demolished in the mid-seventeenth century so that its materials could be reused elsewhere: traces of its west wall, however, can still be seen outside the east side of the north transept.

By far the most memorable feature of Peterborough, however, is its really magnificent west front built in the early thirteenth century, the three giant arches of which, with fine decorated gables above, make an even more monumental entrance than that at Lincoln minster (see chapter 2). No doubt, it was the Romanesque west front at Lincoln which gave the Peterborough designer his basic idea. A small galilee porch in the centre of the west front built in the late fourteenth century, has above it a Trinity Chapel. Although dwarfed by the west front, it fits in very well with the overall design.

Peterborough cathedral's sufferings in the Civil War have already been mentioned, but its interior was to be even more radically altered during the nineteenth century. The building had unfortunately been allowed to fall into a bad state, and the restorations were very drastic in several places. The whole of the central crossing area, and tower above, were rebuilt between 1883 and 1886, and J. L. Pearson, the architect responsible, even suggested adding a lofty central spire. The west front was restored more sympathetically in the 1890s.

Peterborough had featured on Henry's original list. So, too, had Westminster. His plan here was for a new and very small diocese of Middlesex, cut out of the mediaeval diocese of London, and against its name in the list, the king had written 'Hilby', indicating that at an early date he had wanted Dr Thomas Thirlby as the first bishop here. A protegé of Archbishop Cranmer of Canterbury, Thirlby was a civil servant and diplomat rather than a churchman. He became bishop on 20 January 1541 and managed to remain a bishop under four successive sovereigns – largely because he was overseas at the critical times between reigns. In this he was similar to Nicholas Wooton, the first Dean of Canterbury, who was also a diplomat and Dean of York, at the same time. Remarkably Wooton survived as dean from 1541 until his death in 1567.

Bishop Thirlby was an old-fashioned Catholic, and disapproved of Edward VI's new prayer book. Nicholas Ridley, at that time Bishop of London, was determined to get rid of him and to re-absorb the see into his own diocese, and in 1550 he succeeded, becoming Bishop of both London and Westminster. Thirlby was translated to Norwich shortly afterwards. Interestingly, Westminster then survived until the reign of Queen Mary as 'a cathedral church and episcopal see to the bishop of London', as the Act of Parliament of 1550 puts it. She turned it back into an abbey in 1556, and finally in 1560 it became a royal collegiate church with a dean and twelve prebendaries, exempt from the jurisdiction of the Archbishop of Canterbury and the Bishop of London. To this day it continues with the chapel of St George at Windsor, as a royal peculiar, answerable only to the sovereign.

This book is not the place to look in detail at the long and intensely interesting archaeological and architectural history of Westminster abbey, as it has been a cathedral for only sixteen years of its life. However, it is certainly clear that Henry VIII wanted Westminster to be a cathedral because of its exceptional royal associations. The Anglo-Saxon abbey, which was probably founded by St Dunstan over a thousand years ago, was entirely rebuilt by King Edward the Confessor, and much of the new church was completed by the time of his death. His funeral, held there at the beginning of 1066, is depicted on the Bayeux tapestry. The church was over 300 feet long and was probably the first 'Norman' great church in England. At the end of 1066 William the Conqueror was crowned in Westminster Abbey, the first in a long line of coronations that have taken place in the abbey since. Edward the Confessor was canonised in 1161 and his body translated to a new shrine in the abbey two years later. It was not, however, until Henry III began rebuilding the abbey on a massive scale that it started to acquire a greater importance.

Between 1246 and Henry III's death in 1272, the colossal sum of about £45,000 (equivalent to hundreds of millions of pounds today) was spent building a really large new eastern arm to the church. This work was very much in the French idiom, and was clearly inspired by places like Rheims cathedral, where the French kings were crowned. It has exceptionally high vaults, standing 103 feet tall – higher than any other English church, though a little lower than Rheims. It also has double flying buttresses to support the vaults, and a characteristic French east end with a radiating group of chapels around the outside of the ambulatory, known as a chevet. Many other features like the bar tracery in the windows, were new in England at the time, and had a strong influence on other great buildings.

In 1269 St Edward the Confessor's body was translated yet again to another new shrine at the abbey. This was the most sumptuous shrine yet created in England, following the form of the great shrine of St Thomas Becket in Canterbury cathedral: the Italian marble inlay that covered it and the surrounding floor (where it can still be seen to this day) alone made it quite exceptional. Henry III is buried, by his own request, beside the new shrine, and has been followed by many royal burials in the abbey since, thereby increasing its royal associations. (In France two separate churches were always used for coronations and burials; the abbey of St Denis being the church for the latter.)

After Henry III's death, all work stopped on rebuilding the abbey, and the western part of the nave retained its eleventh-century Norman form for another century. The eastern part of the nave, which contained the monks' choir, had been rebuilt in the later part of Henry III's reign – it is a remarkable fact that, unlike many cathedrals, the liturgical topography of Westminster abbey has remained virtually unchanged since the thirteenth century. The choir behind its pulpitum screen is still in the east end of the nave and the high altar and shrine, separated by another screen with doors on either side, are still within the apsidal eastern arm surrounded by royal tombs. St Edward's shrine was taken down by Henry VIII, but it was re-erected under Queen Mary and the lower part has remained *in situ* ever since.

The western part of the nave was rebuilt very slowly after the demolition of the eleventh-century work in 1375. The various stages of rebuilding are remarkably conservative, following the style of the mid-thirteenth-century work carried out by Henry III. A close look at the fabric, however, makes it possible to locate the breaks between all the later stages of work. By 1496 the nave was pretty well finished, and between 1528 and 1534 a final campaign brought the

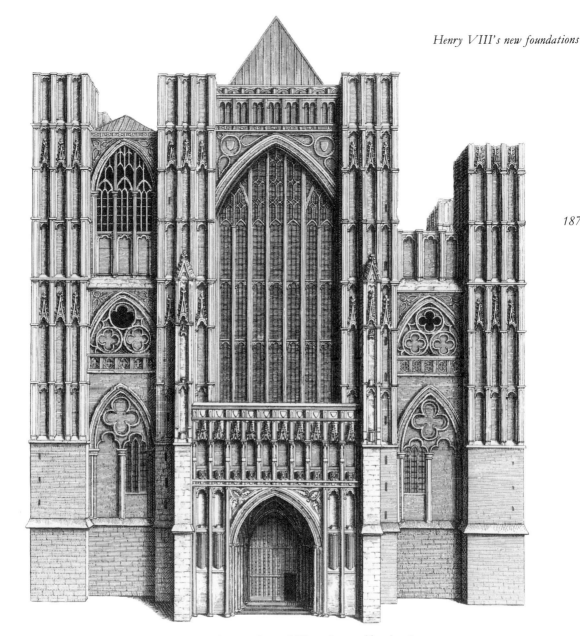

Hollar's view of the west front of Westminster abbey in 1647.

towers up to clerestory level, that on the south-west being slightly higher than that on the north-west. No other work was carried out after this date, and when the abbey became a cathedral six years later it would have looked exactly like the building that we see in Wenceslas Hollar's fine engravings of over a century later. (The western towers were not completed until 1745, to a design of Nicholas Hawksmoor.)

In 1500 John Islip had been elected abbot, and much of his early tenure of that office was spent in supervising the building of the unique new Lady Chapel that replaced an earlier thirteenth-century Lady Chapel at the east end of the abbey. Intended to hold a shrine for King Henry VI, murdered in 1471, it was built and paid for by his Tudor successor Henry VII. However, on the latter's death in 1509, Henry VI's expected canonisation had not taken place, and only Henry VII is buried there, in what is virtually a separate church. The whole building cost about £20,000, another huge sum of money for the time, though nothing to the private fortune Henry had amassed through confiscations of Yorkist property.

Unfortunately the building accounts for this extraordinary chapel are lost, but the recent research of Dr Walter Leedy, who has closely examined the constructional methods used in building the matchless pendant and fan-vaults over the chapel, and compared them to other vaults, attributes the design to Robert Janyns, the royal master mason who was also working at Windsor. Previously it had been suggested that the chapel had been designed by the Vertue brothers, also royal master masons, whom we met at Bath abbey, but this now seems less likely.

This great chapel was finished during Henry VIII's time, and it was quite natural for Henry to think of the abbey, with its many royal tombs, as a future cathedral. Retaining the Benedictine monks and the shrine of St Edward there was another matter. After the death of Abbot Islip in 1532, the writing was clearly on the wall so far as the monastery was concerned, and no further building work took place there, bringing an end to one of the costliest ecclesiastical building projects ever undertaken in Britain. It is ironic that during Westminster's short period as a cathedral from 1540 to 1556, Henry VIII was spending vast sums of money on palaces at Hampton Court, Nonsuch and elsewhere.

Perhaps the strangest of all the new cathedral foundations was that created in Oxford. In 1539, as we have seen from Henry VIII's list, he was planning to place the new cathedral for Oxford in the great abbey church of Oseney, and sure enough Oseney was made a new cathedral in 1542. Today not one trace of Oseney cathedral remains above ground, and the cathedral is at Christ Church College. How did this come about?

Oseney, situated on a large island between two branches of the Thames immediately west of the city, had been founded as the Augustinian priory of St Mary in 1129. By 1154, when it was raised to the status of an abbey, it must have been a large monastery, perhaps the biggest in Oxford. In 1539 the abbey was dissolved and just over two years later, in 1542, the abbot became the first bishop of Oxford, with his cathedra in Oseney cathedral.

Earlier than this the priory of St Frideswide's, another Augustinian house founded in 1122, had been chosen as the ideal site for a vast new Oxford college by Cardinal Wolsey. After obtaining a papal bull in 1524 to dissolve St Frideswide's, Wolsey went on to dissolve twenty-one other small religious houses and use their lands and manors to endow the new college, to be called Cardinal College, with £2000 a year. Work started in July 1525, when a huge base court was laid out just inside the southern city walls – the parish church of St Michael at the south gate, as well as the western half of St Frideswide's (including the west bays of the church) were demolished to make room for it and between 1525 and 1529 up to 500 men were engaged in building a very large great hall and kitchen on the south side of the court. A large new chapel, perhaps to be on the scale of King's College Chapel in Cambridge, was planned for the north side of the court, and it is clear that Wolsey intended to demolish the whole of St Frideswide's to allow for his grandiose scheme. To this end, a special temporary timber belfry was erected in the cloisters in 1528 to hang the bells until the new tower (Tom Tower) had been completed. A year later Wolsey had fallen from favour and all building work stopped. However, the college with its twenty scholars, was already in being and, after a period of indecision, Henry VIII decided in 1532 to refound it as King Henry VIII College with a dean and twelve canons. No more building work was to take place, and the remaining parts of the old church were to be used as the college chapel. In 1538, the shrine of St Frideswide was dismantled (it was reconstructed from fragments in the late nineteenth century), and six years later the college was surrendered to the king. Just over a year later in November 1546, Henry decided to refound it yet again as Christ Church college, but this time with only eight canons and a dean, and at the same time to transfer the bishop, Robert King, from Oseney to St Frideswide's, allowing the king to augment his fortunes even further from the rich estates of Oseney. The abbey there was soon stripped of its lead, and the

189

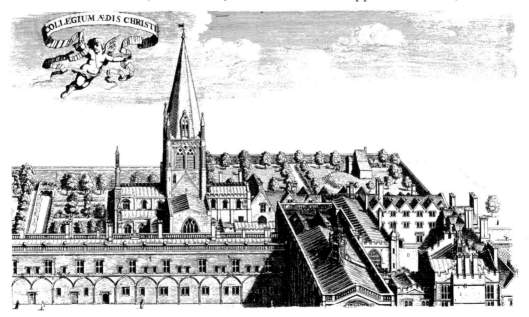

Part of Loggan's view of Christ Church College, Oxford in 1675.

walls were pulled down during the Civil War to use in the city's defences. The site is now covered by the railway just south of Oxford station, and by a nineteenth-century graveyard.

This extraordinary history is still reflected in the present complex of buildings at Christ Church, Oxford. The great quad, with its clear signs of an uncompleted vaulted cloister, and the gateway tower (completed by Wren in 1681 when the 'Great Tom' bell from Oseney was hung there), are the most obvious signs of

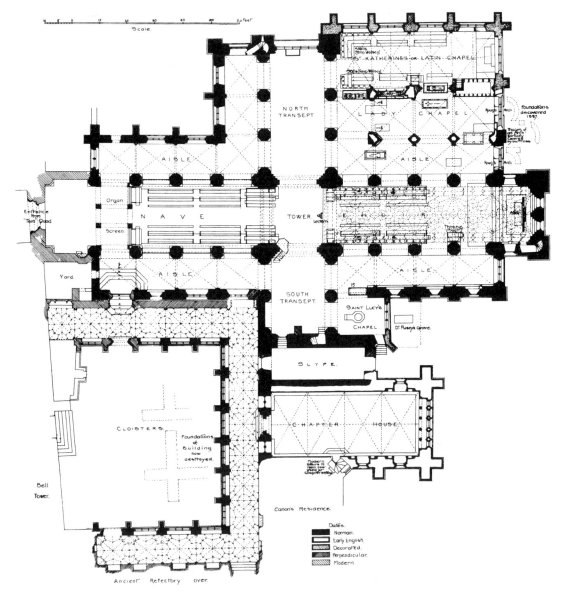

Plan of Oxford cathedral at the end of the nineteenth century.

Wolsey's unfinished work. Tucked away in the south-east corner of the college are the remains of St Frideswide's priory, and it is plain here how far Wolsey's demolitions had gone in 1529. The foundations for the temporary belfry in the cloister (the excavated remains have been left uncovered) are also visible, as are the surviving Augustinian priory buildings (chapter house, dormitory and refectory) around it. Before 1529 the eastern three or four bays of the nave of the late-twelfth-century church had been demolished, and a new solid west wall was built three bays west of the crossing. In the 1870s a further bay was replaced by Gilbert Scott, and a new western entrance from the cloister was created.

Oxford cathedral today is exceptionally small, by far the smallest cathedral in England and Wales. (St Asaph, the smallest of the Welsh cathedrals, is nearly 50 feet longer.) Its length of just over 150 feet is shorter even than the eastern arm and crossing of Bristol. Inside, however, there is much of interest. The main structure was built in the late twelfth century with round pillars and unusual double round arches. On the north side is a large aisled transept with two later chapels to the east (the thirteenth-century Lady Chapel and the so-called 'Latin' – earlier St Katherine's – chapel). Over the crossing is a fine tower and stone spire which, although much restored, is one of the earliest in Britain. The most splendid feature, however, is the magnificent, very late-fifteenth-century vault over the choir which was perhaps designed by William Orchard (though no documentation exists to prove this) who had earlier (1480–3) vaulted the nearby Divinity School, and was buried here in 1504. Orchard was another of that exceptionally brilliant group of master masons which included John Wastell, the Vertue brothers and Robert Janyns. Here the oblong compartments have been turned into squares by pushing out 'hammer-beams' with pendants and transverse vaults between the latter. In the square central vault are the most beautiful lierne star-vaults covered in bosses. The way the thick arches at the side disappear behind the main vault is very reminiscent of the great pendant vault in Henry VIII's chapel at Westminster abbey. Unfortunately, the large fourteenth-century window in the east wall was replaced by Scott in the 1870s with two 'Norman' windows and a wheel window above. This, unlike the true Romanesque arcading, does not fit with the vault.

To this day Oxford cathedral has continued as part of a unique double foundation, serving also as the chapel for Christ Church college. It has, however, always been only a single foundation but serving two functions; a memorial, if nothing else, to Henry VIII's parsimony.

Apart from the six new cathedrals, Henry VIII also created eight new cathedral foundations from the dissolved cathedral priories. There was almost certainly continuity of use of the buildings between the last days of the monasteries and the setting up of the new secular foundations, although a period of time

elapsed between the two events. In every case except Canterbury, the old prior became the first dean, and a group of senior monks became canons (or prebendaries as they are invariably called). Junior monks became minor canons, and no doubt many of the old monastic servants continued in their posts. We should not forget that much of the communal life of the monasteries had already disappeared before the dissolution, and most senior monks already had their own private chambers. Only the junior monks had a more communal life, and this continued in the 'petty canons' hall' often created in the new foundations.

193

At Canterbury, for example, the 'petty canons' hall' was contrived within the huge monastic reredorter (communal WC) and in 1546 the old communal buildings (dormitory, kitchen and refectory) had their roofs stripped of lead and were left as shells. The dean was given the prior's complex of lodgings, and all the other major canons, twelve in number, were given houses and gardens created out of the old monastic buildings. Only one new house was built, in 1547.

Just before the dissolution, the aged prior Thomas Goldwell, who was anxious to become dean, wrote to Thomas Cromwell:

I have been Prior of the seid church above xxii years, wherefore it should be moche displeasure to me in my age to be putt from that my levying or from my chamber and lodgying which I have hadd by all the seid xxii years.

Archbishop Cranmer, who disliked the septuagenarian prior, would have none of it, and Goldwell was 'put out' of his lodgings, but with a good pension. 'No one has hindered the word of God so much as he, or maintained superstition more' wrote Cranmer to Cromwell. The new dean was to be the eminent ecclesiastical lawyer and diplomat Nicholas Wooton who, as we have seen, was also to hold the deanery of York.

Unique to the new foundation at Canterbury, and surviving to this day, was the provision for six preachers as well as twelve canons and twelve minor canons. The preachers were provided with a horse and a house, and were expected to deliver sermons in Canterbury and the surrounding parishes, and in 1544 Archbishop Cranmer had the huge chapter house at Canterbury turned into a 'sermon house', fitting it out with pews, pulpit, galleries and so on. The chief gallery on the north was called the royal gallery and had latticed casement windows. Whether Henry VIII or any other monarch ever used it is unknown but, sadly, all traces of these later fittings have been totally destroyed.

At about this time a new two-tiered gallery was built outside the north choir aisle of St Paul's in London so that people could listen to sermons preached from St Paul's Cross. The upper tier here contained a royal box. Other cathedrals also made provision for preaching at this time, and we know that Bishop Knight (1540–7) had a fine stone pulpit erected in the nave at Wells which was entered

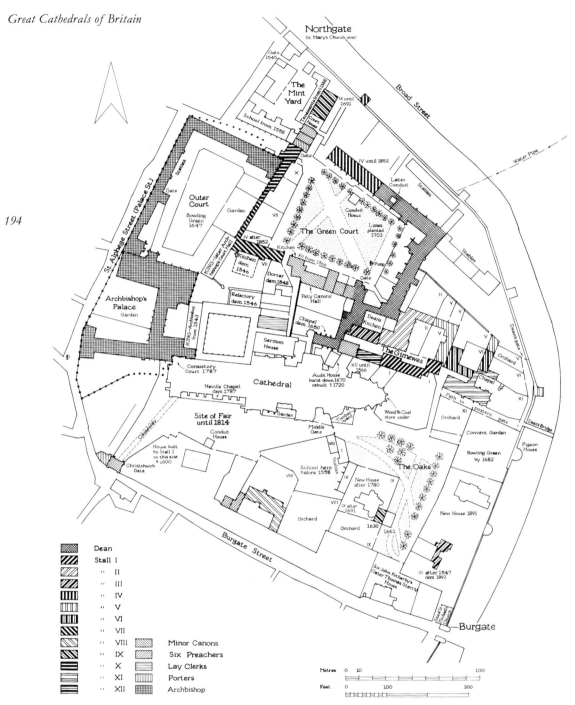

*The precincts around Canterbury cathedral as adapted
for the new dean and chapter after 1541.*

through Hugh Sugar's chantry. Sermons are also known to have been preached
at an early date in the naves at Chichester, Bath, Ely and Worcester.

During the last months of 1539, when the last of the great monasteries were
being dissolved, various plans were being discussed for the new foundations.
Cromwell was anxious to keep down costs, and so only four of the new foun-

dations, Canterbury, Winchester, Durham and Westminster, were to have as many as twelve prebendaries. The rest were to be smaller. Worcester, for example, had ten, while Ely had eight and Rochester six, with Carlisle only having four. The most important element in these new foundations was the provision for students and scholars. At Rochester, for example, apart from the dean, six prebendaries and six minor canons, there were to be a deacon and sub-deacon, six lay clerks, a master for eight choristers, four divinity students, twenty-three grammar scholars, six poor men, a porter/barber, and a butcher and cooks. In many cases it is the cathedrals' schools, the 'King's schools', which have flourished most, though alas, with the reforms of the nineteenth century, they have all become fee-paying private schools.

The century following the dissolution was to be a time of neglect for the English cathedrals. Little actual destruction occurred, except for such things as shrines and images which were described as 'objects of superstition'. At Winchester, however, the puritanical Bishop Horne (1560–80) pulled down the cloisters and chapter house as well. In some places in the first half of the seventeenth century some new work was undertaken. Again at Winchester, for example, the last vault in the whole cathedral, a wooden one, was put in under the crossing tower in 1634. This very late fan-vault is decorated with carved bosses and with medallion portraits of King Charles I and his French queen, Henrietta Maria. The work was carried out under Bishop Curle (1632–47), and was to be followed in 1637 by the erection of a new front to the pulpitum screen in the classical manner. Designed by Inigo Jones (1573–1652) it was nevertheless unfortunate enough to be described by John Britton as a 'bad and unsightly object', and this encouraged its demolition in the 1820s. The central part of the screen was re-erected in the Cambridge Museum of Archaeology in 1909. The statues of Charles I and James I, from the screen, still survive in the cathedral, after being hidden in the Cromwellian period.

However, by far the most famous cathedral work by Inigo Jones was at St Paul's cathedral in London. The magnificent spire had fallen in 1561, causing much damage. This was repaired, though the spire itself was never rebuilt, and further restoration campaigns were proposed. Nothing was achieved, however, until 1631 when Bishop Laud (1628–33) appointed Inigo Jones as architect. Between 1633 and 1642 much repair work was carried out, financed by a national appeal. Jones was, of course, a classical architect, and he therefore reclothed the outside of the nave and transepts to make them look like a Renaissance building, refacing them in Portland stone and adding volutes and obelisks to the gable ends. Particularly fine and striking was the great portico with Corinthian columns 45 feet high that he added to the west front. On top was a large balustrade surmounted by statues of King James I and his son Charles I who paid for the

Hollar's view of Old St Paul's from the south-west in the mid-seventeenth century.

portico out of the privy purse. Hollar's fine engravings are our only graphic evidence for this work. They show how skilfully Inigo Jones had contrived to add another style of architecture to this magnificent building. It is, therefore, all the more tragic that this, the largest of all our British cathedrals, should have been totally destroyed in the Great Fire of 1666. A drawing by Inigo Jones preserved at Worcester College, Oxford shows that he intended a new arcaded loggia and ogival dome with spirelets to be erected on top of the great tower – a tantalising proposal.

All work on St Paul's came to an end with the outbreak of the Civil War in 1642, when the cathedral was desecrated and used as a 'Horse-Quarter' for soldiers. The eastern retrochoir was walled off and made into a preaching house. After the Restoration in 1660 the mess was cleaned up; repair work was restarted, with the central tower receiving particular attention. In April 1663 a Royal Commission was set up with the aim of getting surveyors to 'search, discover,

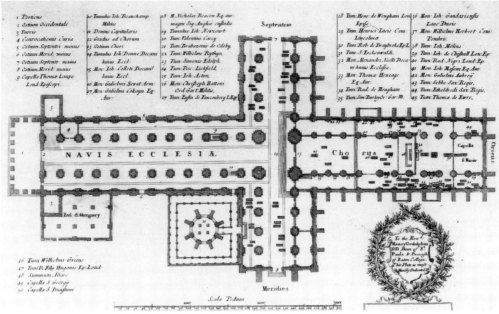

Hollar's plan of Old St Paul's cathedral.

try and find out the true state of the said church and the particular decays thereof'. Having done this, they were to carry out the repairs needed. Their most important finding was that the central tower would have to be demolished and rebuilt from the foundations.

It was at this point that Sir Christopher Wren appeared on the scene for the first time. Aged just thirty, he was the Savilian Professor of Astronomy at Oxford and had been recommended to the dean and chapter by the new Archbishop of Canterbury, Dr Gilbert Sheldon, for whom he was just starting to build the Sheldonian theatre in Oxford. Wren carried out a detailed study of the mediaeval fabric of the cathedral, and of its many structural problems, making an 'exact Plan, Orthography, and Section, upon an accurate Survey of the whole Structure, even to Inches; in the Prosecution of which, he was astonish'd to find how negligent the first Builders had been'. In 1665 the Great Plague hit London and Wren departed for Paris to study the buildings there. On his return, in the spring of 1666, he wrote a report for the commissioners in which he suggested that the inside of the Norman nave should be recased 'after a good Roman manner' (just as Inigo Jones had done on the outside), and that new vaults of brick and stucco (for lightness) be built. He preferred this to 'the Gothick Rudeness of ye olde Design'. Wren then went on to agree with the earlier commissioners' drastic solution for demolishing and rebuilding the crossing area, but instead of having a new tower he wrote:

I cannot propose a better Remedy, than by cutting off the inner Corners of the Cross, to reduce this middle Part into a spacious Dome or Rotundo, with a Cupola, or hemisperical Roof, and upon the Cupola (for the outward Ornament) a Lantern with a spiring Top, to rise proportionably tho' not to that unnecessary Height of the former Spire of Timber and Lead burnt by Lightning.

The structural base for this brilliant new idea must have come from Wren's examination of the cathedral at Ely, where his uncle, Matthew Wren, was bishop. The sacrist, Alan of Walsingham, had rebuilt the crossing area there in a similar way 340 years earlier, as we have seen in chapter 4. On 27 August 1666 Wren's report was accepted, but six days later the Great Fire of London started. Within a couple of days St Paul's was a gutted shell.

Thus came to an end the largest Romanesque and Gothic building in Britain. The story of Sir Christopher Wren's new cathedral, built between 1675 and 1710, is beyond the scope of this book. His new building was a great masterpiece, but the building techniques that he used were quite different from those of his mediaeval predecessors – for example, for vaulting he used brick and stucco saucer domes 'in the Roman manner' – and, despite eventually being planned as a new 'Gothic' building with nave, choir, transepts, etc., the overall effect of Wren's new cathedral is classical, with splendid façades and much use of beautiful carved details in stone and wood.

At the time that the finishing touches to the lantern above the great dome at St Paul's were being carried out early in the eighteenth century, no other cathedral in Britain had had any real building work done to it for nearly two centuries. Repair and maintenance of all these buildings had been sporadic, and many cathedrals were decaying rapidly. The £736,752 that was spent on building the new St Paul's cathedral was a quite exceptional sum of money, not least in that much of it had been raised from a coal tax. Although elsewhere the damage caused by the Civil War made it necessary to carry out some repair work after the Restoration, this was mostly on a small scale and the £9000 or so raised by Bishop Hackett for the repair of his cathedral at Lichfield was unusual: the damage here had been very great, and the bishop was an extremely zealous fund raiser. He was also able to persuade the king to grant him a hundred trees from a nearby royal forest to help with the massive campaign of re-roofing that was needed. In general, though, most cathedrals had reached a low point in their long histories by the middle of the eighteenth century. In the next few decades many of them were to receive some of the most unsympathetic restoration and alteration work ever carried out. At the same time, archaeology was to make its first appearance, and this will be the subject of my last chapter.

8

DESTROYERS AND RECORDERS

Restoration and archaeology

On Easter Monday 1786 the western tower of Hereford cathedral collapsed and reduced to rubble the two western bays of the building, destroying at a stroke the beautiful Romanesque west front. (As a result of this tragedy Rochester cathedral is the only high Romanesque west front surviving in England.) The situation at Hereford was made worse when the dean and chapter invited James Wyatt (1747–1813), one of the leading architects of the day, to be responsible for the rebuilding. Between 1788 and 1796, with the chapter's full support, Wyatt proceeded to remove the entire west bay of the nave and went on to demolish the whole of the Norman triforium and clerestory, leaving only the arcades. He then took down the spire from the central tower. The west front was then rebuilt, without a new tower – to save money and achieve a more 'uniform' appearance – in a debased form of 'Gothick' architecture which was more classical than mediaeval. Cathedral building had reached its nadir in England. His very feeble west front was replaced early in this century.

The west front of Hereford cathedral in the early eighteenth century, drawn by Browne Willis.

Following a survey Wyatt had done a few years earlier for the dean and chapter at Lichfield, in 1788 he started to restore that cathedral too, using Roman cement (a hard hydraulic cement invented at the end of the eighteenth century) as a patching-up material rather than stone, and the next year he began work at Salisbury for the bishop there, Shute Barrington. By the early 1790s the drastic nature of Wyatt's 'restorations' were becoming apparent and his critics named him 'the destroyer' (later 'the vandal').

Wyatt's work was indeed very destructive, but we should not forget that many cathedrals in the mid-eighteenth century were in a very poor condition. Very few people had any interest in Romanesque and Gothic architecture, except for such men as the novelist and antiquary Horace Walpole (1718–97) and his lifelong friend, the poet Thomas Gray (1716–71). The essential object of these later eighteenth-century 'restorations' was to tidy up the cluttered mediaeval interiors of the cathedrals and create long, clean 'vistas' – after all, this was the glorious age of English country house architecture, based on the classical principles of symmetry and balance. Hence Wyatt's demolition of two chantry chapels on the north-east and south-east sides of Salisbury, and his rearrangement of most of the mediaeval monuments in neat rows in the nave. Outside, the close was tidied up and the cathedral was treated like a great country house in its own park, a landscape which entered the romantic imagination through the painting of John Constable, the most English of painters, early in the next century and is still admired today. Wyatt's work reflected the taste of the time, and we should perhaps look upon the bishops, deans and chapters of the eighteenth century as 'the destroyers', as it was they who commissioned and approved his schemes.

Apart from Wyatt's now well-known and infamous restorations not only at Hereford, Lichfield and Salisbury but also at Durham, many other cathedral authorities were also carrying out their own destructive restorations. At Canterbury, in 1787, the old floor was ripped out and all the 'untidy' leger-stones (flat gravestones) with their incised effigies of archbishops, priors and so on were removed from the nave, and a new floor in Portland stone was laid (luckily a plan of the floor was made before its removal). A small chantry chapel on the south side of the nave was also demolished at this time. Half a century earlier, at York minster Lord Burlington, the Palladian architect whose most famous building, Chiswick House, had popularised the new classical style, had designed a new black and white marble floor for the whole building which, laid a foot above the old floor, meant that the top of virtually every tomb in the nave, choir and transepts was destroyed.

At Ely large-scale restorations were carried out between 1757 and 1771 under the supervision of an architect from Cambridge called James Essex (1722–84). It was at this time that the octagon was first restored and the monks' choir stalls were removed from their original site to the east end. Sadly, the twelfth-century pulpitum screen was destroyed at this time, though Essex did make a sketch of some of its details which reveal how fine it was. More fortunately, his proposed demolitions of the south-west transept and the Galilee porch were not carried out.

Soon after work got under way at Ely, Essex travelled to Lincoln to survey the cathedral for the dean and chapter, and between 1761 and the end of the century much restoration was carried out. Here, too, a reflooring took place, with the destruction of many monuments. We know where these had been sited, though, from a plan made by Lincoln antiquaries before they were removed. (Earlier – in 1641 – Sir William Dugdale had made drawings of many of the fine shrines and monuments in the cathedral just before their destruction during the

Civil War in 1644.) In 1772 the large chapel of St Hugh in the north-east transept was demolished. Not all was destructive, however. Essex did provide fine new pinnacles and a traceried parapet on the central tower, and Gothic canopies on the strainer arches in the eastern transept, as well as a new bishop's 'chair' and a three-gabled reredos for the high altar. It is interesting to note that half a century before this, in 1725, when the dean and chapter, on the advice of the architect James Gibbs, proposed removing the two western spires a riot broke out among the people of Lincoln. Gibbs, who had just rebuilt St Martin-in-the-Fields in London, described the spires as 'so many Extinguishers set upon great candles'. They survived, but were eventually demolished in 1807 without protest.

I don't propose in this book, to look in detail at the many large-scale restorations that were carried out in the cathedrals of Britain in the later eighteenth and nineteenth centuries. Rather, I want to show how this work of restoration was accompanied by the first real archaeological studies of cathedrals, which led in turn to the first academic studies of Gothic architecture, and ultimately to the Victorian Gothic revival.

As a result of his work at Ely and Lincoln, James Essex became very interested in the fabric, and not just the decoration, of the cathedrals. For example, he studied the geometry of arches and windows and looked carefully at the structural problems of Gothic vaulting. Towards the end of his life, after collecting much material, he was proposing to write a book on the history of Gothic architecture. Unfortunately, when he died in 1784, this had not been achieved, though he did read a paper (subsequently published) on 'Some observations on Lincoln Cathedral' to the Society of Antiquaries in March 1775 and, as Dr Thomas Cocke has shown in several recent studies of Essex's work, there are some important manuscript drawings by James Essex in the British Library.

A century earlier, the antiquary John Aubrey (1626–97) had compiled a *Chronologia Architectonica* in which he made the first attempt to work out a chronology of English architecture. Unfortunately this, too, was never published (the manuscript is in the Bodleian Library at Oxford), and it was not until after the foundation of the Society of Antiquaries of London in 1717 that a body of people got together to compile a collection of drawings of major architectural monuments in Britain and publish them. Here we have a more ordered continuation of the process of 'preservation by record' that was first started in the mid-seventeenth century by Aubrey's contemporary Sir William Dugdale. He used the services of the brilliant draughtsman Wenceslaus Hollar (to whom we owe so much of our knowledge of London's Old St Pauls) and the far less able Daniel King to illustrate his two great books, the *Monasticon Anglicanum* (published in three volumes, 1655–73) and *The History of St Paul's Cathedral* (1658). Both were splendid, but isolated achievements, and it was not until 1727 that J.

Browne Willis started to publish his *Survey of Cathedrals*. This included a good plan, as well as the dimensions and one or more elevations of every cathedral in England and Wales – his published elevations of the west front and north prospect of Hereford cathedral are now unique records of the building before the fall of the west tower in 1786 (see p.199).

By the middle decades of the eighteenth century many drawings of ancient buildings had been published – particularly by the Buck brothers – and men like Horace Walpole and Thomas Gray were feeling their way towards a better understanding of Romanesque and Gothic architecture, though it remained largely unappreciated by popular taste.

In 1753 a remarkable book was published entitled *A Series of Particular and Useful Observations made with Great Diligence and Care upon that Admirable Structure, the Cathedral-Church of Salisbury*. The author, Francis Price, had been surveyor and clerk of works at Salisbury since 1734, and was well known for his standard manual *The British Carpenter*. His book is the first detailed account of the fabric of a cathedral ever written. Earlier books like Dugdale's, admirable though they are, were about history, heraldry, sepulchral monuments and so on. Price examined Salisbury's foundations, building materials, and masonry techniques and was the first to suggest that the tower and spire at Salisbury had never been intended by the original builders – as we saw in chapter 3, his description and understanding of the spire are still unrivalled. The plates in his book are equally important (see p. 98). They are there to illustrate and elucidate his text, not just as pretty views and prospects. His drawing of the detached bell-tower is another unique record, as this splendid structure was demolished soon after Price's time.

In 1771 another important book, *The History and Antiquities of the Cathedral Church of Ely*, was published by a minor canon there called James Bentham who was greatly helped in this work by Thomas Gray and James Essex. The former contributed a detailed study of Romanesque decorative work to the introduction of the book, while Essex was actually the 'archaeologist' who had explained the fabric of the cathedral to Bentham, passing on what he had learnt of the chronology and constructional history of the building during his work there as cathedral architect, and providing accurate plans, sections and elevations for the book.

One of the most vociferous of the people who were beginning to criticise savagely the destructive restorations of James Wyatt and others by the end of the century, was a man called John Carter. He was the draughtsman to the Society of Antiquaries, and his very detailed plans, sections and elevations of cathedrals are some of the finest and most beautiful drawings ever made (see p. 181). They deserve to be much better known today. Attitudes to Gothic were by now beginning to change and John Carter's protests were instrumental in saving the magnificent late-twelfth-century Galilee (the Lady Chapel) at Durham which was

The detached bell tower at Salisbury, drawn by Francis Price
in the mid-eighteenth century before its destruction.

to be demolished to make way for a carriage drive around the west end of the cathedral – named 'St Cuthbert's Promenade' by Carter.

By now the first stage of the 'Gothic revival' was in full swing, and Gothic architecture was as much admired as classical. A mass of books was published, including the most influential book of all, Thomas Rickman's *An Attempt to Discriminate the Styles of Architecture in England, from the Conquest to the Reformation*. This first appeared in 1815 and then went through many editions over the next few decades. It was Rickman who invented the classification that we still use today of Early English, Decorated and Perpendicular. He also used terms like 'geometrical tracery', 'four-centred' arches, and 'water-holding' bases (an early Gothic base with a deep internal hollow capable of retaining water). His analysis of both architectural style and of the individual parts and details of mediaeval buildings produced a framework that is still of use to this day. The influence of his book was to be very great and certainly prepared the way for Robert Willis' great studies of cathedrals later in the nineteenth century.

The year before Rickman's book first appeared, a man called John Britton published the first of his splendid volumes of engravings entitled *Cathedral Antiquities*. These included plans, elevations, sections and architectural details, as well as general views (see pp. 61 and 138). Over the next twenty years, six volumes were to be published covering many of the English cathedrals. There was clearly now an excellent market for books with fine illustrations of the great cathedrals and many rival volumes soon followed, particularly those which between 1814 and 1842 published a mass of excellent engravings of the English and Welsh cathedrals by James Storer, J. C. Buckler and B. Winkles. These drawings, which can still be acquired today, though sadly they are usually ripped out of their original bindings, are in no way 'archaeological' records of the fabric, but nevertheless are important as views of the buildings before the Victorian restorations got under way. Additionally, large numbers of unpublished drawings of this period exist in various collections. John Buckler (1770–1851) and his very long-lived son J. C. Buckler (1793–1894) made tens of thousands of drawings many of them including important details of cathedrals; J. C. Buckler's measured drawings of the north-west tower of Canterbury cathedral, which are a meticulous record of this early Norman structure just before its demolition in 1832, have already been mentioned in chapter 2 (see p. 52).

The turning point in the Gothic Revival, or its *annus mirabilis* as Professor Pevsner has called it, came in 1841 when Augustus Pugin (1812–52), the architect responsible for much of the detailed design of the rebuilt Houses of Parliament, published *The True Principles of Pointed or Christian Architecture*. Pugin told people that it was their duty not only to build in the Gothic style, but also to record mediaeval buildings and study them in every detail, just as his father had done.

Pugin senior's two volume *Specimens of Gothic architecture*, published in 1823, contain some of the finest drawings ever made, and his son had no doubt been smothered in Gothic from an early age. Partly as a result of these well-intentioned words, thousands of churches in Victorian Britain were restored in the following half-century, many of them very destructively. The great cathedral restorations of the mid- to late-nineteenth century did as much harm as those of the eighteenth century. 'Restoration' meant the purging of a cathedral of anything that was not Gothic (Inigo Jones' screen at Winchester, for example) and – even worse – replacing late mediaeval features, particularly windows, with the 'ideal' Gothic style of the thirteenth and early fourteenth centuries, often called 'Middle Pointed' architecture at this time. The arch-restorer of the later nineteenth century was Gilbert Scott (1811–78) who was responsible for many very bad restorations, as well as some more sympathetic ones.

It was not until towards the end of the century that a vociferous voice of protest arose against these activities. 'The first step to restoration is to dash the old work to pieces', said the writer and critic John Ruskin (1819–1900). 'The second is usually to put up the cheapest and basest imitation which can escape detection, but in all cases, however careful, however laboured, an imitation still...Do not let us talk of restoration. The thing is a lie from beginning to end.' In 1877 the Society for the Protection of Ancient Buildings was formed by the poet and painter William Morris (1834–96) and others. They declared that 'these last fifty years of knowledge and attention have done more for their [buildings'] destruction than all the foregoing centuries of revolution, violence and contempt.'

The Church of England was itself undergoing great turmoil at this time. A body called the Ecclesiastical Commission was set up in the 1830s, and in its first report recommended that several dioceses (particularly the huge diocese of Lincoln) should be reorganised, and that two new sees should be created at Manchester and Ripon. They also suggested that the large incomes of the richest sees such as Durham and Canterbury should be reduced. In a second report published the following year in 1836 they further suggested that each cathedral chapter should be reduced to a dean and four residentiary canons only. This was indeed a major reform, long overdue. At Canterbury, for example, the number of canons in 1841 was twelve; by 1852 this was reduced to six, and later the number came down to four.

The reform of the Church of England went hand-in-hand with the restoration of its buildings. The Gothic revival soon found itself caught up in the heated religious controversies that overtook the church following the publication of Pusey's and Newman's *Tracts for our Times* and the birth of the High Church Oxford movement. The analytical and archaeological approach to Gothic which had been pioneered by Thomas Rickman and his successors, particularly William Whewell (Master of Trinity College, Cambridge from 1841) and Professor Robert Willis (1800–75, the great architectural historian) was soon in conflict with the romantic views of mediaevalism held by the High Church wing of the Victorian Gothic revival. 'Poor Whewell and Willis', wrote Professor Pevsner, 'were soon to find their clear world of scholarship clouded by the passions of Catholics and Anglo-Catholics and Anti-Catholics and Ruskin.'

Again, it is not my purpose to look in detail at these controversies. I do, however, want to consider the work of Professor Robert Willis with whom I began this book, as it was Willis above all others who made cathedral archaeology a science.

In 1841, Pevsner's *annus mirabilis*, Robert Willis wrote not only his first paper on cathedral archaeology, on Hereford cathedral, but also one of the largest and most important papers he ever wrote, entitled 'On the Construction of the vaults of the Middles Ages'. This is a masterly analysis of the geometrical and technical skills used by mediaeval masons when planning and building vaults. Willis starts by looking at the relatively simple groin-vaults and ends by discussing the extremely complicated late mediaeval vaults in St George's chapel, Windsor, the 'New Work' at Peterborough, and in Henry VII's chapel at Westminster

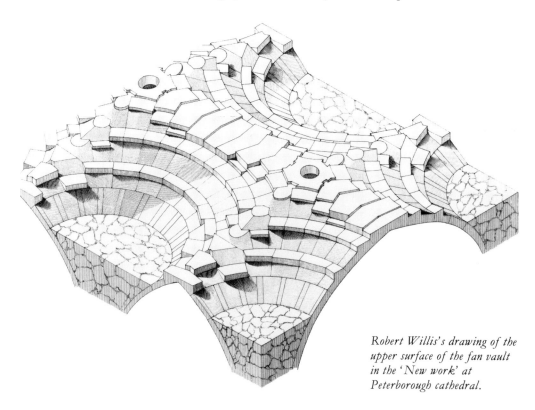

Robert Willis's drawing of the upper surface of the fan vault in the 'New work' at Peterborough cathedral.

Abbey. His drawings of the vaults at Peterborough and Westminster are particularly fine. He also shows how rib profiles were actually set out with lines cut on certain stones. He did this by examining the nave demolition work in 1839 at Southwark priory (later cathedral) and at the north-west tower at Canterbury cathedral, 'The best instructor of all' in studying vaults he says, 'is a building which is being pulled down, but such opportunities are always to be regretted.'

Willis's paper on Hereford, which was written for the dean and chapter there, is entitled 'On the present state of the cathedral of Hereford and on the causes which have led to it'. It is both a technical report and an archaeological analysis of all the settlement problems in the cathedral. At the end are three diagrams (a plan and two sections) of the central crossing area which show for the first time in a cathedral a sequence of archaeological stratification – that is, a chronological succession of different areas of fabric, including the sequence of later 'casings and repairs' of the tower piers.

In 1843 the British Archaeological Association was founded, and the following year, after a split among its members, the Archaeological Institute of Great Britain and Ireland (later the Royal Archaeological Institute) came into being. The formation of these bodies (they are still flourishing today) was of great importance for the study of all aspects of the material remains of the past. Large annual meetings were held in different historic cities, and the proceedings of these meetings were published soon afterwards. At the first meeting of the British Archaeological Association held in Canterbury in September 1844 Robert Willis gave the first of his great cathedral lectures. I have already had frequent cause to mention his account of Canterbury cathedral, which was published the following year, and it was to set a standard that has hardly been bettered since. The following year Willis turned his attention to *The Architectural History of Winchester Cathedral*, and the year after that to York minster. Both papers were published soon afterwards. He then went on to read papers in Norwich (1847), Salisbury (1849), Oxford (1850), Wells (1851), Chichester (1853), Gloucester (1860), Peterborough (1861), Worcester (1862), Rochester (1863) and Glastonbury Abbey (1865), but unfortunately his busy schedule meant that he did not always find time to write them up for publication. His lectures on Salisbury cathedral were first published in 1972. His examination of the York minster crypt discoveries and his investigation of the 'foundations of early buildings recently discovered in Lichfield Cathedral' show that the below-ground remains of cathedrals were also beginning to provide clues to the earlier history of their fabrics. An understanding of below-ground archaeological stratigraphy, however, was still a long way off.

Willis also published important papers on the monastic buildings at Worcester and Canterbury, and in the last years of his life he was preparing a monumental architectural history of the University of Cambridge. This was eventually completed and published in 1886 by his nephew J. W. Clark. It is an astonishing body of work for a man who was also a busy professor of engineering. One of Willis's most remarkable papers is his essay 'On the fall of the tower and spire, February 21st 1861' at Chichester cathedral. His description of the events leading up to the collapse are both a careful analysis of the causes of the failure and a very gripping narrative. Here is the climax:

On Thursday, the 21st, before daylight, the work was resumed. Seventy men working with most commendable enthusiasm and courage, under great personal risk, made strenuous efforts to increase the number of shores, under and around the tower; for those applied only the night before were bent and the danger became more and more imminent. The workmen were only induced to quit the building by the inevitable dinner hour of noon. But, by this time the continual failing of the shores, showed, too plainly, that the fall was inevitable. Warning was given to the inhabitants near the building, on the south-west, and the workmen, returning at one, were prevented from re-entering it. Anxious groups, outside the cathedral enclosure, stood gazing at the tower, and in less than half-an-hour, the spire was seen to incline slightly to the south-west, and then to descend perpendicularly into the church, as one telescope tube slides into another, the mass of the tower crumbling beneath it. The fall was an affair of a few seconds, and was complete at half-past one.

After the collapse Willis made careful drawings of the crossing area, showing the breaks, and indicating where the earlier fissures had been. These accompanied his published account (see p. 210). He then analysed

more minutely the history of the failure of the south-west pier, which was weakest. It began slightly to bend to the south in the middle of February last: this was shown by the closing up of the old fissures, which divided it from the transept... The eastern respond of this pier, belonging to the south tower arch, began to split from top to bottom (CD, plate B), and a fissure extending into the nave arch became manifest. On the Sunday preceding the fall, the bulging of the facing of the pier was observed to increase so alarmingly, that men, as already stated, were set to work to apply shores, during the service in the nave. This bulging increased on the succeeding days, rapidly, and the arches of the triforium assumed gradually the peculiar elliptical form, which is produced by the unequal settlement of the piers of a semicircular arch. On Wednesday, the facing of the pier, about seven feet from the ground, bulged out about three inches on the south side, and strained and bent the timber struts, which connected it with the north-west pier. The pier then settled down about three-quarters of an inch, crushing in the centre, in such a manner, that, on its north face, at about four feet from the ground, the front of the stones stood at their original height and perfect, while the back part of the same stones was crushed and pressed downwards three-quarters of an inch. On Thursday morning, the upper part of the pier was found cracked, and audibly cracking in many directions, flaked stones fell from it, whole stones burst out and fell. Finally, at half-past one, the whole gave way, as above related.

Here we have, for the first time, a detailed account of what we have seen was a common occurrence in the Middle Ages.

Chichester cathedral in 1861 just after the collapse of the central tower and spire.
(A contemporary engraving in The Illustrated London News.*)*

Robert Willis not only understood the structural problems of cathedrals better than anyone else at the time, he was also unsurpassed at sorting out the stratigraphical sequences within the buildings. We have already seen how he made sense of the very complicated sequences in Canterbury, York, Winchester, Chichester, Lichfield and Worcester. To this can be added his mastery of the documentary sources. His translation from the Latin of Gervase's account of the rebuilding of Canterbury cathedral after the 1174 fire is still the most used version. In 1844 he published a little book entitled *Architectural Nomenclature of the Middle Ages* in which he brought together a wide variety of terms used in mediaeval documents in England, France and Italy. Very few architectural historians and archaeologists today have anything like Robert Willis's skill at mediaeval Latin and palaeography. He was also the first to publish in English (in 1859) Villard de Honnecourt's unique thirteenth-century notebooks with their fascinating

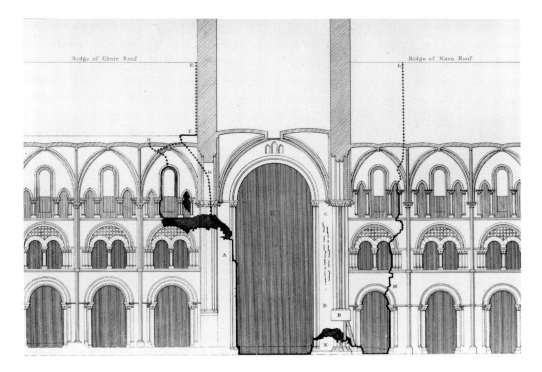

*Robert Willis's longitudinal section (his plate B) of the tower area,
looking south, in Chichester cathedral, showing the
cracks and fissures of 1861.*

diagrams of machines and tools, and their contemporary plans and elevations of various French buildings. Honnecourt's architectural drawings are of immense importance as they are the only contemporary drawings of a mediaeval architect to survive.

As an example of Willis's great understanding of the complicated fabrics of cathedrals, let us return to Chichester. In describing the original apsidal termination of the Norman church, Willis illustrates part of the south-east side of the cathedral (in the cloister garth area), and describes how the masonry changes in the middle of a bay. The masonry to the west, of the early Norman church, is slightly curved for an apse, while to the east the wall for the later squared east end begins. He then goes on:

But [the wall] evidences more than this, as I shall proceed to show. As an apse, it may either be the remains of a small apsidal termination of the aisle, or a portion of the curved wall of a semicircular aisle embracing the great apse of the Norman presbytery, and connecting the north and south aisles, so as to form a procession path [ambulatory]. Its slight curvature indicates that it belonged to the latter arrangement, and the necessity of providing access to the Lady-Chapel has already shewn us that the procession path must have existed. But in this short portion of curved wall, one of the triforium windows appears; exactly similar to those in the neighbouring compartments, only that it is placed close to the buttress. This indicates that a very narrow compartment was made the beginning of the circular wall. Such a compartment could only have been occasioned by the presence of a chapel radiating outwards from the procession path ... And thus it appears that the Norman Cathedral had three radiating chapels and a procession path.

In 1966 when a new concrete foundation was placed around the east end of the cathedral, a brief rescue excavation found part of the foundations of the curved chapels on the north and south, proving beyond doubt Willis's surmise of over a century earlier.

After Willis's death in 1875 other scholars carried on his work on cathedrals, particularly W. H. (later Sir William) St John Hope, whose two volumes on Rochester cathedral and its associated priory buildings, published in 1898 and 1900, are masterly combinations of documentary and architectural history. By this time the publication of large coloured fold-out plans was becoming common, and St John Hope's plans are particularly fine. Sir Harold Brakspear was another scholar who produced beautiful coloured phased plans. Elevation drawings and sections were, however, much more rarely produced, and to many the plan alone was all important. One should add, however, that the very detailed plans of our cathedrals made at the end of the nineteenth century, particularly those published in *The Builder*, are often still the best in existence.

Another careful recorder was J. T. (later Sir James) Irvine, who had been Gilbert Scott's on-the-spot clerk of works for many restorations (see p. 54). In 1890 he published his 'Description of the remains of the Norman cathedral of [Bath] exposed during the repairs made between 1863 and 1872'. The information he recorded below the present floor level is still a prime source for reconstructing the Norman abbey church. Irvine also published a useful paper on the west front of Lichfield cathedral in 1882 and did recording work at Rochester cathedral.

By the beginning of the twentieth century this first phase in architectural and archaeological investigation within our cathedrals was coming to an end. At the same time some excellent general works of synthesis were published. The best of these were Edward Prior's *History of Gothic Art in England* (1900) and *The Cathedral Builders in England* (1905), and Francis Bond's *Gothic Architecture in England* (1905). Francis Bond followed this book with some excellent volumes on screens and galleries, fonts, woodcarving and other furnishings as well as a book on *The Cathedrals of England and Wales* (1912). At the same time some important new work was done by Dr John Bilson on the vaults in Durham cathedral and later, as we have seen in chapter 3, on the elevations and building history of Wells (see p. 93).

At Lincoln John Bilson's investigations followed on from the work of J. T. Smith, who, as clerk of works at Lincoln from 1870 to 1901, had recorded various details and in 1905, had drawn up reconstructed plans and elevations for a paper entitled 'Architectural drawings of Lincoln Cathedral in Norman times'. Bilson's paper called 'The plan of the first cathedral church of Lincoln', written in 1910, was based on a series of small-scale excavations he had carried out within the present minster to find the plan of the original Norman cathedral. These excavations were, as usual at the time, limited to a search for earlier walls only, and were done as a series of key-hole trenches.

With the cessation of most large-scale restorations at the beginning of the present century, the attention and efforts of many antiquaries and architectural historians now turned to the great ecclesiastical ruins and to large-scale uncoverings of the ruined walls of some of the great abbeys like St Augustine's in Canterbury and Glastonbury. Unfortunately these excavations were carried out by paid labourers using miniature railways, and the excavation directors, men like W. H. St John Hope, came only at intervals to view the work and make plans. Vast areas of archaeological deposits were thus stripped off and destroyed without record. This is sadly what happened at Old Sarum between 1912 and 1915 when the late-eleventh- and twelfth-century Salisbury cathedral and its associated buildings (cloister, bishop's palace, canons' houses, and cemeteries) were uncovered for the Society of Antiquaries by St John Hope and others. A very large number of most important discoveries were indeed made, but this was achieved by stripping the whole church to locate only the walls and floors.

Old Sarum is a unique cathedral site because it was abandoned in the thirteenth century and then demolished in about 1331. The excavators found most interesting remains of twelfth-century floors, mostly made of green and white squared blocks of Hurdcote and Chilmark stone, decorated stone tombs, some of which bore inscriptions, and a mass of Romanesque architectural fragments which are now in Salisbury museum. In the church two main phases were noted, and it was observed that the first Norman cathedral (started in c.1075) was constructed with a white mortar, while the enlarged twelfth-century cathedral used a bright yellow mortar. Although the walls had been extensively robbed, the complete plan of the cathedral was recovered as well as the plan of more ephemeral things like altar bases and the pulpitum screen. It has recently been suggested that the early twelfth-century presbytery originally had a central chapel at the east end on two levels with the main altar above a ground floor crypt containing relics. This was then replaced in the late twelfth century by a chapel at only one level (with an elaborate new floor), which may have been a prototype for the new Lady Chapel that was to be built half a century later at the new cathedral down in the valley.

To the north-east of the cathedral was found a cloister, the earliest yet known from a secular cathedral. On its west side, and adjoining the large aisled north transept, were the massive remains of a large rectangular building on a vaulted crypt. This could have been the vestry or just possibly the chapter house, with the treasury in the crypt. To the north of the cloister was another large building complex around a courtyard. This was the new palace of Bishop Roger (1102–39). It had a large aisled great hall on the east and a domestic range on the

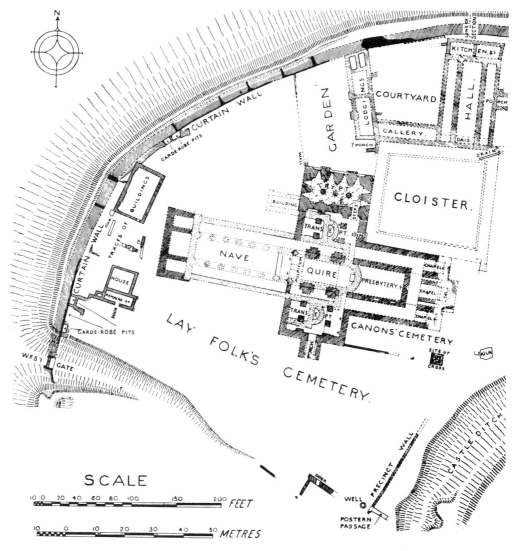

Plan of Old Sarum cathedral made by Sir William St John Hope
at the end of the 1914 season of excavations.

west with a covered passage on the south joining them together. All in all the excavations, which ground to a halt during the First World War, uncovered an immensely important complex of buildings which now badly needs re-excavating and interpreting. Sir William St John Hope died in 1919 and no final excavation report has ever been published.

The First World War marked the end of almost all cathedral archaeology for about half a century. A small amount of work was done in the inter-war years, for example at Wells where the dean, Armitage Robinson, and John Bilson published very important papers on the documentary and fabric evidence for the late-twelfth-century cathedral, but on the whole there was no major new work. The most useful books of the period were Sir Alfred Clapham's two volumes on *English Romanesque Architecture* (before and after the Norman conquest) published in 1930 and 1934. Clapham's synthesis of the Norman cathedrals was particularly useful, though it tended to concentrate most on the plans of buildings, several of which (Lincoln, Old Sarum and St Augustine's abbey, Canterbury) had only recently been uncovered. Two other important books of the period were Professor A. Hamilton Thompson's *The Cathedral Churches of England* (1925) and D. Knoop and G. P. Jones's *The Medieval Mason: an Economic History of English Stone Building in the Later Middle Ages* (1933). The former is a historian's approach but very useful to the architectural historian and archaeologist. (The part of this book dealing with the secular cathedrals has now been superseded by Kathleen Edwards' excellent survey *The English Secular Cathedrals in the Middle Ages* (1949).) Knoop and Jones's book for the first time put the mediaeval master mason firmly on the map. Since the last war Dr John Harvey, in his many published works, has made detailed studies of all known master masons in England, and has tried to relate them to surviving works of architecture. The culmination of this work was his magisterial *English Medieval Architects: A Biographical Dictionary down to 1550* (1954, second revised edition 1984).

Perhaps the principal reason for the cessation of cathedral archaeology after the First World War was the passing of the Ancient Monument Act of 1913 which, for the first time gave ancient ruined buildings statutory protection. The exemption of cathedrals and churches in use from its stipulations meant that deans and chapters could carry on as before in a closed world from which most archaeologists felt excluded. For example, when a new chapel was built onto the east end of Norwich cathedral in 1930–2, no proper investigation was carried out beforehand. During this time, as it happened, archaeological excavation was at last becoming a scientific discipline in England, thanks to the work of Sir Mortimer Wheeler and others. The stratigraphical sequences found below ground were at last being understood, so that 'finding walls' was no longer the principal reason for uncovering buildings.

When Martin and Birthe Biddle carried out their great campaign of excavations on the north side of Winchester cathedral between 1962 and 1969, a new era dawned for cathedral archaeology. Here for the first time was the proof that a very great deal could be found out about a major building, in this case the Anglo-Saxon cathedral, even if all the walls and most of the foundations had been robbed out. The results of these excavations have been discussed in chapter 1, but it should be stressed here that before this work started virtually nothing was known about Anglo-Saxon cathedrals. The meticulous care with which the site was excavated and recorded was also an eye-opener, and heralded the beginning of a new age in large-scale area-excavations, and for Anglo-Saxon archaeology in particular.

In 1966, as a result of a detailed structural survey, the dean and chapter of York minster were told that unless remedial work was undertaken straightaway the central tower of the minster would probably collapse within a decade or so. An appeal for £2 million was launched in May 1967 and work was immediately put in hand. Archaeological excavation was included as a major element in the restoration programme with important results. Not only was an immense amount of new knowledge gained, mainly about the Norman cathedral (see chapter 2), but the discoveries of the archaeologists, led by Derek Phillips, were of great use to the engineers who were engaged in underpinning the four piers of the tower. Virtually all the uncertainties remaining from John Browne's nineteenth-century excavations were sorted out. The only thing still missing was the Anglo-Saxon cathedral. Other excavations have subsequently been carried out inside and just outside the minster, and further investigations have also continued on the upstanding fabric, making York minster by far the best studied cathedral in the country.

One or two other small-scale excavations have been allowed in and around English cathedrals in recent years, at Canterbury, Worcester, Lincoln and most recently at Carlisle in 1988. Two other larger excavations, those carried out beside Exeter and Wells cathedrals, have thrown new light on the Anglo-Saxon cathedrals that preceded the neighbouring twelfth-century and later structures (see chapter 1). Both have led to above-ground archaeology being carried out on the present cathedrals during extensive restoration campaigns. At Exeter this continuing campaign, which started in 1981, has involved the detailed drawing and study of the great west front image screen, and the Norman south tower. Other work has been carried out within the cathedral, and the attitude of the dean and chapter there should be a model for other cathedrals to follow.

The most important new work on upstanding cathedrals has, however, been that undertaken by Dr Warwick Rodwell at Wells and Lichfield cathedrals. At Wells the magnificent west front, with its unique sculpture collection, was very carefully cleaned and conserved from 1975 to 1986. From an early stage of this work very detailed records were made of every part of the west front. A huge archive has now been amassed of stone-by-stone drawings, photographs and written reports which not only record all the original building materials, mortars and phases of construction work, but also all subsequent restorations and repairs. The sculpture has been particularly carefully recorded (many traces of the original paint were found), and at last art historians have 'reliable documents' to use when discussing the sculpture. Other archaeological investigations have been carried out inside the cathedral, including the making of a new measured survey of the ground plan of the cathedral to a high degree of accuracy. This last is now an urgent requirement in most other cathedrals.

In 1982 Warwick Rodwell started a new programme of archaeological research in Lichfield cathedral which has already been immensely fruitful. By accurately drawing a new plan of the choir area in 1986–7 and making stone-by-stone drawings of all the walls around the choir, including those under the triforium roof, he has discovered several major areas of masonry of the late eleventh and twelfth centuries that were completely unknown to Robert Willis. The form of the early Norman cathedral, and all the changes that occurred in the twelfth century, are now becoming very much better understood.

In a continuing programme of research at Lichfield, which is fitting in closely with the restoration programme (and hence making use of large areas of scaffolding erected inside the cathedral), Dr Rodwell has now taken us into a 'post-Willis' era of research. To understand our cathedrals fully, we must now make measured drawings of all parts of the fabric. This is obviously an immense job, but if it can be done in conjunction with masonry restoration it will revolutionise our knowledge of the buildings.

At Chichester, for example, a five-year programme of restoration has just got underway on the north side of the nave. As each bay is cleaned, 1:20 scale-drawings of all the external walls are being made before the rotten stone is removed and replaced. The cleaning is essential because the walls are very heavily coated with industrial pollution. Once this has been removed the masonry and

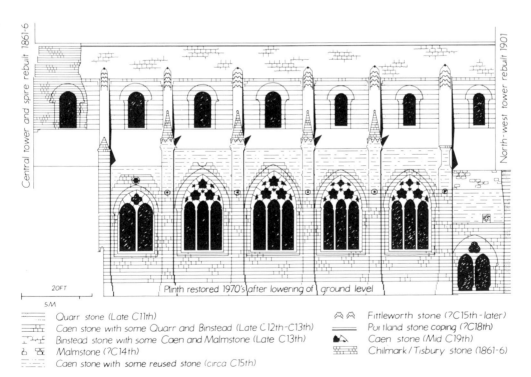

Central tower and spire rebuilt 1861-6

North-west tower rebuilt 1901

20FT

5M

Plinth restored 1970's after lowering of ground level

Quarr stone (Late C11th)
Caen stone with some Quarr and Binstead (Late C12th-C13th)
Binstead stone with some Caen and Malmstone (Late C13th)
Malmstone (?C14th)
Caen stone with some reused stone (circa C15th)

Fittleworth stone (?C15th-later)
Portland stone coping (?C18th)
Caen stone (Mid C19th)
Chilmark/Tisbury stone (1861-6)

Elevation drawing of the north nave area at Chichester cathedral,
showing different phases of work.

mortar jointing look like any newly excavated surface in an archaeological excavation, clearly revealing each period of work. At Chichester these are particularly noticeable because the stone used for each phase is almost always different. The early Norman clerestory walls, which still contain their original windows, are made of Quarr stone. On top of them is a Caen stone string-course surmounted by a double corbel-table of the later thirteenth century made in Binstead stone. Cutting into this work are the tops of flying buttresses made in Fittleworth stone (from near Pulborough) which must date from the later mediaeval period. The top coping on the parapet is in Portland stone (perhaps eighteenth century), while the area of rebuilding after the fall of the spire in 1861 can be very clearly seen. The much more uniform masonry here is in Tisbury and Chilmark stone from near Salisbury. There are other areas of fourteenth-century masonry in a soft upper greensand, which is probably 'Green Ventnor' or Bonchurch stone from the south side of the Isle of Wight. When all of the stonework has been recorded, a series of three-dimensional drawings will have to be made to show how the north side of the nave evolved. Then, using documentary evidence, dendrochronology from the associated roofs, and art-historical studies, a much more detailed absolute chronology of this part of the cathedral should be possible.

In recent years there has been a coming together of all the different scholars working on the archaeology and the architectural and art history of our cathedrals, and in 1975 the first of a new series of annual conferences was held by the British Archaeological Association at Worcester. Papers were read on the history, architectural history, sculpture, manuscript illumination, seals, tile pavings and Victorian restoration of the cathedral. Much knowledge was shared between scholars, who spent much of the conference exploring the building and looking at its treasures, and the subsequent publication marks the beginning of a new era in our understanding of the art and architecture associated with this cathedral. Since then a conference has been held each year in a different cathedral, followed a year or so later by excellent publications.

One other development which has occurred very recently indeed is the publication of a draft 'Care of Cathedral Measure' by the General Synod of the Church of England. This measure, which was first introduced in January 1988, has the overall objective of 'strengthening and extending the Church's existing legal and administrative structures for the care and conservation of cathedrals'. Among other things, it proposes the setting up of 'fabric committees' at each cathedral and the appointment of 'archaeological consultants' to the dean and chapter. Although this measure has not had a smooth ride through Synod (the provisional draft was rejected by the deans and provosts at the February meeting of Synod, and changes are still being debated at the time of writing), many cathedrals have in the last year or so voluntarily put these recommendations in hand. There is, therefore, at last a feeling among many (but not all) deans and chapters that they have much to gain from fabric committees and consultant archaeologists, even if they ultimately lose some of their independence thereby.

Alongside this debate has been the spectre of the ever-increasing need for major restoration programmes at our cathedrals. The estimated cost of these restorations is rocketing, and many of the poorer cathedrals are finding it hard to raise the money required. In recent years Canterbury and York have raised several million pounds fairly easily (as did Ely cathedral in 1987), but Salisbury's current appeal for £6.5 million has to date raised only £3.1 million. The smaller, less-visited and less well-known cathedrals like Rochester and Hereford are now finding it increasingly difficult to raise the money required to make ends meet, let alone pay for new restoration programmes and archaeological recording. This dilemma was brought dramatically to public attention in November 1988 when Hereford cathedral's dean and chapter announced that they intended to sell their unique thirteenth-century *Mappa Mundi* (Map of the World) to the highest bidder. This has now led to increased calls for government funding of restoration programmes at cathedrals, and ultimately this must surely come, though not without much debate in the meantime.

We are, therefore, at the dawn of a new era in our cathedrals' history, an era which will involve archaeologists more than ever before. After more than half a century of comparative inactivity in cathedral archaeology, a great deal has been achieved in a handful of cathedrals in the last decade or so. This new work must now spread to the majority of our cathedrals, and it is to be hoped that by the end of the century the architectural history of many cathedrals in Britain will have been completely rewritten. At the same time, a new system of state-funding for restoration should have evolved alongside a mandatory system for monitoring all proposed restoration and conservation work. For archaeologists – and for cathedral chapters and ultimately the general public who benefit from their work of interpretation – it is essential that, if nothing else, every cathedral should have started to amass an archive of measured drawings, photographs and written reports about its fabric and fittings. Total preservation of a cathedral can never be possible, but 'preservation by record', so that no detail, however small, disappears without being drawn and photographed as has happened so often in the past, must be the goal of the future.

Glossary

Bold type indicates terms explained in detail elsewhere in the glossary.

ABACUS the slab making up the top member of a **capital**.

AMBULATORY a processional walk around the eastern arm of a large church, especially the aisle enclosing an **apse**.

APSE a semi-circular recess, usually for an altar.

ARCADE/ING a series of arches.

ASHLAR regular squared stonework.

BALLFLOWER DECORATION lines of carved small round projecting flowers used as decoration. It is found only in some areas, and dates to the very early fourteenth century.

BAY a section of wall between external **buttresses** or internal **piers**.

BLIND ARCADE an **arcade** cut into the surface of a wall.

BOSS a prominent knob, usually at the intersection of the ribs of a **vault**.

BUTTRESS

    CLASPING stonework encasing the corner of a building (or tower) to strengthen it.

    FLYING an open-arched structure built from a **pier** to an external upper wall. It transmits the outward thrust from a stone **vault** to a **buttress**.

    PILASTER tall strip of stonework built against a wall to strengthen it.

CAPITAL the top section, often decorated, of a column.

CAPSTONE a stone which caps or crowns a spire, **vault**, etc.

CHEVRON V-shaped incised decoration common in the twelfth century on arches, **piers** etc.

CLERESTORY the windowed upper part of a wall above the aisle roofs.

CORBEL a large projecting block, usually of stone.

CROSSING the area, often under a tower, between north and south **transepts**.

CROCKETS leafy projections on the edges of sloping gables, pinnacles, etc.

CRYPT a space below a church, usually in the eastern arm.

CUSHION CAPITAL a **Romanesque** capital cut from a cube by having the lower angles rounded off to a circular base.

DECORATED STYLE a formal division in English mediaeval architecture c.1290 to c.1350, taking its name from the type of window **tracery** that is used at this time.

EARLY ENGLISH a formal division in English mediaeval architecture c.1180 to c.1250 when the pointed arch makes its first appearance.

EFFIGY a figured sculpture, usually horizontal, on top of a tomb.

FINIAL decorative topmost feature on a gable, pinnacle, etc.

FLAMBOYANT a formal division of French late Gothic where the **tracery** is full of wavy undulating lines.

GEOMETRIC a formal division of English mediaeval architecture c.1250 to c.1290 taking its name from the form of the tracery used at this time.

GOTHIC the name given to mediaeval architecture after c.1180 when the pointed arch was first commonly used: corresponds with **Early English, Geometric, Decorated,** and **Perpendicular**.

KEYSTONE the stone at the top of an arch.

LANCET tall late-twelfth to early-thirteenth-century window with a pointed head.

LAP-JOINT a carpentry joint where one timber is joined to the side of another.

LIERNE (see **vaulting**).

LOZENGE diamond-shaped decorative motif.

MISERICORD carved bracket on the lower side of a hinged stall seat to support a standing occupant of the stall.

MORTICE-AND-TENON JOINT joint made by making a hole in a piece of wood (mortice) to receive the end of another piece (tenon).

NAILHEAD DECORATION decorative motif of small pyramids in a row, usually **Early English** in date.

OGEE an arch shaped like two long S's, i.e. with convex and concave curves.

PARAPET a low wall on top of a large wall at the base of the roof.

PERPENDICULAR STYLE a formal division in English mediaeval architecture c.1340 to c.1530.

PIER a supporting pillar in an **arcade**.

PISCINA a shallow basin with a drain for washing vessels used during Mass, usually in a wall to the south of an altar.

PRESBYTERY the area of a church east of the choir containing the high altar.

QUATREFOIL ornamentation of four lobes or leaves.

QUOIN dressed stones at the corner of a building or **buttress**.

REREDOS a screen or wall decoration at the back of an altar.

RETROCHOIR the area of a church behind the high altar.

RIDGED RIB a horizontal rib in a **vault** running along the centre or at right angles to it at the highest point of the vault.

ROMANESQUE name given to mediaeval architecture in the eleventh and twelfth centuries, when the round arch is used, often called 'Norman' in England.

ROOD crucifix on top of a screen, usually at the east end of the nave.

SACRISTY room used for keeping vestments and sacred vessels.

SEDILIA seats (often three) for priests on the south side of the high altar.

SQUINCH ARCH an arch across the corner of two walls to support a higher (sometimes octagonal) structure.

STRING COURSE a horizontal line of stones (sometimes with a moulding) in a wall.

TENON-AND-MORTICE JOINT (see **mortice-and-tenon**).

TIEBEAM large horizontal beam running between two walls.

TIERCERON (see **vaulting**).

TRACERY intersecting ribs on **vaults**, blank arches or in the upper part of a window.

  BAR TRACERY slender bars used in the window head which continue the mullion lines c.1250.

  PLATE TRACERY earliest tracery with decorative openings cut through solid stonework.

TRANSEPTS north and south projections of a church.

TRIFORIUM a gallery, usually above the aisles.

TRUSS triangular-shaped group of timbers making up a section of a roof.

VAULT/ING arched ceiling of stone or timber.

  FAN vault of concave semi-cones without ribs.

  GROIN vault with four curving surfaces without ribs.

  LIERNE vault with extra small ribs in the upper part.

  PENDANT vault with large hanging **bosses**.

  RIBBED vault with ribs dividing it into four (quadripartite) or six (sexpartite) sections.

  TIERCERON vault with extra ribs springing from the corners of the **bays**.

VOUSSOIR one of the stones making up an arch.

Index

Picture credits

TERRY BALL page 55; BRITISH LIBRARY page 23 (Westminster Psalter MS2A XXII FF21); PETER BURTON & HARLAND WALSHAW page 142 inset; CANTERBURY ARCHAEOLOGICAL TRUST pages 13 & 194; CITY OF LINCOLN ARCHAEOLOGICAL UNIT page 28; NICOLA FOOT page 88; J.H.P. GIBB pages 45 & 46; GUILDHALL LIBRARY pages 71 & 197; CECIL HEWITT pages 92 & 104; CLIVE HICKS pages 11, 70, 103, 107, 114, 132, 139, 154, 169 & 182; ILLUSTRATED LONDON NEWS page 209; ROBERT KILGOUR page 121; LINCOLN CIVIC TRUST page 15; MUSEUM OF LONDON pages 187 & 196; NATIONAL MONUMENTS RECORD page 64; OXFORD COUNTY LIBRARIES page 189; WARWICK RODWELL page 44; ROYAL ALBERT MEMORIAL MUSEUM pages 116 & 118; SALISBURY CATHEDRAL page 98; SCOTTISH DEVELOPMENT DEPARTMENT pages 159, 162, 163, 165, 168, 169 & 172; SOCIETY OF ANTIQUITIES pages 40, 52, 61, 68, 86, 87, 93, 95, 124, 128, 134, 181, 183, 190, 192, 199, 203, 206, 210 & 213; WEIDENFELD pages 16 & 17; YORK CITY ART GALLERY page 140.

Drawings by John Bowen

Pages 22, 35, 36, 62–3, 76, 79, 80, 81, 98, 111, 120, 152 & 216.

Maps by Line & Line

Pages 20, 25, 30, 34, 39, 126, 156, 179.